METAMORPHOSIS

HERMETIC SCIENCE AND YOGA POWER

ORDO ASTRI

METAMORPHOSIS

HERMETIC SCIENCE
AND
YOGA POWER

OLIVER ST. JOHN

Metamorphosis
Hermetic Science and Yoga Power
© Oliver St. John 2024

Cover design and graphics © Oliver St. John 2024

ISBN 978-1-7391549-5-0

ORDO ASTRI IMPRIMATUR
www.ordoastri.org

In this terrible *kali yuga*, all beings generally obtain *asura* traits. What is the supreme path that can cure them of this? What is that supreme object that ensures the best of the best? At present, what is the means that is the purest of the pure? In particular, what means can be used to swiftly purify one's *atma*? O father with a sparkling mind! How can one always obtain Shiva?

Skanda Purana, Shiva Purana

CONTENTS

Concerning Metaphysics

Before metaphysics can be explained by discursive means, the terms used must be redefined. Metaphysics is meant here in the etymological sense of the word, which is to say, 'beyond the physical', and so nothing to do with the chemical state of the body or brain, or the psychological domain. Metaphysics refers to the infinite, unlimited universal doctrine that can only be known metaphysically. As it depends from a supra-human source, it can never be a branch of philosophy or some other science. Indeed, philosophy and the other modern theoretical sciences were originally derived from metaphysics and not vice versa.

Symbolism is the only way to convey metaphysical reality without direct knowledge; language itself comprises a set of symbols. Ancient languages, with all their subtlety of etymology, roots of words and phonetics, are nonetheless well equipped to symbolise metaphysics, which is solely concerned with principles that amount to pure knowledge. Such principial knowledge is most adequately set down in the Hindu Vedas and Vedanta. Such knowledge is not in any way derived from an individual author, as is the case with all Western philosophical theories. With the Vedanta, the goal is always that of pure knowledge: untransmissible, infinite and absolute reality. That is what we mean by 'metaphysics'.

This knowledge is not then in any way apprehended by reason or argument as it is derived from a supra-human source. All dialectics of the ancient sciences, including Hermeticism for example— something that in itself has been confused with profane science— form only an outward veil of that which is truly esoteric, which is inevitable. The ordinary meaning of the term 'dialectic', derived from Greek (διαλεκτικη), means 'a discussion', and that word derives from analysis, which is necessarily confined to the domain of reason. The limitation imposed by this is such that the conventional modern dictionary definition, 'enquiry into metaphysical contradictions and their solutions', is confused in its very nature and rests on total misunderstanding of the word's meaning. Such an enquiry removes the enquirer from anything metaphysical, even in the etymological sense. There can be no contradiction in metaphysical or principial reality, which is infinite and contains all possibilities within Itself without any disharmony entering therein. The dictionary will even inform us that metaphysics is concerned with 'abstraction' that has 'no basis in reality'! This owes to the fact that modern science imagines 'concrete existence' to be the only reality.

Some scholars have even attempted to reduce the meaning of metaphysics to the level of the utterly inane, until it becomes no more than 'in addition to' or 'after', as with the appendices of a book![1]

Inevitably, some Sanskrit terms must be used when expressing a metaphysical idea, for there are no words in modern languages to describe Atma or Brahma, for example, let alone the vast array of other technical terms and their different contextual uses. Sanskrit has the vocabulary of a complete science of consciousness itself; this is better understood if the universe is considered as ontological and not material; unfortunately even that completely escapes the grasp of ordinary rational comprehension and is only truly conveyed by direct knowledge. The means of acquiring such knowledge is the subject of the *Yoga-Sutras*, for example, but few are prepared to make the intense and prolonged effort that is needed.

We must then rely on symbolism and language, whatever its shortcomings, if we are to communicate anything at all. That limits our scope to a few that are prepared to work diligently towards an understanding, putting aside any preconceived notions they might hold. It is these few persons that we are addressing, for the rest are as in a deep sleep, lacking the strength or will to awaken. In fact, these sleepers are even the enemies of the knowledge that is our subject and our ultimate goal, which means they will never acquire it. As it is put very succinctly in the alchemical text *Aurora Consurgens*,

> Fools despise this glorious Science of God, and the Doctrine of the Secrets, and the Secret of the Philosophers, and the Medicine of the Physicians, because they do not know what she really is. ... And nor is this kind of wisdom suited to the ignorant because everyone who is ignorant of her is her enemy, and not without cause, as the Observer of All Things says. ... Nor will the spirit of this Wisdom enter into a coarse body, and nor can a fool ever grasp it, due to the poverty of his reasoning, because the wise have not spoken to the foolish, for he who speaks to a fool speaks to someone who is asleep.[2]

---

[1] We refer to S.M. Cohen, 'Aristotle's Metaphysics' [Stanford Encyclopaedia of Philosophy, California].

[2] Book I: III.

Preface

Sophia is our Guiding Light.

Our books published since 2021 map out a journey away from occultism and towards pure metaphysics. That is to say, not metaphysics as in the Greek scholastic sense or the modern dictionary sense but as indicative of the Vedanta, for example, where the goal is that of pure knowledge: untransmissible, infinite and absolute reality. Metaphysics in the particular way that we use the term refers to the infinite, unlimited universal doctrine, which, as it depends from a supra-human source, can never be a branch of philosophy or some other science.

Metaphysics is veiled in the symbolism and scriptures of all ancient traditions but two things are needed to make any effective use of its study: firstly, the works of René Guénon on the Hindu doctrines and esoteric symbolism. After that, the translations of source texts by Swami Gambhirananda are not in any way diluted.[3] There are many more but none can be recommended without some reservation as distortions come about through translations and commentaries made for Western readers outside the tradition. Even modern Hindus use Theosophical inventions such as 'reincarnation', which has no place in the Vedanta, because they think that English-speaking readers will believe in this. They also refer to the Hindu tradition as a 'philosophy', which it is not; philosophy is a Greek and European convention that owes to rational argument and theories produced by individuals. It is not in any way comparable to the ancient doctrines, which are derived from a supra-human source.

Likewise, those with a modern education will refer to all ancient traditions as 'religion', which is impossible. Religion is relatively modern and particular to exoteric doctrines and theologies; it must include sacraments, ritual and dogma. Hinduism, for example, does not depend on the latter and has no exoteric aspect. These errors are by now widespread and are used by translators and publishers alike. And yet the mind is shaped by its own cognitions and so the terms we use are important; this is not a matter of semantics.

---

[3] *The Bhagavad Gita*, *The Upanishads* and the *Brahma Sutras* commented on by Shankaracharya—the core doctrine of Advaita Vedanta. For example, the correct term 'transmigration' is used, not 'reincarnation'.

'Metamorphosis' also happens to be the title of our monthly *Journal of Metaphysics*.[4] If we turn to a dictionary for the meaning of 'metamorphosis' we get an explanation that is either incomplete or even the total inverse of the etymological sense of the word. A 'change of the form or nature of a thing or person into a completely different one' takes no account of the metaphysical sense of this, where the change in the state of the being passes completely beyond the previous. Such a change is permanent; there can be no passing back to former states.

Although the details of spiritual organisations are of little interest to the wider public, some general facts are warranted here, for an operational collegium was always the foundation of our writings. The Order was founded in 1996 and it was not until August of 2022, with the retitling of our Journal to *Metamorphosis*, that the description Universal Gnostic Collegium was introduced. This allowed a wider net to be cast, so to speak. Previously, there was a highly specialised focus on what was defined as 'Esoteric Thelema'; much of our earlier work consists of commentaries on key verses from the (Egyptian) Book of the Law that was part 'received' mediumistically and part composed (fabricated to a certain extent) in Cairo in the spring of 1904. We always strove to distance ourselves both in theory and practice from the mainstream interpretations, which rest on neo-spiritualism and all its falsehoods of progress, evolutionism and reincarnationism and the inversion of all esoteric symbolism—a subject well covered in our most recent works.

By late autumn of 2019 it became obvious to some of us at least that what Guénon termed the 'Reign of Quantity' and the 'System of Antichrist' was about to crystallise or harden, and that our exterior world would never be the same again. And furthermore, that we have entered the final phase of what is called the Kali Yuga or Age of Darkness in traditional Hindu doctrines. It became very clear to us that two centuries or more of ignorant occult experimentation and evocation have played a part in bringing in what may well be a premature close to the present humanity. This has been aided and abetted by the anti-initiatic and anti-traditional beliefs that have become part of a wider culture as a consequence of the extraordinary success of neo-spiritualist propaganda.

---

[4] The name has been used from 21st August 2022, to reflect a radical change of perspective that took place after the covert global coup d'état of spring 2020. The *Journal* ran for seven years from May 2015 to July 2022 as *The 93 Current* and existed under various titles since the year 2001.

Quite a struggle can take place until a butterfly emerges from the cocoon. The metamorphosis is not accomplished without a good deal of effort. The first twenty-two years of our development could be summarised as an ongoing critical study of Thelema and magick, placing it in the context of the Hermetic and other traditions. We have produced a moderately large number of books on the subject. *Nu Hermetica* was comparable to entering a new state of being. With the next, *Way of Knowledge*, we redefined the path, as is needed in the present times. The latter brought in for the first time traditional yoga practices such as exist, though are little known of in the West, within the initiated Patañjali lineages in India. Yoga—in the true sense of the word, not 'yoga for health' or any of the fake versions that are found in the market place—began to take on a far more central rôle. *Thunder Perfect Gnosis* included ten chapters on the practice of concentration essential to real yoga meditation. This book marked a complete departure from our previous attempts to link the cult of Thelema with authentic tradition, and contains no reference to it or the book that was received in 1904 through a combination of spiritist techniques and magical evocation.

With the present work we continue to look at subjects of Gnostic and Hermetic interest that were previously left unexplored from the metaphysical point of view, while at the same time going further into details of the practice of yoga and meditation already introduced. Part Two of the book, 'Yoga Power', is a continuation of the very practical instruction on the yoga of Patañjali that took up a large part of *Thunder Perfect Gnosis*. Having there set down the essential requirements for yoga, including a concise account of the cosmology of Shankhya plus intellective process, devotion and concentration, we now look more deeply into the subject, covering such little known or understood aspects as the Supernormal Powers.

Sophia be-with-us forever.

Oliver St. John

Land's End Peninsula Sol in ♌ Luna in ♌ 2024

PART ONE
HERMETIC SCIENCE

Can God be Plural?

Much of our instructional writing assumes that the student or practitioner knows what a deity actually is, at least in theory. In that case, the question does not arise of how it is possible, for example, for there to be so many names of God or Deity in the Egyptian and other ancient traditions. However, given the extent of the distortions that prevail around all matters spiritual, often resting on a real hatred of tradition, and the confusion that automatically arises therein, it would seem worthwhile to say here more on the subject than has been said previously.

The equivalent for 'Deity' in Sanskrit is Deva, Devi, *devas* or *devis*, and we can easily see the etymological link with 'divine' in our own language. Unfortunately, the dictionary is only a place to discover false knowledge when it comes to anything that touches on the esoteric or metaphysical, let alone the sea of ignorance that one encounters on websites and the like. The word 'deity' is from the Latin *deitus*, from *deus*, from the Greek *theotēs*, 'divine'. Taking the list of errors that is given in our standard dictionary, we first have 'a god or goddess in a polytheistic religion: a deity of ancient Greece.' Polytheism is a notion completely unknown and irrelevant within any ancient tradition. It is only applicable, and at that approximately, to the later and more degraded stages of the Greek and Roman civilisations. As for a 'polytheistic religion', religions are necessarily monotheist! God cannot be a plurality as that would be pure self contradiction. The different names and appearances of Deity are descriptive of multitudinous attributes of the principle of universal manifestation or Pure Being.

The dictionary next goes on to define Deity as 'the creator and supreme being in a monotheistic religion such as Christianity.' The notion of a 'creator' is indeed exclusive to Judaeo Christian theology. Something cannot be created from nothing, or from 'outside' as it were. The universe is ontological in nature. 'Monotheism', while true of some theologies, only means anything at all in relation to the invented notion of polytheism. As previously explained, polytheism has never existed in India, for example. It is likewise with ancient Egypt, although all these errors and slurs are placed upon her by scholars and the 'man in the street' alike, for both reach no further than what is called profane ('ignorant') from the point of view of initiated tradition.

There is even worse, much worse, when we consider the populist psychological thinking that relegates everything supernatural to a theoretical 'subconscious', which then results in the quite fantastic absurdity of God or gods reduced to an aspect of an individual or collective, which is no less limiting. Effectively this reduces Deity to nothing more than a figment of imagination. That kind of thinking, based on purely theoretical invention, has led to the vanishing away of God altogether from modern civilisations, so that it is by now very commonplace to hear it affirmed as though it were a fact. Occultists will always claim to hold some special kind of knowledge, yet in propagating such theories they have only succeeded in making what little they know the domain of the most ordinary intelligence. Sri Ramakrishna once remarked to a sceptic more than a century ago that God looks very small when seen from far away. His meaning was that the person he was addressing was very far from the knowledge of God, and that furthermore, his whole disposition barred him from ever knowing it.[5]

The way of real knowledge and spiritual realisation involves ritual (*karma*), devotion to deity (*bhakti*) and vigilance of discrimination or intellective process (*viveka*, that leads to *jnana*).[6] Taken together this is the special form of Raja Yoga that forms the core of our practical work. Deity is integral to the essential practice of faith, love and devotion. It is needed in the practice of real meditation (*dhyana*).[7] However, it is true that the Advaitans, when teaching those qualified for the ultimate liberation (*moksha*), correctly pointed out that the worship of Ishvara ('the Lord') is secondary from the point of view of the supreme principle. There is thus a lesser and a greater path even as there are degrees of reality, relative to the state of being; yet even Shankara himself, the foremost advocate of Absolute Non-Dualism, composed beautiful hymns of devotion to Mahadevi Shakti, the Goddess of the Tantras.[8]

---

[5] Ramakrishna was a devotee of Kali Ma and lived much of his life at the temple of Dakshiniwara in Bengal.

[6] Viveka is, properly speaking, a modification of the *boddhi* or supra-human intellectual intuition. This is how discrimination is possible. The term Viveka-Khyati means 'realisation through discrimination', and this leads to *ynana*, metaphysical knowledge or truth, which is the goal of yoga.

[7] By 'real' meditation we do not include the practices of non-traditional modern developments of Buddhism, for example, where atheism is not regarded as an affliction and, on the contrary, is even considered in some schools to be a necessary qualification for tyros at the entry level.

[8] See *Hymns to the Goddess*, Sir John Woodroffe.

2

It is well known within Hinduism that according to the doctrine of the Cosmic Cycles, we are now in the dark age of Kali Yuga.[9] The Tantras and the way of devotion, which is integral to them, are deemed to be very efficacious in these times. Thus even two thousand years ago when the Patañjali Aphorisms were written down from the previous oral tradition, devotion to God, Shakti or Ishvara was placed in a position of central importance, even when the goal was pure knowledge, and the means not in any way incompatible with Advaita Vedanta. It is worth repeating then that the different names of Deity are descriptive of attributes of the principle of universal manifestation or Pure Being. Any multiplicity of Deity would be a contradiction in terms, as well as a refutation of the metaphysical supreme principle, which, while containing all possibilities within Itself, is not in any way divisible into parts.

The very ancient Sekhmet usually takes the form of a lioness with a woman's body, though she is not limited to that and is able to appear as Hathoor, the woman of love. Both Sekhmet and Hathoor are closely associated with the sun as solar principle. Isis, as is clear from her hieroglyphic name, is associated with what is better known in Hinduism as Hiranyagarbha, the cosmic 'world egg'. The latter is frequently confused with a representation of the cosmos itself but it is in fact the principle by which the cosmological sphere comes about. Each year, a ritual and festivity was celebrated where Isis was united with Neïth, a union that also symbolised the indivisible nature of the land of Khem, or Egypt. All these names and forms express principles that can be symbolised in nature. The cat goddess Bast was variously associated with both Ra and Sekhmet.[10] Bast is well fitted as a household deity of the fireplace or home shrine, whereas Sekhmet, as having more to do with the cosmic order, is a deity better suited to the temple, whether that is to be taken literally or figuratively. Sekhmet, like the Hindu Durga, is 'hard to approach', as her way concerns knowledge only accessible to very few.

In Hinduism, Saraswati or Parvati are better suited to the householder or lay practitioner, though they are equally deserving of respect, for Parvati can manifest as Durga if she chooses to do so. It should by now be clear as to how the Egyptian Neïth of the Delta can take the form of a lioness, in which case she is indistinguishable from the goddess Sekhmet.

---

[9] That is to say, it is well known within Hindu tradition although nowadays, owing to the all-pervasive Western influence, even many Hindus doubt it. It is scarcely known if at all within the general milieu of modern thought.

[10] See 'House of Bast', *Thunder Perfect Gnosis*.

3

Ra can take the form of a lion or a cat, and both Sekhmet and Hathoor are called the 'Eye of Ra', and can be the 'daughter of Ra' and at the same time his mother. If symbolism is understood in relation to the principles it points to, there needs be no confusion at all. All deities, or gods or goddesses, are particular symbol forms of one Deity, and this is why the scholarly and dictionary notion of polytheism, which they level at all ancient traditions, is hopelessly wrong.

It remains for something to be said regarding angels, which though these are best known within the Judaeo Christian tradition are also well known within other traditions such as Islam, where they frequently have the same or very similar names. In Hinduism, the word *deva* or *devi* is equally applicable to deities or what are otherwise called angels. Many of the better-known angels such as Michael, Raphael and Auriel are found in the Hebraic tongue, which facilitates the ancient science of numbers. For example, when Michael is spelled in Hebrew (MIKAL) it can be calculated as 101. The title of the last book of Prophets is Malachi (MLAKI), also 101 and a rearrangement of the same letters. Malachi, from the root *melek*, means 'Messenger'; all angels are messengers in that they function as intermediaries by which man is able to know God through his attributes. All names of angels end in AL, or El, which is a name of God that was once used throughout the Middle East. Thus any difference between angels and deities is only a matter of differing traditions that veil the principles in different clothing. There are four worlds or levels of being in the Hebraic tradition; while Metatron is usually 'located' in the world of emanations (Atziluth), Michael is usually placed in Yetzirah, which corresponds to the level of subtle form. And yet these 'positions' are as interchangeable as are the Egyptian and Hindu deities, as according to context.

All angels, properly speaking, belong to the celestial and formless level of manifestation. As such, neither angels nor deities have an individuality, which is something very particular to the human being. Angels are not human, in spite of the anthropomorphic forms often given them, and they could not be what they are if they had their origin in the human psyche, the content of which is even inferior to ordinary reason.

The forms by which we know angels, as with deities, are handed down through ancient tradition, and were conceived to assist us with concentration of the mind and meditation, so that it is possible to know God. Thus we know them by name and form, Sanskrit *nama* and *rupa*, but in reality what they are is more than that as ultimately they are not separate from God, Mahadevi, Shakti or by whatever name is afforded to divinity. It can then be seen how fatuous it is to pitch one deity against another, or to fear that worshipping Isis might give offence to Neïth or Hathoor, especially if one of the latter were a tutelary deity. Having said that, in practice one does not 'choose' a deity according to the neo-spiritualist notion of 'intuition'. On this, it is worth repeating what was said in *Way of Knowledge*:[11]

> One of the most subversive notions of the postmodern fake spirituality is that a person should be guided by their 'intuition'. This conveniently rules out completely any need for study and learning of wisdom texts, affiliating with orthodoxy or initiatic organisations, or the performance of any devotional rites and observances other than devotion to the ego-self, which is always the primary objective.

It is more the case that one is blessed to be chosen. When the name of a tutelary deity or particular aspect of the divine is known, then obviously there are good reasons for being consistent. To a follower of Tahuti (or Thoth), Tahuti is God and verily God. To a worshipper of Parvati, she is supreme Mahadevi.

The tutelary deity brings us to the notion of a Holy Guardian Angel; the word 'tutelary' carries every meaning of association with a particular place or location, and also of protection or guardianship. The tutelary deity has the angelic attributes of both messenger and instructor. In Hinduism, the Shakti can personify the supra-human faculties, to the extent of acting as 'inner guru'. It is always worth repeating that the feminine powers Shakti, Shekinah and Sekhet carry the same meanings in Sanskrit, Hebrew and ancient Egyptian. The Guardian Angel is not by any means unique to the Western Tradition, if it may be called that (it is more a lost tradition), but the term is most often found in occult writings where it has suffered obfuscation and even abuse by those with a psychological bent. The latter reduce this, in the same way that they reduce and simplify everything to the utterly commonplace, to the level of a kind of 'psychic' apparition, or even a purely imagined thing such as a 'spirit guide'.

---

[11] *Way of Knowledge*, 'Postmodern Shamanism' p. 98.

And there, abuse is not too strong a word, for such 'spirits' are fondly believed to be higher intelligences, or otherwise, and as is more usually the case, a higher aspect of the individual self. In truth, these so-called spirits, whether imagined or not, link the profane practitioner with *sub-infra* or demonic forces, or otherwise the discarded remnants of former human beings.[12]

However, be that as it may, in reality a Guardian Angel, if it is really that, is no different from a tutelary deity, as we hope by now to have explained in clear terms. It remains to be explained as to why it is that a teaching exists in occultism that is the exact opposite of what has been said here regarding the Guardian Angel. However, that is a whole subject in itself and involves historical and other references, so it will be dealt with in the next chapter.

---

[12] See René Guénon, *The Spiritist Fallacy*, which deals with all aspects of the occult and its various notions concerning the 'afterlife', spirit mediumism, clairvoyance (so-called) and much else besides.

Shadow of the Wings

I t has been established that there is no real difference between a tutelary deity and a Guardian Angel. How did it come about then that a teaching exists in occultism that is the exact opposite of this? The instruction has it that the Holy Guardian Angel must not be confused with a deity. As with all the teachings arising from neo-spiritualism, it is conveyed with convincing authority, yet has almost no real knowledge to support it. The ideas of the occultists of the late nineteenth and twentieth century emerged from spiritism, which is the name given it by the French although it was first promoted in America in 1848.[13] Other movements swiftly developed and spread, including the influential Theosophical movement; spiritism, which involved supposed communications with the dead, once taken up by the Americans and British soon spread to the rest of the world along with the Theosophist's pet theories, especially reincarnation and evolutionism. Neo-spiritualists and occultists, outwardly at least, had a kind of reverence for the late nineteenth century Order of the Golden Dawn, as it has come to be known.[14] The Order was allied to the London branch of the Theosophical Society and yet opposed to it in other ways—a contradiction that is commonly found among occult groups. Curiously enough, the Order expressly forbade experiments in passive psychism. Yet much of the teaching was derived from 'table-turning' and other parlour favourites of the time, so it is impossible not to think there was quite a level of deceit involved.[15] The deceit was continued in various ways long after the ignominious breaking up of the Order of the Golden Dawn into dissident factions, and was magnified by some of its most notorious former members. The latter achieved the notoriety through a strange combining of 'secret societies' with initiatic pretensions and populist propaganda; this was never adopted with much enthusiasm by the French but had great appeal for the British and American public.

---

[13] There were earlier forms of spiritism, thought to have originated within German Masonic groups; these 'secret societies' did not promote their methods but the Fox family, who introduced spiritism to America, were of German origin. In England and America the method of séances is usually called spiritualism, which is a misnomer. See René Guénon, *The Spiritist Fallacy*, Part Two, chapters two and three.

[14] Isis-Urania Lodge was founded in London, 1888; the name 'Golden Dawn' seems to have become attached to the Order in more recent times.

[15] The sheer extent of the deceit involved is revealed in René Guénon's factual book on the subject, *Theosophy: History of a Pseudo-Religion*.

There was much rivalry between different groups of occultists. The power and influence of the Theosophical movement rested on 'Hidden Masters', called 'Secret Chiefs' by the Golden Dawn. These communications were derived from spiritist experiments combined with sheer fantasy and lies—letters or messages supposedly written by such 'Masters' were deliberately faked. However, the 'cause' was powerfully persuasive enough to gain a following that included some very wealthy persons, prepared to provide considerable funds, so it was possible to stage large scale international public events. The speakers would consist of a strange mix of spiritists, occultists and those who, like the Theosophists, aimed to promulgate a 'new world religion' as a cover for certain political aims. One such speaker was Swami Vivekananda, who was among the first of the new breed of Hindu apologists. The upholding of the Theosophical main agenda, however vague, which required belief in reincarnation, evolutionism and scientism, was an article of faith that opened many doors in the way of sponsorship and a credulous following among spiritists.

It then follows that others wanted to join in the lucrative game and out-do the Theosophists.[16] As this may appear overly cynical, it is worth saying that the sincerity of many of the adherents is not in question although one really has to wonder when it comes to some of the leaders of the organisations, who made it quite clear that they considered any means to be justified for the end they had in mind.[17]

We need to look now at how the occultists worked in order to prove their theories, which were perhaps unsurprisingly reflective of the milieu of the times. Although the Golden Dawn and its offshoots strictly forbade, even by dint of oath, any passive involvement in séances or mediumship, it is where their interest in the occult was fired in the first place. It is also quite plain that they continued their spiritist experimentation even while condemning other persons and organisations that did the same! René Guénon has explained much on how spiritists went to work to 'prove' their theories:[18]

---

[16] See Guénon—the evidence was produced by the hands of the fraudulent mediums themselves, for they produced many letters and publications, often with frank disclosures [*ibid*].

[17] As to precisely what that end was, it goes far beyond the present study to provide even an overview and we have to recommend the work already cited above by Guénon, plus *The Spiritist Fallacy*, as these are comprehensive and very thorough.

[18] *The Spiritist Fallacy*, 'The Influence of the Milieu', p. 116.

If such results [for example scientific discoveries] have never been obtained by the mediums it is because, even if they receive an idea in this manner [through a group subconscious ambience], they are incapable of drawing the proper conclusions. All they can do is express it in a more or less ridiculous, almost incomprehensible form, but one which will be enough to excite the admiration of the ignorant among whom spiritism recruits the great majority of its adherents. This explains 'communications' of a scientific or philosophical allure, which the spiritists present as proving the truth of their doctrine when the medium, being either ignorant or unlettered, seems obviously incapable of having invented such things. ... The ideas or mental tendencies of which we speak act somewhat like 'wandering influences', a term so comprehensive as to include in its scope the former as a special class.

Thus it seems that to work a way around the apparently strict rules against passive mediumship that were held by occult organisations by the end of the nineteenth century, members and in particular the leaders of groups would seek to use the services of others that had the mediumistic ability they scarcely if ever possessed themselves. In the case of some of the more notorious charlatans of that era, the medium would be drugged or made drunk (or both) so as to facilitate an even greater degree of 'receptivity'. This was simply to make the medium even more prone to accepting the auto-hypnotic suggestions made by the operator, who kept more or less sober—or at least not so intoxicated as the psychic medium—so as to control the operation and the medium. Thus what was 'received' in this manner was nothing more than a sort of subconscious mirroring of the ideas held in the mind of the operator, or ideas existing in the milieu of the times or of a group, and which the operator or magician wished to prove through what would appear to be supernatural means.[19]

So it is that certain occultists, seeking to out-do their rivals, promulgated the idea of the Guardian Angel as though it were almost something of their own invention, although it is part of the Judaeo Christian tradition. Occultists are passionately anti-traditional and seek every means possible to subvert traditional knowledge so as to replace it with pretended inventions; that is to say, not of their own conception as they wish to make it known but merely part of the milieu of general socialistic and spiritist 'plans for humanity'; they were thus compromised when it came to explaining what they meant exactly by the term 'Holy Guardian Angel'.[20]

---

[19] Thus it can be seen in what manner the 'Great White Lodge' went about its business!

[20] Cf. 'Satanic Inversion of the Angel', *Thunder Perfect Gnosis*.

They planted a trail of obfuscation, in the first place insisting that the Angel was too holy and mystical to be explained; they confused the Guardian Angel with the notion of Secret Chiefs or 'Hidden Masters' that was so successfully used by Madame Blavatsky and others who continued Theosophy after her. An instruction thus came about amidst these pseudo-mystical writings that the Holy Guardian Angel must not be confused with a deity as it was after a different nature and order of things, although precisely what nature and order could not of course be divulged. All this was further confounded by the 'personalisation' of the Guardian Angel, so it was supposed to be unique and special for each individual, which means that effectively such an entity is a kind of 'little helper' that everyone could acquire. This use of the Guardian Angel as a kind of helpful commodity became central to the rather unholy advertising campaign of one charlatan in particular who did not shirk from declaring himself the prophet of a New Aeon and indeed, in his own words, a New World Teacher!

If an Angel of any kind were so particular to an individual then it would have to be in some ways attached to an individuality, which means that it would be no more than a kind of extension of that individuality. This left the field wide open for the psychological mind-programmers to come in later and relegate the whole business to the subconscious mind, which is where they relegate everything of the supernatural order. This is how traditional knowledge becomes mutated and twisted by the profane: an attribute, messenger or function of God becomes no more than an echo of a person's own mind, a product of sheer fantasy or dreaming. Perhaps we should not even be surprised that this has proved to be a very saleable package in some quarters, to the present day.

Having now disposed of some erroneous notions concerning the Guardian Angel, it remains to say something about what that figure is in actuality. The subject has been covered in previous works.[21] However, we have said that the Guardian Angel, far from being an invention of occultists, has always existed in the Judaeo Christian tradition. There is nothing that can be explained or set forth in discursive writing that is 'too holy' to be written of. In fact nothing that is written is in any way holy in itself, as all speech and writing is by its nature secondary or reflected knowledge. The knowledge sought is inexpressible but can be symbolised in form, hieroglyphs or words.

---

[21] See *Nu Hermetica—Initiation and Metaphysical Reality*, pp. 122–137. More specifically, *Way of Knowledge* pp. 45–78.

It will be helpful to give at least one key Christian text and then go on to place the Angel in a cosmological perspective, something almost entirely lacking in those today who develop an interest in such things. According to the book of John,

14: 26 But the Comforter, which is the Holy Ghost, whom the Father will send in my name, he shall teach you all things, and bring all things to your remembrance, whatsoever I have said unto you.

14: 27 Peace I leave with you, my peace I give unto you: not as the world giveth, give I unto you. Let not your heart be troubled, neither let it be afraid.

14: 28 Ye have heard how I said unto you, I go away, and come again unto you. If ye loved me, ye would rejoice, because I said, I go unto the Father: for my Father is greater than I.

14: 29 And now I have told you before it come to pass, that, when it is come to pass, ye might believe.

14: 30 Hereafter I will not talk much with you: for the prince of this world cometh, and hath nothing in me.

Those words reported by John were of Jesus addressing his disciples close to the end, which meant the re-ascension of Christ Jesus and his withdrawal from the earth and the company of men. This 'end' can also symbolise the end of the world or end of time, when all of manifestation is withdrawn in the *mahapralaya* dissolution. It is here clearly explained that the Comforter or Guardian Angel is the Holy Ghost, as it is termed in the Christian tradition, and this Angel is sent in the name of Christ. For, with the departure of the son of God, who is the intermediary between heaven and earth, all men, even the elect or the faithful followers of truth, would descend into utter darkness in the final phase of Kali Yuga that was to come. It is therefore a part of divine ordinance that there should still be a way, even in the darkest hour. For when that hour comes, and the 'prince of the world cometh', which is the System of the Antichrist as known by a few in the present day and age, that ruler of the temporal world, in all its great material wealth and seeming power, has absolutely nothing with the way, the truth and the life; for it knows nothing of it and that truth causes the prince of the world to vanish away to nothing, seeing as that power is ultimately only the power of a great illusion.

There are some who will read this and yet not understand at all, because it is couched here in Christian terms, which are always somewhat offensive to the deeply held prejudices of the modern mentality. For the benefit of those—for it will benefit them if they can think deeply and long upon these matters—we will now put this in the terms of pre-religious Gnosis and traditional Hindu cosmology.

11

There is an Oracle of Isis, called 'oracular' because it is a *shruti* or direct knowledge text as opposed to that which is a product of discursive reason; we presented this previously so will only give part of it here:[22]

I am Pure Being,

And I shine by my own light; I am not Reflection.

Even the light of the Sun is derived from mine, yet to some I am like one single drop of Dew. And this I have given to you.

It is alike and the same

To the knowledge of my Name.

These are the recorded words heard from the Guardian Angel known as Isis, who in other terms is the Mother of God (Horus in this case). Here, Isis assumes the role of intermediary and so the Holy Ghost, which is called Shekinah in Hebrew and Shakti in Sanskrit, as the feminine divine presence and power, is sent from her, in her name.

Pure Being is called Ishvara in Sanskrit, the Lord, or Isani, the Lady, Mahadevi or Mother of the Gods. Properly speaking, it is not being as such, as that is involved with manifestation, but is the principle by which being is able to be produced. That which shines by its own light, not reflective, is the Witness, Atma or Purusha. And this, which we shall call Atma so as not to overcrowd the terms, is the Real that is no different from Brahma supreme. Atma is 'knowable' but even that, which still implies a knower and a thing known, can take many years practice of devotion and yoga concentration of the mind. There is however an intermediary between the supra-human and the individual state, known as *boddhi*, otherwise the higher intellectual intuition, not under any circumstances to be confused with the popular and very much degraded notion of 'intuition'. Even this apprehension of *boddhi* as a meditation 'object' requires that the practitioner be capable of reaching to the pure I-sense, unqualified or conditioned by thought, image, recollection, testimony, inference or any secondary knowledge. That which Isis terms as a 'single drop of Dew' is this *boddhi*, which is as a ray of sunlight. The ray is not the sun itself but by analogy it can produce a reflection in water that is the appearance of the sun. When the thoughts and mind are made absolutely pure then this ray can be perceived as the true source of the individuality, which is a reflection of the real Self or Atma.

---

[22] See *Way of Knowledge*, p. 79.

Herein is the key to the sayings of Christ Jesus given earlier, and the Oracle of Isis and indeed the whole matter of the Guardian Angel. It is given here as explicitly as language allows. That should be sufficient but to be thorough we will quote from our commentary on an ancient Egyptian ritual 'Journey of the Soul' that corresponds to the seasonal rites of Samhain or Halloween every year.

Firstly, one must ascend or pass through the psychic realm, which finds its limit at the 'holy horizon'. The 'flame coming forth in splendour' on the holy horizon is that very 'first light' of a new day, exactly as symbolised by the 'Sun rising above the Waters of Space', which is also figured by the hexagram of water and fire triangles. The Sun in the centre, the spiritual Sun, rises above the lower or inferior waters when we reach the 'centre of all', which is the primordial or 'Heart girt with a Serpent', the abode of the Holy Guardian Angel. For it is only there that the human can even reach or be touched by the solar ray and the spiritual influence. In the Aphorisms of Patañjali this is described in III: 33 as 'First knowledge known as Prātiba, where everything becomes known'. The sage Vyasa commented on the aphorism thus: 'Prātiba, *i.e.* Tāraka knowledge is the state of knowledge before attainment of discriminative knowledge, like the light of dawn preceding the sunrise. By that also, *i.e.* when Prātiba knowledge is attained, the Yogin comes to know everything'.

The Evil Genius

Following the personalisation of the Guardian Angel within the Western Mystery Tradition, another term was used for the Adversary or opposer to spiritual knowledge, namely, the 'Evil Genius'. This seems to have been derived from the Golden Dawn, where the resultant dualism of a 'Higher Genius' and 'Lower Genius' was referred to in lecture papers. The dualistic notion was probably adapted from the theories of German philosophers such as Arthur Schopenhauer, which, as with Blavatsky's Theosophical teachings on the nature of the self, was a distortion of the Eastern doctrines re-invented to suit the Western mentality.

It is not possible to speak of the Evil Genius without dealing at least briefly with its imagined counterpart, the Higher Genius. This, sometimes called 'higher self' by some occultists, is not in any way to be confused with the Guardian Angel that was discussed previously.[23] This term is a corruption of the Atma Self in Hinduism, a corruption that reduces the supra-human principle of the individuality to a mere extension or even a 'development' of that individuality. Some of the worst rubbish imaginable has been said publicly of this Higher Self, including the identification of it with spiritist practices or séances, 'mystical' states, consciousness 'expansion'—the exact opposite of the concentration of mind that is really needed—and 'psychic' training, whereas in fact the Atma is not in any way knowable from the psychic domain, which by its very nature is subject to modifications and determinations of the mental faculties at a relatively gross level.

Both the Higher and Lower Genii figured in the most important ritual of the Golden Dawn, which was to inaugurate a Neophyte by a formal ceremony with all the current members present.[24] Having said this, we should first make it clear that we are not intending here to deny the potential efficacy of the ritual when it is done with proper knowledge and understanding. It contains universal and traditional elements, especially in the adaptation called *Phoenix*.[25]

---

[23] See 'Shadow of the Wings'.

[24] This 'introduction' was later transposed as a ritual for the initiation to the first degree proper by some dissident factions, in which case it was either done with two officers only or was worked on by the Neophyte in private. The 'current members' are those who know the Order password, which is changed seasonally or periodically so as to exclude any excommunicants or those who have lapsed in their obligations.

[25] See *The Phoenix and other Stellar Rites of Initiation*.

Central to the Neophyte ritual, which is formularised as 'light descending in darkness', was the part when the Neophyte was sworn in by oath. At this juncture, a monstrous form of the Adversary was seen (by the operators) as arising from the base of the cubical altar. This was immediately trodden down by the hierophant or officiant, who literally stamped his foot to reinforce the intention, replacing the hybrid form Omoo Szathan with that of the Egyptian God of Silence, Harpocrates.[26] The idea is that this moment poses a critical point in the life of the candidate for initiation; for we must choose by our own will to put the darkness and ignorance of the profane world behind us. All the fears and doubts of the candidate thus rise up at this moment and threaten to undo the operation. He naturally lacks the strength to overcome this antagonism himself, for he is veritably a beginner on the path, symbolically taking the first stumbling steps; the hierophant thus takes the part of intermediary on his behalf and supresses the reaction by sheer force of will. At least that is the ideal; in practice where such ritual is used there is rarely any preparation as will be demanded within a real initiatic organisation. Those who have experience of the operation of initiatic rituals know very well that a person may swear a mighty oath, pass through the gates of such a ritual, and at a later date quit the path through inability to relinquish or even recognise egotism, or otherwise holding to the anti-spiritual ideals of the 'worldly wise'—and that really amounts to the same thing. In such cases obviously no initiation can take place; if the seeds were cast then they were cast on stony ground.[27]

The Eight Limbs of Yoga precepts of the Patañjali aphorisms are more than enough to frighten adventurer's away from initiation, to go hot-foot in search of some counterfeit that may be gained with far less trouble.[28] Only a person suffering the utmost delusion arising from ignorance would imagine that simply performing a ritual or participating in one could wipe out all the afflictions, which are called *kléshas* in Sanskrit. In fact, if we take the Adversary—even a personal one—as a composite of all that opposes spiritual realisation, then this includes more even than the afflictions held in common with all men. For example, there are *karmasayas*, ongoing actions of past deeds, and countless mental impressions retained by the memory, some of them harmful to the path.

---

[26] See p. 29 *Phoenix* [ibid] for the description of Omoo Szathan (the name is transliterated from Coptic).

[27] See Matthew 13: 20–22 for the Parable of the Sower.

[28] See 'The Eight Limbs of Yoga', *Thunder Perfect Gnosis*.

While such a ritual as has been referred to offers for most persons only a 'virtual' initiation, it can nonetheless be made effective if the candidate is a recipient for real spiritual influence, such as is figured in the symbolism.[29] In reality all this takes time, exactly as it does with the inner alchemy of traditional spiritual yoga. And yet it is surprising, given the warnings that exist in literature, that many will come to this expecting some miracle to take place that requires little or no effort from their selves. This is all the more so with what are described as 'magical' organisations. Desire for a real change in the being that can come about as if 'by magic' is rarely admitted by tyros but if the notion is nonetheless there, whether realised or not, it will certainly amount over time to a formidable bar to real initiation ever taking place no matter what rituals have been done. The devil is a master of disguises.

It is clear from the Neophyte ritual context that the Evil Genius is a name for a collection of afflictions—all the doubts and fears that assail one who seeks the truth—and that is assuming they really want truth, given that it always contradicts any ideas or imaginings one might have previously held; the real difficulty is that some afflictions pass by completely unnoticed by today's practitioners, who may not even recognise them as afflictions given that the corresponding mental states are considered normal, or even worthy of admiration, by the profane world. Taking what has been said as a workable definition of the Evil Genius, there is no entity involved as such, and the Evil Genius is in no way any part of the Self or even the creature 'self' or ego-sense. It is a collection of errors and as such is no more than a phantasm that vanishes as soon as the Sun of the spiritual Self arises—if the practitioner should be so blessed with perseverance, faith, strength and endurance.

It follows that if the personalisation of the Guardian Angel is a false notion, or at least an error coming about through gross over-simplification, then the Evil Genius is likewise a personalisation of Satan. The primary error is to imagine the Guardian Angel as having an opposite—there is no duality in the spiritual world. But once it is made personal it becomes something other than what it truly is; the whole matter enters duality and so we have this personalised evil. It is very divisive to the soul, though, so long as this is in any way thought to be the Self.

---

[29] This also requires that the organisation can transmit such an influence.

16

The difficulty with the personalisation of these two seeming 'entities', Angel and Devil, is that attachment follows. And certainly, given how the mentality of most people goes to work on such things, if the Guardian Angel becomes a 'desirable object', as though it is something that one could possess, the Evil Genius can easily become a useful scapegoat for all perceived shortcomings. While the harmful impressions of the mind arising from dormancy will always take one by surprise, thus giving a semblance of an autonomous and ever-present intelligence, the only intelligence is that of the afflicted, who is able to cognise such impressions and associate feelings such as pleasure or pain to them, thus forming attachment.[30]

There is no equivalent for an Evil Genius in the Hindu doctrines, which is perhaps rather telling. Quite often the Evil Genius is written off by 'occult scholars' and the like as 'the ego', which is a very vague term usually used nowadays for the errors or vices of the self. The Sanskrit *ahankara* equivalent is simply the sense of 'me', which does not necessarily carry any negative associations unless from the point of view of *paramatma*; even then, one who truly knows *paramatma* (in the way of direct knowledge) has transcended *ahankara* as well as all notions of good and evil that afflict the soul. The Hindu doctrines include the *asuras* or demons, and these, in a way similar to the 'war in heaven' and subsequent fall in most if not all traditions, began as *devas* (or 'angels') but became drunk and fought among themselves. Those *devas* unaffected by the poisons threw the *asuras* from the top of mount Meru. They fell all the way to the bottom and were unable to rise again. The *asuras* signify all afflictions such as lust, anger and greed and yet they are in no way 'personal demons'— a term quite often used in ordinary parlance and a kind of oxymoron in a way, for anger, fear and so forth might influence the person but they are hardly 'personal', and in fact they are better understood once they are realised as truly *impersonal* forces. Through attachment, the person may identify with them, but that is the error of ignorance that is spoken of exhaustively in Advaitan texts and commentaries.

It seems that the notion of an Evil Genius has its uses, especially in ritual, but it is a blanket term for something only described in detail in the *Yoga-Sutras*, covering hundred of pages, and that also requires a knowledgable teacher in order to practice and understand correctly. A practitioner should exercise caution, therefore, in using the term and bringing it into his practice without knowledge.

---

[30] See Part Two, *Thunder Perfect Gnosis*, on the yoga of Patañjali.

Reincarnationism

Reincarnation is an entirely modern invention. It consists of the theory that individuals are reborn in a succession of earthly lives for perpetuity, following a historical time-line. Reincarnation has been falsely ascribed to the Hindu doctrines, whereas it simply does not exist there. It has been used to explain metempsychosis and the transmigration of souls as also found in other traditions, for example the Orphic Mysteries and the ancient Egyptian tradition. The notion has become so deeply ingrained one might say that it is by now embedded at a deep stratum of modern thinking. Reincarnation is accepted without question and even if not believed, is falsely ascribed to all ancient civilisations and what are typically and insultingly called 'ancient beliefs' by those supposed to be experts in such studies.

The term 'reincarnation' thus frequently appears, and without any explanation, in commentaries and translations of Vedic source texts—the latter being all the more possible owing to the fact that translations from Sanskrit to English are necessarily more in the way of paraphrasing; a literal translation makes no more sense than the Egyptological renderings of the ancient Egyptian Pyramid Texts and others. Reincarnationism was originally unique to modern Europe until it spread to America and Britain and from there to the world. In the first half of the nineteenth century French Socialists, who sought an explanation for social inequality, persuaded Allan Kardac, the founder of the French School of Spiritism, to accept their theory of souls being born into a succession of lives taking place in the same 'world' following a time-line through 'history'.[31] The Spiritists made a dogma of reincarnation. They extended the notion from inequality of social conditions to include even physical and intellectual inequality. Given the pervasive moralistic tendencies of socialistic thinking, it is perhaps hardly surprising that the reincarnation theory implied the punishment for wrong-doing in past lives being carried over to the present. In more recent times this notion has been modified by its adherents so that the progression of lives is compared to life seen as a 'classroom', learning 'lessons' along the way and improving always; this is of course reflective of the academic background of many of today's alternative therapists and entrepreneurial healers, who go so far as to attach 'spirituality' to what they do.

---

[31] A detailed account of this is given in *The Spiritist Fallacy*, René Guénon, Part Two, Chapter Six.

The Theosophists took the notion from the Spiritists (also called spiritualists in America and Britain)—a collection of groups involved with séances, who believed they were in communication with the 'spirits' of deceased human beings. The Theosophists developed this idea, little known at the time, alongside two others of their own invention and now common among neo-spiritualists: Evolutionism, based on popular scientism and 'progress', and a completely false idea of Hindu *karma*—a word that only means 'action' but to which the Theosophists ascribed sentimental moralist valuations, which they pushed to the level of total absurdity. Reincarnation, evolution and 'karma' became veritable articles of faith within the movement, and they wasted no time in working tirelessly, using every means at their disposal, to spread the propaganda. The campaign has been remarkably successful.

The theory, in essence, rests on the absurdity of the ideal of equality, which inevitably rests on all being the same, which is a natural impossibility. While today's version of the theory insists that equality is about 'respecting the differences' between people, it also insists ferociously that all people must accept the same ideals and values, which then automatically suppresses real individuality and most especially, all traditional civilisation. The idea of 'progress' built into this presupposes that one must accept every new scientific theory and its applications as inevitable and necessary, however destructive that may be. In the present times we see compulsion now brought to a level that can only be described as totalitarian.

The fallacy of reincarnation can easily be shown. There must be a starting point for the projected 'evolution' of lives but if the starting point is not the same for all, so that some men have passed through more lives than others and have made more 'progress', then this is an injustice, and so the theory itself has inequality built in to it. Further, if the differences between people are accepted, then there must have been a point somewhere in the supposed evolution where inequality was begun, which must have a cause. Given that the cause is put down to actions done previously then an explanation is required as to how they behaved differently in the first place. Self-contradiction is implicit in the theory for if perfect equality was the rule then people would be alike in every way. For inequality to come about then the potential for it must have pre-existed latently within the person, thus they were not equal from the very beginning.

The point of view accepts, necessarily, that there are inequalities between species in nature while other differences are not seen in that way. Therefore some inequalities are acceptable while others are not. No being is exactly like any other being in nature, and so to question the equality of beings is to question the difference, which is absurd. So long as there is a multiplicity of beings then there must be as much difference, otherwise beings would comprise a single entity. To see injustice in this is to superimpose sentimental or arbitrary moral concerns on reality. There is no injustice, in fact, in the truth of the matter, which is that each being carries its own possibilities within itself, as inherent in its own nature. According to René Guénon,

> The notion of justice stripped of its sentimental and specifically human character is in fact that of equilibrium and harmony in the universe [that is to say, all manifestation taken as totality]. Now, in order that there be total harmony in the universe it is necessary and sufficient that each being occupy its proper place as an element in the universe in conformity with its own nature. And this means precisely that the differences and inequalities which one is pleased to denounce as real or apparent injustices necessarily and effectively contribute to this total harmony. And this total harmony cannot but be; to wish it otherwise would be to suppose that things are not what they are, for it would be an absurdity to think that something can happen with a creature that is not a consequence of its own nature [that is to say, the moral and sentimental view that it must come about from the result of past actions].[32]

Total harmony is total possibility and it is in fact unjust to steal this away from people, as is now happening everywhere in the world.[33] One of the many damaging consequences of reincarnationism is that it has been used to interpret the Hindu doctrines, even though reincarnation has never had a place within them. It is not only a misinterpretation but also an obscuration—carried out with relentless thoroughness, so that even those who have read the modern language translations of Hindu texts would be astonished to learn that reincarnation is simply not there. Reincarnation supposes that a being has previously been embodied and upon death takes a new body, returning to the same state it has already passed through. This is not in any way the same as transmigration, which is part of Eastern doctrine and is found in other traditions. Transmigration involves a change of state in the being; it is a passage to completely other worlds of existence, not returning to the same one.

---

[32] *The Spiritist Fallacy*, p. 172.
[33] See 'Uniformity against Unity', *Thunder Perfect Gnosis*.

By different states (Sanskrit *avasthā*) is meant entirely different conditions than those of the commonly accepted human world, though in the Hindu doctrine 'man' can adopt different forms in different worlds or through the Cosmic Cycles—these forms differing because they do not have the same spatial or bodily parameters that are defined by the terrestrial ones. This is held in common with all ancient traditions and not only the Hindu one; for example, the Orphic and the Egyptian. A being cannot have two existences in the corporeal world when considered in its fullest extent and this applies equally to any supposed existence on another planet or a distant star system—the corporeal world is not limited to earth but is a very particular state of being. There is no repetition in the universe, and it might as well be noted here that the monstrous 'eternal recurrence' of the philosopher Nietzsche was a purely imagined theory, resting on his incomprehension of Eastern texts.[34]

From a metaphysical point of view, universal and total possibility is infinite and must include all, leaving nothing outside of itself. There is no repetition in infinity, which would otherwise be limited and so not infinite. Repetition can only take place in a finite grouping or 'set' (as in mathematics), and even those elements could not be absolutely identical.[35] There are no closed cycles in the universe when seen as absolute totality—an identical possibility would be the same possibility. This concords with the Hindu doctrine, where for anything to exist (to emerge from undifferentiated *prakriti*) it must have at least one change in characteristic.

The human individuality includes the gross and subtle states of form and there is no return to these states; yet it is these states that the Spiritists and subsequent reincarnation theorists are exclusively concerned with. To return to this world would mean never leaving it. To quote René Guénon once more,

> Nothing can ever return to the same point, even in a system that is only indefinite (and not infinite), as for example the corporeal world. While tracing a circle, for example, a displacement is effected and the circle is not closed except in an entirely illusory manner.[36]

---

[34] Nietzsche took years working up 'eternal recurrence' in notebooks before tagging it into his *Thus Spake Zarathustra*, in an attempt to fill the vacuum left by his general theory, which itself rested on a negation of Christianity.
[35] The Zermelo–Fraenkel 'set theory' is used in modern mathematics.
[36] *The Spiritist Fallacy*, p. 180.

The hub of much common confusion over the 'cycle of births', in common with all ancient traditions, rests to a certain extent then on metaphysical incomprehension. A cycle of births does not mean returning to the same state and can be regarded as both macrocosmic and microcosmic. For example, there are cosmic cycles, which from our point of view look like great aeons of time, and which can be understood analogously not as closed circles, as in a sphere with a central point, but as open spirals. There can be no closed system.[37] It is naturally likewise on the microcosmic scale, where there can be countless births without ever returning to the same state. The states of being in their multiplicity, as with the cyclical manifestation of the worlds of being, which we see as 'cycles of time', are simultaneous in reality and may be viewed in this way as well as a succession, relative to the human point of view. Time is only a condition of one of these states, viz., the human state; duration only takes place in some of them, so succession is best understood as symbolic rather than actual.

A further distortion rests on confusions of metempsychosis, where it has been supposed, owing to a misunderstanding of the analogies used in Hindu and other texts, that a man or other being will pass through forms of life such as mineral to vegetable, to animal and then human, a notion that was also formed from the popular evolutionist theories. The true doctrine is that an individual, when taken in its entirety, already includes all the possibilities of terrestrial life forms, though not in the physical sense. Thus reincarnationists have seen ancient texts and superimposed the theories they already want to prove, and which have nothing to do with the sources they use as 'evidence' of the same theories. The Spiritists, who developed reincarnationism in the first place, failed to understand—or did not want to understand—that metempsychosis means that after death fragmented components, physical or psychic, may form other bodies, but these elements do not in any way constitute a human being, whether that is called 'soul' or 'spirit'.

There is more to be said on metempsychosis, which along with transmigration is the fundamental basis of ancient teaching on the cycle of births. The word is rarely if ever used in translations, however, though it is frequently alluded to in the texts, including the Yoga-Sutras. Following death, the psychic elements in man are dispersed and it is possible for them to enter other living beings, whether human or animal, in the same way that the elements of the physical body dissolve and some of these serve to form other bodies.

---

[37] One must study René Guénon's The Multiple States of Being and The Symbolism of the Cross to gain a complete idea of all that is implied here.

The real being, its imperishable, immutable essence, cannot be in any way affected by the mutation of the aforesaid psychic elements. It is these dissociated psychic remnants that sometimes occur as the phenomena thought by Spiritists to constitute whole human beings, which they call 'spirits'. Thus reincarnation rests on a confusion of two distinctly separate aspects of ancient teaching, metempsychosis and transmigration, in which they perceive no difference. The psychic elements may include the mental images that are retained in the memory, and which are sensorial impressions. Such faculties are formed by attachment to the corporeal state and are perishable, and not in any way immortal. Memory itself is a defining characteristic of the corporeal state as it is allied to time, which is a conditioning factor of the human. The transmission of psychic elements to another being still living can take place. This also occurs in the ordinary way of hereditary line; as physical characteristics are normally passed on to children from their parents, so are psychic characteristics. Guénon defines these phenomena as 'physical seed' and 'psychic seed'. The psychic elements when latent in the subconscious are also what are called 'latent impressions' in the Hindu doctrines, and these can even be passed across cycles of birth. Such characteristics may find outward expression or remain dormant until activated by something, be it a memory, circumstance and so forth.[38]

Anti-spiritual forces can make use of these dissociated psychic elements. For example, in recent times mass hypnotism through technological means has been successfully employed to implement sweeping social, economic and financial agendas under the pretext of 'health and safety', which operates on the base level of the survival instinct. Once the threat—even a continual threat that changes in its form—finds its sympathetic ground in the subconscious of a whole people, almost any other suggestion will be accepted as the condition of that collective mind has been weakened; compliance is made easy.[39]

---

[38] See Part Two, 'Transmutation'.

[39] During the lock-step strategy, radically and visibly implemented between 2020 to 2022, 'war' conditions were made use of without the necessity of an actual war, which would have been financially unsupportable at that time. There was much use made of helicopters, continually patrolling civilian areas where no real threat existed; memories of the Second World War were evoked by various means, including the propaganda used by all sides in that war. Even though only a tiny minority of the populace remembered that war from direct experience, the psychic elements subsisted across generations and the fear of 'plague' was enough to re-activate them.

Posterity is the pseudo-immortality of the ordinary person, or the person without knowledge, and which constitutes the great majority in the present times. Nothing of the individual being is truly 'passed on' to future generations, only physical and psychic dissociated parts. In fact most persons by now can only imagine immortality in terms of posterity, seeing in this a kind of prolongation of their self.

Rarely, a considerable collection of dissociated psychic elements can be transferred from a deceased person to a living being, and this can convey the illusion of reincarnation.[40] This is one reason why the use of funerary rites with proper religious foundation has always been, until very recent times, considered so important. It was known by the ancients that prevention of haunting and other kinds of phenomena could only be ensured by the correct procedures being observed. It has become increasingly the case in secular societies that there is a total abandonment of all religious factors, and only some form of remembering the person as they were when living is carried out. This does not only leave the field wide open for the transmission of dissociated psychic elements to the living, which can lead to all sorts of morbid and other ill consequences, but also encourages it, as the whole concentration of the congregation is placed on the recollection of the same dissociated psychic elements or memories. While religious rites, notably Christian ones, allowed the first part of a service to include a memorial, it was not for a long time framed in sentimental terms and was superseded by the doctrine of salvation and the recollection, instead of that of the person's life, of the life of Christ Jesus, so that participation in his resurrection might remain a possibility. Thus the traditional funerary rites act directly upon the psychic elements in question. The abandonment of orthodox funeral rites is already having very far-reaching consequences but the real cause of such malign resultants will never be suspected.

The ancients never envisaged such a thing as reincarnation but in order to convey certain ideas that are beyond normal imagining—for example we can only imagine other states of being as somehow modelled on terrestrial life—symbolism and analogy is used that can easily be misconstrued. Ancient teaching on cycles of birth always amounts to either transmigration or metempsychosis, and once this is understood then the meaning of the texts becomes clear—though the reincarnationists will never accept this.

---

[40] One most notable case is that of Dorothy Eady and it is perhaps equally notable that Eady herself always denied that reincarnation was involved. See *Omm Sety's Egypt*, Hanny el Zeini and Catherine Dees [St. Lynne's Press].

Unconscious Spiritism

Spiritism, or 'spiritualism' as it came to be known in Britain and America, continues to flourish and spread its evil influence long after René Guénon wrote his very substantial work, *The Spiritist Fallacy*, exposing the total absurdity of spiritist doctrines. One might have thought that spiritism would be scarcely as popular today as it was at the time when Guénon felt it imperative to warn of the dangers, for at that time the proliferation of the practices rode on the back of the occult revival and early formation of neo-spiritualism. It was quite shocking then to learn that there are no fewer than twelve 'Spiritualist Churches', one even calling itself Christian, in our local vicinity—and that only includes such groups as have registered or publicly declared their activities.

Spiritist propaganda permeates the most surprising domains. For one example alone, an academic work bears the title *All Catholics are Spiritualists*, a monstrous lie based on complete ignorance of what spiritism really involves, not to mention ignorance—perhaps wilful— of Catholic doctrine and practice.[41] The fact that even the title of the book is extremely anti-Catholic is probably not even recognised by those who manage such things. The position of the Catholic Church, in fact, has always been identical to our own, and that should be enough to prove there is not a 'religiose' or even a moralistic side to the condemnation of spiritism. The Church has never denied the phenomena involved but sees its source in diabolical forces, as opposed to what the spiritists fondly imagine to be departed relatives and 'loved ones' calling from beyond the grave. The problem is not that diabolical forces exist, or that such can produce a wide range of phenomena through willing human mediums; the problem is with the practice of spiritism itself.

It is not the intention here to even summarise Guénon's thorough refutal of spiritism, based on expert doctrinal knowledge, hundreds of testimonies from the spiritists themselves in their own words, and his own unique insights into the practices. It must suffice to say here that the absurd and dangerous notions that form the doctrine of spiritism are purely a modern invention.[42]

---

[41] Mary Gove Nichols and Thomas Low Nichols, Cambridge University Press— published on the Internet 30th July 2018.
[42] Dating from 1848. See 'Shadow of the Wings'.

There is no real purpose to spiritist practices other than mawkish curiosity and sentiment combined with serious ignorance; the fact that 'anyone' can learn it or participate accounts for the popularity with the uneducated.[43] The phenomena produced by mediums is real enough, as recognised by the Church, and it was the fascination with any kind of phenomena whatsoever in the nineteenth century that drove the spiritist cause—a cause put forward with fanatical enthusiasm.

There is no real or true relation between spiritism and magick, or at least the relation historically was due to unsavoury alliances formed between co-conspirators in the anti-traditional cause rather than in the doctrines or practices, apart from the indulgences of some of the early founders of organisations such as the Golden Dawn and some of the later dissident offshoots.[44] Spiritists believe, with an unnatural ardour, that they are in communication with 'spirits' of the dead, which is an impossibility that is not in any way supported by any ancient or traditional doctrine. What they are really in touch with is very complex but can owe to metempsychosis, which is not in any way known or understood by spiritists, and what can best be described as degraded psychic remnants of former human beings— such remnants are perpetuated by the practices, whereas in the normal case they would not persist long.[45]

There are also what Guénon terms 'wandering influences', which can amount to artificial thought-forms (elementars) created for the most part unintentionally from the minds of individuals or a group. It is for this reason that when the messages, usually of an incoherent nature, are 'received', they nearly always reflect exactly the intentions of those who lead the groups and exert control over the mediums. In spiritist circles anything whatsoever is eagerly accepted without discernment so long as it provides some material phenomenal effect or 'voice' that can be relayed by the medium.

---

[43] The history of spiritism or of the Spiritualists proves that the movement was always popular with uneducated persons, to the extent of being semi-literate. Some early exponents of the movement had not even read the Bible, yet this did not prevent them from putting forward a strongly anti-religious outlook. Nonetheless some scientists and clergymen were persuaded—so by 'uneducated' we can include a very narrow, modern schooling.

[44] The mediumism of Rose Crowley that produced the 'Book of the Law' in Cairo, 1904, was a result of the application of both spiritist and occult techniques. Her subsequent nervous collapse was no doubt due to it. There were many hundreds of cases of madness, death and illness among spiritists at the time Guénon wrote his book on the subject.

[45] See 'Reincarnationism'.

26

It is a completely passive mode of operation, where human beings place themselves under the control of *sub-infra* forces, some of which are not a great deal unlike the Spirits of the *Goetia*, the evocation of which traditionally requires utmost care and a great deal of technical knowledge.[46] Those who control the spiritist operations are themselves controlled by forces of which they know nothing at all, since their doctrine is complete fiction.

However, the purpose of this present writing is not to expose the perilous practices of spiritists but to draw attention to what might best be termed 'unconscious spiritism'. As said before, the occultist or magician should properly speaking be far removed from any such practices, which involve no real knowledge of anything. Magick at the very least requires ordinary knowledge of principles—or it should do. But today the situation is even more degraded than it was, say, a century ago. Some of the larger organisations founded on the works of relatively modern charlatans permit almost anything, at least among the practitioners at the lower levels of their system. There has been a general and insidious merging of the occult with some things that would normally be seen as pure fantasy, or sub-genres in the pop music world such as 'Gothic Witchcraft'. Over time these have increasingly joined forces with some of the most perverted factions of our deeply sick society, and this kind of thing has gained a modicum of respect in the world of art and graphic design.

It would not be at all surprising then to learn that what passes for magick and occultism can rub shoulders with spiritism of one kind or another. The influences extend with multiple tentacular grasping in every direction, while the real source of suicides, madness, death and disease is never suspected. This, which we know to be a fact, when combined with the readiness of individuals with almost total lack of any knowledge to take on operational procedures and even to guide other fools, means that whether phenomena is produced by magick or not, unconscious spiritism can be at work. Thus, the 'wandering influences' that are the source of spiritist phenomena can attach themselves to the participants in occult experiments with a deadly and fulminating effect, all the more so because the real nature of the forces involved remains completely unknown to the gullible—even when the latter includes those who proclaim knowledge they most certainly do not possess.

---

[46] Nonetheless, anyone that had real knowledge in the metaphysical sense would never wish to perform an evocation of infernal forces; the use of ceremonial evocation was always something of an anomaly.

There is little if anything we can do to prevent diabolism from gaining an increasing foothold in today's world but to be vigilant and to know the real facts. Those who fall victim to such practices usually do so out of their own will and nothing can be done to 'improve' them in the moralistic sense or even to help them at all while that is the case. The best advice is to stay well away from those who practice such odious pursuits. They will not listen to reason, which they are in fact opposed to in every way. It is plain enough from the historical evidence of the spiritist movement that the founders were strongly opposed, sometimes expressing hatred, to anything of even the most ordinary intellectual nature unless it was conventional science, which they sought to harness in the form of pseudo-science.

Psychic Residues and Symbolic Weapons

Psychic residues are known to permeate ancient sacred sites or 'centres' that have been long abandoned, their legitimate purpose completely forgotten so that anything written down or said about them is pure supposition.[47] The same can also be said for statues and even small figures. As we are entering an area that is very little understood today, it will be helpful to quote from the Hermetic scripture known as the Prophecy of Hermes. This is thought to date from the 2nd century and consists of four chapters from the Perfect Sermon.[48] Before the discourse enters sacred ground, Hermes speaks against the profane or uninitiated:

> The knowledge of the immortal nature is conveyed only to a few. These are chosen through the devotion of their heart. Still, of the rest, the vicious folk, we ought to say no word, for fear that our sacred sermon should be spoiled by even thinking of them.

While some could easily take the last few words as figurative, the power of thought to shape the mind and the minds of others is taken as understood. So it is in fact meant quite literally. The word 'vicious' was well chosen by the translator, because it has an etymological association with 'vice'.[49] The same word 'vicious' is sometimes used in translations of Hindu sacred texts. The exact meaning of the word is 'in place of', that is, a substitute or superimposition. In the *Yoga-Sutras* this is called *viparyaya*, 'false cognition' by covering what is real with something unreal or imagined. This is, in effect, a kind of poisoning or pollution of the mind as it prevents the mind from cognising a real thing or a truth. For this reason every ritual begins with some kind of symbolic banishing away of profane influences to clear the ground so that a spiritual influence is even possible. When the discourse turns to statues, by which is meant specifically the large and small figures of Gods in the temples, which to the ancient Egyptians were not Gods but *neteru*, 'principles', even Asclepius the initiate is without comprehension.

---

47 René Guénon first used the term 'psychic residues' to explain degraded former spiritual centres of influence. See *The Reign of Quantity and the Signs of the Times*, chapter 27 [Sophia Perennis].
48 See *Nu Hermetica*, 'Prophecy of Hermes'.
49 Latin *vitiosus*, from *vitium* 'vice'.

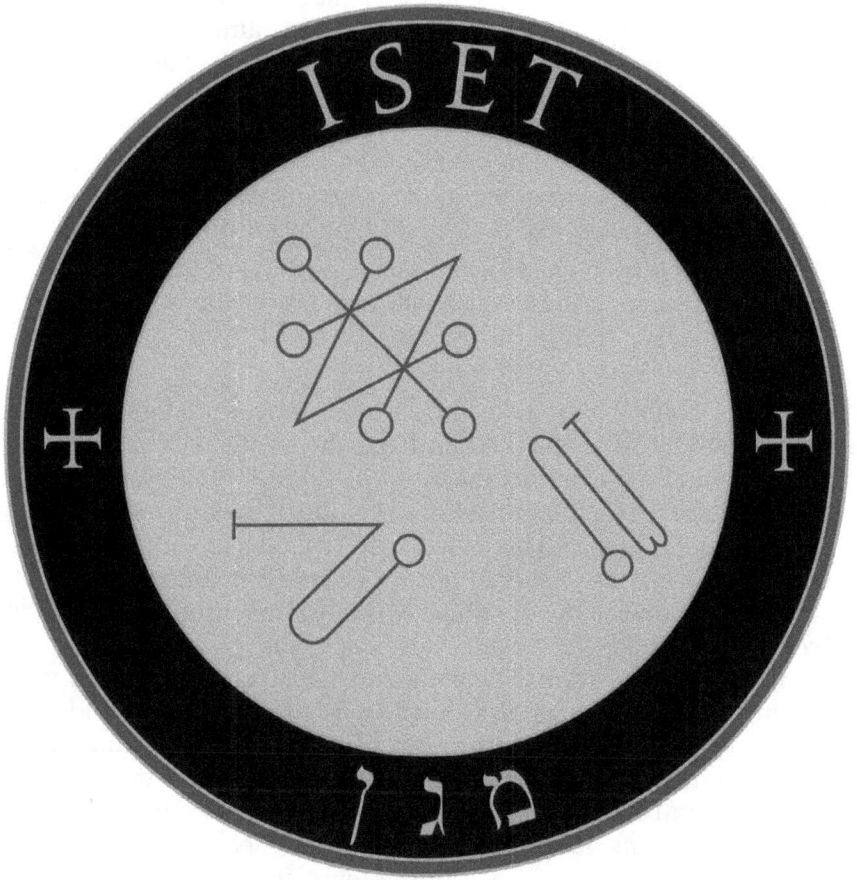

Reverse side of a talisman depicting the Intelligence and Spirit of Saturn

By that time what was once common or ordinary knowledge was fast being forgotten or relegated to the field of esotericism. In fact at that time initiatic rites were often continued not on mountains or in temples but in caves or subterranean labyrinths. This was not only to protect from physical intrusion but also to shield off the rites and the places from malefic forces in the Age of Kali Yuga.

> As the Most High God created the Gods in Heaven, so man is the maker of the gods who, in the temples, allow all to approach, and who not only have light of blessing poured on them, but who also send forth their light on all; thus the devotee does not only go forward towards the Gods but also confirms the Gods on earth.

> Are you surprised, o Asclepius? I see that you—even you!—do not believe.

Now we begin to construe the nature and origin of psychic residues. As the figures receive the light of blessing, the gods in the temples pour forth their light upon all who approach them. Once again, the use of a word, 'light' in this case, is not figurative. Neither is it literal but in Hermetic writings light does not signify that emitted by the Sun or a lamp, but rather a special kind of intelligence, and so it is a technical term.

While the word 'transmission' is used to denote such a ray being sent and received, thought or 'mind' does not occupy space. What is being described owes much more to a likeness or similitude that subsists in the mind of the recipient. We have already said that cognition shapes the mind; it makes a sort of mould or receptacle that can be filled with that which is alike, and which is frequently compared with either fire or liquid.[50] When a cognition is held in the memory it is called a latent impression, for it rests dormant until recollected, when it once more has the power to move or influence. Thus such impressions may be helpful (to spiritual practice) or harmful. Now if a recollection is often evoked then its power is strengthened. It is only by the practice of yoga and discriminative knowledge that harmful impressions are weakened and helpful ones strengthened. We can compare this intellective process with what takes place over time with statues, temples and places. Through repeated use, especially over very long ages in time, there is a build up of what can best be termed as 'forces'.

---

[50] In alchemical or sacred texts, for example.

31

When knowledge is lost or forgotten, traces nonetheless subsist as an imprint or invisible footprint even in physical objects. It will be explained how a once helpful and benevolent influence can become degraded and evil in times of great ignorance. But firstly there is a difficulty in the discussion that must be resolved, owing to the very loss of knowledge previously mentioned. With all this talk of thought and mind, it is too easy for those with a conventional education to relegate all of it to the realms of psychological process. That is not in any way even near to what is meant here as intellective process. Psychological thought cannot admit to intelligence that is beyond the human reason or what it terms the 'subconscious', a theoretical term of very ordinary convenience, and that relegates everything of the spiritual realm to a degree more inferior than reason, whereas in fact the spiritual is far beyond the reasoning and other faculties that are adjunct to the mind. For this reason the word 'forces' is used; while language is imperfect to express metaphysical truth, by choosing words carefully we can at least avoid some unnecessary errors.

We can also put it like this: no one will dispute the existence of, say, a church building. It is made of stones or bricks, wood and other materials. But if someone with technical knowledge remarks that the church is consecrated—and so might be subject to desecration—we begin to lose the attention of the 'ordinary person', through more or less total incomprehension of the meaning. At best, the person may think consecration owes to something psychological or otherwise imagined. Even if they admit that such an imagining might have power attached to it, their belief in psychology limits this very strictly to human feelings and emotions, which are *emotive*, but which only lead further away from the real source of perception. Psychology is a theoretical system composed of false cognitions, in which everything is sourced back to the individual, each according to his own, as though the soul was a self-contained unit. Spiritual reality is utterly denied as it can only be seen as that which originates in the psyche. Unless the person is capable of admitting the possibility even of the *supernatural* that is not an adjunct of individual minds or what is termed 'belief', they will never understand what we have to say here and they are in fact the vicious ones referred to by Hermes, for all they know is in fact a superimposition upon the real and a rejection of all traditional doctrine.

Supposing a drunk wanders into a temple, perhaps one of those great stone-built Indian palaces built to the honour and glory of God in one of the countless names of God, such as Kali. The drunk begins to shout or behave in a lewd or otherwise disgusting manner. Sooner or later the attention of the guards will be drawn by the noise and they will seize the drunk, carry him out a long way from the temple precinct and hurl him into a ditch. They might even beat him up a little bit to teach him a lesson. When the guards return they will inform the priests so the place is cleaned up then libations poured, prayers recited to Kali and fresh offerings made of incense, flowers, water and unguents. It is fully understood that a temple can be consecrated and re-consecrated as necessary following some violation. While the feelings of the guards might have been outraged, human emotions are by no means at all the limit of what is taking place here, and in fact are no more than contingent or circumstantial.

Now we can go further into how it is that a spiritual centre may transmit a helpful or a harmful influence, and that if it is abandoned and its rites forgotten, the psychic residue subsists though it tends to become degraded for all sorts of reasons. In modern times ancient centres will often become part of the tourism industry. Shops and recreational facilities are built nearby or even adjacent or *inside* the ancient buildings. Those who visit are for the most part merely curious; they want to photograph themselves in these places and let their friends see it; they are unaware of any influence of a supra-human or infra-human nature. They pay more attention to their cell phones and camera equipment than they pay to the place and what they 'see' is for the greater part no more than a virtual electronic representation.

Thus the *viparyaya* 'superimposition' is carried forward from mind to physical activity and from there to representation twice or three times removed even from the concrete fact of existence, let alone any subtle reality. There is worse than this for such a place can have an effect comparable to a condenser or capacitor, and where at one time it had what might be called built-in insulation, owing to various rites and practices, in the present time that will not be the case. Any harmful consequences will not of course ever be realised as owing to the juxtaposition of ignorance with a complex bank of powerful but invisible forces.

A further, more modern example applies to many churches today, where custodians have either succumbed to pressure from the church authorities to develop the use of the places as sources of revenues or are themselves simply ignorant as any man in the street. It is sadly quite common now to visit a church and find that a café has been established in one corner complete with jazz music. Such music has nothing sacrilegious about it as such but it is wholly against the spirit of the place that was previously built up over centuries of prayers, hymns and rites including baptism, weddings and funerals. The profane is here brought right into the heart of what was once sacred. And there are even worse things permitted than small cafés with secular music to help customers pass the time without any thought at all of spiritual things. Churches can be hired for adult parties and children's recreational activities, all of which involve a great deal of noise and confusion. The subtle fabric of the prayers, hopes and aspirations of the centuries, is shattered. That Light of the Intelligible alluded to previously is then replaced with the glare of electronic confusion and noisome babble. Even when the church is empty and not out for hire, walking into its space no longer conveys tranquility; yet it is not simply an absence of presence, there can even be an accumulation of 'positive evil' that might be detected by a sense of emptiness and despair, for example, or otherwise confused thoughts entering the mind for no apparent reason. It does not stop there, however, for an old building conveys its influence to the surrounding locality, though the source of disturbance will never be suspected.

The same considerations apply, on a smaller scale, with all kinds of magical or consecrated talismans including statues, figures and symbolic weapons. This is being referred to artefacts of recent make and use, not the vastly ancient ones, which we have already covered. To quote from one of our books on ritual practices:[51]

> A temple is a living symbol of the Great Work, and is dedicated to a particular aspect of deity such as Kali or Sekhmet. Each piece of furniture or equipment used solely for spiritual purposes has a Ka (strength or force) and a subtle counterpart. Even if we have an improvised temple that can be unpacked from a box, we need to take care when moving house that we break it down carefully. We will then be sure to take the Ka and *genius loci* with us when we go. When we rebuild it in the new location there will be much less work to do in forming the unique presence.

---

[51] *Ritual Magick—Initiation of the Star and Snake*, 'Temple Observances'.

One very well known occultist wrote that consecrating a magical or symbolic weapon is really no different than using a favourite set of golf clubs often, so that over time 'something' is put into the object that assists the magician—or player. That person wished not to discern any difference between a profane or ordinary activity and a sacred one, which was part of his overall strategy. There is a large difference, in fact, but this cannot be understood at all unless one has knowledge of a more than ordinary kind, which we call metaphysics. The difference can also be due to the method of consecration used, and there are considerations as to how effective that consecration is, as depending upon the skill of the operator or other conditions, which can be indefinite. As with most talismans, if done with a more or less classical method, celestial and other forces are invoked with the purpose of controlling a 'spirit' that is closer to the earth, so as to indwell the object and imbue it with a particular kind of magnetic (or attractive) power. Such agencies or intelligences are first and foremost non-human, as should readily be understood—and if it is not well understood then such a person should stay well away from such practices. A link is thus made between the individuality of the magician and a non-human intelligence. Planetary spirits, as one example, do not have an individuality; they are an aspect of being that is beyond the human scale and that normally has nothing at all to do with human consciousness. With a talismanic operation, the invoked intelligence assumes a temporary individuality through its relationship with the operator, and for this reason one must always be aware of the higher principle holding governance. If the operator is ignorant or careless, however, then the intelligence becomes easily separated from the higher principle and governance, so that only the inverse or infernal reflection manifests in the human state.[52]

It should by now be well understood that the use of talismans as merely mechanical or auto-hypnotic devices for some imagined self-improvement, gain or other personal goal, is a degradation of the art and necessarily divorces the highly specialised kind of intelligence involved from its principle; such grave injunctions are in no sense at all moral but are based on spiritual realities; the fact most persons do not believe in the latter does not cause those realities to cease to exist. In the same way, the sky still exists even when a blind man is unable to see it. Thus much care is taken over the preparation and consecration of talismans.

---

[52] This paragraph is paraphrased from *Nu Hermetica*, p. 61.

In the case of relocation or removal, transmutation is integral to metaphysical doctrine. Moving a thing from one place to another initiates a change of state or at least modality. This then leads us on to the consideration of operational procedures. It is by one change alone that any object is able to emerge from the undifferentiated and unmanifest ground (*prakriti*) into manifest existence in the present. So it is that simply moving something from one place to another can be what might be termed a magical act. Any person that is innately qualified to be a practitioner of the science of magick already has the sensitivity that implies knowing something of transmutation, even if that idea is not clearly formed. They only need to have it explained to them to fix the knowledge securely, and that in itself may effect a change in the state of the being, however subtle, and that may lead on by 'following' (*savichara*) to further knowledge.

To return then once more to the matter of psychic residues: it has been explained that while effective at what might be called the psychic level, or in a more exact sense the subtle realm, the source or origin is not psychic, and in fact if it was self-contained in that way, and not adjunct to a principle higher than itself, it would have little if any power to move anything. In fact, it could not exist! As for any desecration, whether by loss, abandonment or profane act, it will now be understood as to the full extent of the mischief, indeed real harm, that can be done. There is one thing more. Certain human agencies can, usually in a way that is completely unconscious (or nescient), manipulate and make use of psychic residues so as to bring about illusionary effects that are nonetheless very evil in so far as they can condition and influence human behaviour and thought.

Persons that unknowingly desecrate talismans simply through their own ignorance are susceptible to such malefic manipulations, and that means that they are also very good hypnotic subjects, accepting even the most fearful, irrational suggestions put into them from governmental or corporate agencies, or from other individuals. The widespread use, to an excessive extent, of hypnotic electronic devices, computers, cell phones, television and the soft applications that drive them, increases this passive acceptance of subliminal or even blatant commands, even when those commands are contrary to physical and mental survival.

The combined effect of electronics and the subtle fields of force from centres retaining psychic residues is fulfilling very rapidly a design for destruction that itself has a non-human origin. In this case it is certainly not a celestial source or a spiritual one, but is what can only be termed as *sub-infra*, which is to say it is below the level of ordinary manifestation and in that way barely existent and yet carrying immense power through its ability to rend the fabric that once protected the earth from influences hostile to it.[53]

On the other hand, it can be seen from all this that intentional uses of magick, whether to consecrate or deconsecrate (i.e. neutralise), very much have their place in this present time, near the end of the Age of Kali Yuga. A person that has been trained in magical arts, which are traditional sciences, cannot afford to be forgetful of what they have learned, or to neglect to do what is necessary to maintain equilibrium, and to be in every way vigilant. In that way, the science of magick and that of yoga, whether it be devotional or for pure knowledge, are not in any way incompatible and in fact should be used together to counteract and in every way neutralise the forces that are by their nature hostile to all real spirituality.

---

[53] This is fully explained by Guénon in *Reign of Quantity*, Ch. 8.

Telesma and Familiar Spirits

W hile there is plenty of literature with instruction on how to consecrate talismans, some of it going into utmost detail, there is almost nothing on how to *deconsecrate* such an item.[54] As to why we might want to go to all the trouble of preparing and making a talisman, completing the operation through magical manipulation of the life-force, and then undo that work at a later date, we will look at that later. In the meantime, if it was really a matter of expediency then we would adapt the ritual that was used to consecrate the talisman in the first place, so the same powers are invoked. Instead of charging with the Oath and so forth, the spirit is given a blessing in the name of the powers and asked to return to its natural abode and habitation. When the charge has definitely left, the ritual is closed and—if really needed—the talismanic object destroyed (depending on what sort of object it is). There would be no need for any 'banishing' ritual added at the end of proceedings if that were seen to be accomplished, unless the talisman was made for some evil purpose involving demons. In that case a blessing would not count for anything and the devil might be hiding in your hat or a favourite piece of ceramic art.

That is the simple expedient solution, but as indicated in the previous chapter, 'Psychic Residues', the matter is far from being that simple in reality.[55] Assuming the ritual of consecration was done effectively: by the will of the operator, a non-human intelligence has become part of his human individuality. It thus gains an individuality it would not otherwise possess. If that were not so then no result could be obtained. Taking the consecration of a planetary talisman of Mercury, for example:

> I shall consecrate and charge a talisman so as to form a true and potent link between my human soul and the wisdom of TAHUTI. To this end I have brought into this circle a talisman, covered with a veil and bound thrice with a cord, so it shall not move until it be duly consecrated...

---

[54] Cf. for example our *Ritual Magick—Initiation of the Star and Snake*, where instruction is given on the theory and method of consecrating a talisman plus five illustrated examples, one of each of the four elements and one of a planetary intelligence.

[55] See especially p. 35 on 'non-human intelligences'.

Furthermore, it is declared towards the end of the ritual:

> May the spirit Taphthartharath charge this talisman with mighty force! Thus may his nature become illumined and glorified, even as the crown is placed upon my head, and the knowledge received in my heart that abideth forever and forever.

That is a mighty spell! The oath declares that this spirit has become part of the soul of the magician and so when the magician achieves salvation, or liberation, then naturally the spirit achieves it too. It has become absorbed into the individuality, as was explained previously, and even the integral individuality. Is it the will of the magician at a later date that this should not be the case, having declared such a solemn oath? A father can legally revoke an inheritance afforded his offspring, but can he revoke all the elements that clothe that soul that are the inheritance of metempsychosis? It is true that such elements are strictly temporary and are as 'clothing', so not forming part of integrality.[56] But in the case of the talismanic operation divine power has been invoked so the talisman enjoys human life for the duration of that life and even beyond, so participating in the spiritual destiny, be it heaven or hell. The term 'familiar spirit' is derived from the Latin *familiaris*. It has intimate implications and is related to trusted household servants. The earliest known Egyptian kings arranged it so all their family and very extensive retinue and domestic servants could be buried in, or otherwise around and nearby, their very elaborate and astronomically constructed tomb—a temple that was in every way a talisman intended to endure for thousands of years, and millions of years in the hereafter.

The word 'talisman' is derived from the Greek *telesma*, which shares a root with 'Tetelestai' said at the conclusion of a Mass, 'It is complete, it is accomplished'. Then how can it be undone? Taking this further along, *Nescit Vox Missa Reverti* (NVMR) is inscribed on the Ace of Discs in our Tarot, 'a word once uttered is irrevocable'. No past deed can be undone in reality because the past does not exist, it has returned to the undifferentiated *prakriti* ground substance. It can only exist as *smrti* retained impressions, in the memory. What is done is done. And yet human beings put themselves through endless suffering when they enter into the delusion that thoughts and actions can be undone or 'put to rights', which also leads to seeking revenge in the name of 'justice', and which only perpetuates the vicious nature of sin, bearing forth more and more poisoned fruits from the same poisoned tree of afflictions.

---

[56] See 'Reincarnationism'.

Talismanic operations are a willed production of *samskara* latent impressions. Those are sometimes referred to as 'indelible' in the *Yoga-Sutras*, and while the use of the latter term is not absolute as such things are subject to mutation over time, there comes a point, from the human perspective, where the *karma* has reached the end of its *karmasaya* cycle and is exhausted. By the law of *apurva*, the knowledgeable relation between two things, Nuit (as Shakti power) is not only the 'cause' that is in itself causeless, and unaffected by anything, but is also present in the resultant.[57]

Certainly, one must give very careful thought to such a matter as the deconsecration of anything, before going to action over it. This is not to say that it cannot be done, only that it needs thinking through as to whether it really needs to be done and if so, to know exactly *what* is being done. Supposing, for example, the object itself was imperfectly made. This is comparable to making a bad drawing that one wants to dispose of. Likewise, potters smash up pots when they come out of the kiln a bit wonky. The pot is a very useful analogy and we will return to it.

This brings to mind the whole question of what is a talisman and where is it really, if it has a location? That touches on the nature of being and how we perceive reality. The Golden Dawn very usefully provided the Z 'lightning flash' formula for talismanic and evocatory operations. They had a very peculiar notion about talismans though. They obviously thought it was about 'bringing life and movement to inert matter'. Aside from the fact that both 'matter' and 'inertia' are modern concepts unknown to the ancients, it is impossible to make a non-sentient object 'come alive'. A pot is a pot and while a pot can undergo changes of state—as for example when someone smashes it—no amount of saying magical spells will change the pot to such an extent that it will get up on legs and dance around the room. It is true that in ancient times there were magicians or fakirs that were so skilled they could produce illusions that would be very convincing, but it is unlikely anyone can do that now. The modern conjuror is no more than a clever engineer.[58]

---

[57] See 'I Am That', *Way of Knowledge*.

[58] Such engineering can be extended to modern governmental and corporate campaigns in the 'public interest', especially where 'safety' is concerned.

The ancient Egyptians had no concept of 'matter' and their view of objects was very different from ours. It was less removed from the idea of consciousness itself. So in their art they depicted pots on legs and there are no 'inanimate' objects in their works. The boat has a face on it, the oars and rudder are creatures, and so forth. We must not suppose that the Egyptians imagined that pots really get up on legs and dance around while we are asleep at night—although if we bring the dreaming realm into it then that is much less restricted than the corporeal, so almost anything can happen. The figures were to communicate principles. So the pot walking about on two legs was to indicate 'bringing forth'.

To get back to the absurd notion of 'bringing life to inert matter', we have to recollect, as within the bounds of ordinary physics, that nothing in nature is really inert. We know the talismanic object itself, as exterior to our perceptions, is neither inert nor sentient, so where does a creature of talismans reside? It is the space occupied by an object that is the ground for the Samyama Yoga meditation.[59] If a pot, for one example, is destroyed, this does not alter space in any way. Also the fact that there are multitudes of pots, each a container or envelope of space, does not change space, apparently contained by them.

While air or *vayu* is not the same principle as space, the *vayu* principle is very much involved in talismans.[60] The character of *vayu* is movement, and to move anywhere there must be space to move in. All talismans, whether their *telesma* finality is deemed as one of the four elements, seven planets or twelve signs, are of the nature of *vayu*. The latter is a modification of *prana*, the essential substance of 'life', or 'breath', of which everything is made. It has a quite exact relation with the Hebrew *ruach*, mind, spirit, and breath of life. The Ruach Elohim is said to have brooded upon the waters of the deep and Being was produced therein. This is why we have the saying that a talismanic operation is to give life and movement to something, even when we know that 'something' is not truly inert and cannot become sentient, as exterior object, however much we will it to be so.

---

59 See 'Power of Knowing Distant Objects'.

60 Akasha is really what fills or pervades all of space, and not space itself, though it is sometimes used as a term for 'space', especially when that is used by way of analogy for something that is not an object as such.

The *vayu* principle is the key to knowing how aspiration, inhalation and expiration take place with regard to assimilating unindividualised elements from the cosmic environment and then sending them back out in a changed form, so they become a part of the integral being, which is vastly more than the individual human modality.[61] This has its correlation with *pranayama* and the ritual movements that follow the motions of stellar bodies as about the Pole star.[62] Aspiration, inspiration and expiration are also mirrored in a Mass. The chalice is raised, and then brought back down, a cross signed and marked in the centre and then the contents consumed. Although the Mass is then done, accomplished in the Greek word *Tetelestai*, it does not stop there but goes on and is able to effect transformation in all states of the being.

To return once again to the question, 'where does a creature of talismans dwell?' We infer that the creature of the *telesma* does not actually dwell in a piece of parchment paper or some other housing. At the same time we are careful to wrap the talismanic object in a covering of cloth. The consecrated object is a type of condenser for the storing of a particular kind of force, as has been determined by the operation of consecration. It requires some kind of insulation, to ensure its effectiveness. It has written on it the name of the spirit, and very likely a sigil or 'signature' formed from the number of the name and letters, especially if it is a planetary intelligence. By the name, Nama, the subtle form, Rupa, is produced. It is a principle not an individuality, until it is joined with the soul of the magician. Thus it is the principle that is wedded to the soul of the operator and assimilated. That is not the end of the matter, however final the word *telesma* is regarding the due actions of the operation; the effect is ongoing and undergoes transmutations that are even able to obtain outside of and completely beyond the human modality. This is, in a certain respect, one reason for doing such an operation in the first place. In the wording of any spell to return a creature of talismans to its natural abode and habitation is then implied the idea of a change of location (and so a change of state). The true location, as has been established, if the consecration was effective, is not only the soul of the practitioner but also the integral being, which is much more than human as it encompasses all states of the being. Such a return of the creature or soul then is not truly feasible, as we have shown by now. Once a change of state has been undergone, there is no return to a previous state of being.

---

[61] See 'The Vayus and Integral Being', Part Two.
[62] The Pole star is called 'fixed' in Sanskrit, as relatively motionless.

42

What then of the talismanic object itself, assuming it is no longer wanted? An amulet is made to ward off undesirable forces, whereas a talisman is made to attract forces that are desirable towards the sphere of the operator. This goes on working in the way of a cathode. The nature of the intelligence in regard to the spirit or *telesma* has been assimilated by the magician—although that is not a foregone conclusion for every time someone consecrates a talisman. For example, one person will hear the words of a guru and get nothing from it at all. Another hears the same words and knowledge is awakened in them. In the case of assimilation, the product of the original operation would not be affected by any kind of removal or 'banishing'. The ritual of deconsecration would amount to simple neutralising of any force, 'magnetism' or residue still active. The blessing to the spirit is really a matter of observance of the principles involved. So long as due attention is given to the powers concerned, there should be no harm done by tracing pentagrams or hexagrams in the reverse direction to that used for invocation. Getting such a procedure in the right order is quite important: One does not close the door on the guests and then, in the way of an afterthought, thank them for their company from behind the closed door!

It remains for something to be said about talismans that are carelessly taken out of their locations, even thoughtlessly unwrapped and exhibited for public amusement. The breaking open of ancient Egyptian tombs and plundering of the treasures sealed up in them was at first the work of tomb robbers, always regarded as criminals by the ancient Egyptians, and was later continued by adventurers and Egyptologists. This pastime was particularly popular in the late nineteenth and early twentieth centuries but no doubt it still goes on. It is ignorance of a magnitude but there it is. The ancient Egyptians were very accomplished at magick and whenever such *desecration* is perpetrated, whether 'in the name of science' or 'for public interest' or whatever, psychic residues break out and cause havoc. The extent of this might even be of the order of major catastrophe sometimes but it is best we do not speculate here.

What we can do is recollect the astonishing (true) account of Dorothy Eady. It is not possible even to summarise the beginning of that story as it is very involved but what is relevant here is that while a child—she was born in 1904 at a time when unwrapping mummies was at its height—Dorothy's mind and body was completely taken over by the psychic remnants, with complete memories, of an ancient Egyptian priestess of Isis. This is not 'reincarnation', as Eady always pointed out, though she was not completely sure what it was.

The Egyptian King Sety I that subsequently visited Dorothy also denied reincarnation as a possibility. And this is completely correct, for reincarnation has no part in any traditional knowledge and is a metaphysical impossibility. Metempsychosis on the other hand does fully explain what took place. A soul that enters discarnate existence after death is no longer human but can retain human memories and desires. Both the king and the priestess entered a part of Amentet that corresponds to the nether worlds—not the darkest hells but far from heaven or the celestial abodes. The priestess had broken her vows of celibacy when she gave way to the desires of the king. On realising that she was pregnant, she committed suicide before the priesthood could find out. King Sety was wrought with grief and guilt, as well as desire for the priestess, and he retained all that in Amentet after the death of his body. He confessed in the narratives that he suffered very greatly. Therefore, by the power of desire and magick, and it seems with the help of a learned priest, he sought to do what is otherwise impossible, to re-enter a human life to fulfil his yearning. This was done by the transfer of the complete memories of the priestess to the mind and body of Dorothy Eady, and then by taking vitality from the latter to build a semblance of a subtle form by which he could enjoy conversation and sexual congress with his former lover. While all of this explanation will seem as improbable to most persons as the highly detailed account of Dorothy Eady herself, if knowledge of the principles involved is gained it is not at all improbable—though no less extraordinary for that.

Aurora Consurgens

The alchemical treatise *Aurora Consurgens* is thought to have been composed in the fifteenth century. The title is given as meaning 'Morning Rising', or 'Golden Hour', and both refer to the dawn and the star of Venus. Book One is a kind of inspired comment on the biblical Song of Songs (or Canticles). Book Two is a commentary on the Latin translation of *Silvery Waters* by Ibn Umayl, a tenth century Arabic alchemist named in *Aurora* as Senior Zadith. Unfortunately the most popular modern editions reproduce the text overlaid with an elaborate Jungian interpretation by the psychologist Maria-Louise von Franz.

It is not intended here to produce a full commentary on *Aurora*, or the extraordinary illuminations that accompany it, as that would require another book of greater size than the one being commented on. We will rest content with drawing attention to some of the symbolism of this fascinating treatise. Something must be said about the illuminations; these have acquired a reputation for their bizarre or otherwise baffling nature. There are various copies of the book and the illustrations, some of which were made at a later date. The original Arabic illustrations, for example as held at Zurich, are in all ways superior to the later ones; they are better drawn, more beautiful and reveal much that is otherwise lost. In some of the watercolours, details portraying graphic sexual imagery were deliberately obscured in the Latin versions or by the collectors. The collectors, as with some publishers of the work, show total incomprehension of symbolism but this did not prevent them from painting out or even scribbling over the parts that offended them; in the case of one publisher, the whole of Book One was omitted as he thought it was blasphemous to explain the science of alchemy using biblical references, and that alchemy could not in any way be explained by key Christian doctrine. It seems that as much as the esoteric meaning of the work was obscure to these profane men, they nonetheless sought in every way to render it even more obscure through censorship.

Aurora Consurgens (Zurich): Lunar Zodiac

46

One of the Arabic versions that has somehow survived without any tampering is that of a woman in the centre of a Zodiac wheel, wearing a typical Arab head scarf and robe, but naked below the waist (see illustration on facing page). The drawing here hides nothing; she is clearly menstruating and so this is a type of lunar calendar based on the Zodiac.[63] She holds up the cloth that she has removed, and her gaze is turned upward towards Leo the Lion; her left foot rests upon the sign of Scorpio while the serpentine plumes of blood below are pouring in the direction of the Archer of Sagittarius. In the language of alchemy, iron may be transformed into gold only during the month of Scorpio; it is the month of Sagittarius in which Sun (Leo) and Moon (Scorpio Eagle) produce the philosophic stone.

Throughout the text of the *Aurora* allusions are made to the union of oppositions, and the illustrations show this in a number of ways. These include the Sun and Moon as male and female figures jousting from the back of hybrid creatures, or a lion (fire) with an eagle's head (water), or a lion with a man's head (Aquarius). None of this symbolism should be taken literally, or indeed psychologically, which limits the meaning to the narrowest definition possible. The Sun and the Moon across all traditions symbolise principles both cosmic and supra-cosmic. While the human body and mind is used analogously in respect of these, higher principles never symbolise the lower and inferior conditioned states, which would be to reverse the natural order of things.

Some of the figures, especially in Book Two, which deals with the better-known physical alchemical symbolism of metals, calcination and so forth, are grotesque. Most bizarre of all perhaps is in Book One, where a hybrid figure with a monkey's head plays a lobster as though it were a fiddle, with a snake for a bow (see the illustration on next page). In later copies this is rendered very obscure, perhaps because the copyists had no idea of what it was they were copying. In the Zurich version it is clear that the snake-bow is actually being drawn by the claw of a large eagle that is situated behind the man-monkey, who nonetheless has all the appearance of playing the violin, or some early form of it.

---

[63] The Moon completes a round of the Zodiac every 28–30 days, which comprises a lunar month. The Arabs and Hindus use a lunar calendar based on these days, called the Mansions of the Moon. Solar and lunar calendars are used to suit different purposes.

Aurora Consurgens (Zurich): Monkey Fiddler

The lobster (possibly a crayfish) is Cancer governed by the Moon, while in alchemy the serpent frequently symbolises Mercury. The lobster-violin is held close to the presumably male figure's heart. The Eagle of Scorpio, also of the lunar type, thus uses the Moon for an instrument on which the work of quicksilver Mercury plays upon the heart of man in a strangely composite state. This might seem more intelligible once it is seen how the various symbols of Sun and Moon or fire and water play the part also portrayed in the old tarot trump of the Angel of Temperance, bearing two jars from which liquids of opposite nature are mingled. The fire heats up the water while the water cools the flames; air, sometimes depicted in the form of birds of various kinds, fans the flames and all of this takes place within a cucurbit (or alembic) vessel. It is also interesting to bring to mind that in the *Aurora* the hierarchy of the principles of air, water and fire is the reverse of what it usually is. Instead of earth being the gross product of the subtler three, through combination, the three principles are said to be produced through alchemical process out of the earth, from which all begins and is the 'first'. So it is that with all forms of alchemy, including yoga or 'inner alchemy', one must begin with man, the microcosm—for unless the principles are found there, no Great Work is in any way possible and all searching is in vain. This view is one that is supported by all other alchemical texts.

The three principles and four classical elements also form the characters of the 'stars' or Zodiac types. One should bear in mind that the twelve signs of the Zodiac are placed under the rulership of seven planets, a number that includes the two luminaries of Sun and Moon, and that the luminaries are placed under the governance of Spirit. The anonymously written alchemical text, no doubt falsely attributed to St. Thomas Aquinas, makes mention of seven stars that must be treated in a special way by the practitioner or Craftsman. Furthermore, Venus, that has the Qabalistic number seven, is the morning star when she rises before the Sun, and is sometimes called the Dawn Herald. In *Aurora Consurgens* wisdom is always referred to in the feminine sense, as Sophia. For this reason alchemy is thought of sometimes as a way of 'warriors' (*kshatriyas*), and which is no different than the way of the lover or poet, so long as that is understood to be analogous with spiritual devotion (*bhakti*).[64]

---

[64] Cf. Fideli d'Amore ('faithful of love'). See *Way of Knowledge*, p. 17.

What that Science is, and what her origin is, I will now declare to you, for I have no intention of hiding these things from you. For she is the gift and sanctuary of godhood, a Divine Work that has been concealed in many different ways by the figurative manner of speech used by the Wise. That is why I intend to shed light upon this Knowledge and why I shall not neglect her, nor shall I go with consuming envy, because ever since my birth I have inquired into her and have not been disregarding of her, because she is the Mother of all Sciences, who has exalted me and showered upon me the most wonderful blessings. She is a Science that I have learned without guile, and which I shall communicate without envy and without concealing from anyone what it is that makes her so wonderful.[65]

One must bear in mind there is a relation between Venus, who also appears as an evening star when her zodiacal position is in front of the Sun, and Nuit, the ancient Egyptian starry goddess. It is Venus, or Sophia, who is depicted as pouring waters from two urns in the traditional image of Aquarius.

For this is the Wisdom, namely the Queen of the South, who is said to have come from the East as the Morning Rising, desiring to hear, understand and see the Wisdom of Solomon.[66]

It is mentioned in the Prologue to the second book that it is needful to explain with what other sciences alchemy is closely related. The following chapter begins with astronomy, which was identical with astrology at the time the book was written down and copied:

The first thing you need to know is that this Divine Science of Astronomy uses a distinctive conceptual framework, namely the course of the planets and their effects, and the number and powers of the twelve signs of the zodiac.[67]

Astrology is ascribed to the path of Aquarius among the (Western) magical powers.[68] A caveat is usually placed next to this, warning against interpreting it according to the modern notion of what astrology is, for there is no power in that other than very commonplace skill to delude the gullible and ignorant.

---

[65] *Aurora Consurgens* Book I.11.

[66] *Ibid* Book I. v. Based on *Songs of Songs*, 6: 9.

[67] *Ibid* Book II.1.

[68] That is, the fifteenth path on the Tree of Life and the letter *hé*, extending from Chokmah, 'Wisdom', to Tiphereth, 'Beauty' (and the Sun).

Astrological symbolism is integral to the science of alchemy but it would be no use applying psychological terms to it, as modern astrologers do, and which is a superimposition, removing the person further and more completely from any chance of knowing the real meaning. It would also be no use trying to construe the meaning of the texts by use of the Golden Dawn system of the magical correspondences as the writers of the texts did not use such a system. Even more ancient correspondences, such as those of the Neo-Platonists, will not necessarily provide a clue.[69]

The Egyptian hieroglyph on which the symbol of Aquarius was modelled symbolises both the sky and water, or more precisely, the 'waters of the firmament' or heaven. The same symbol ≈ is used to depict both fire and light, as radiation or vibration. It forms a part of the Egyptian name of Nuit, goddess of the night-sky par excellence. As such, a natural correspondence, not derived from any system as such, is the dome of the sky or heaven. This has its analogous counterpart in the seventh luminous chakra 'beyond the chakras', referred to in the *Yoga-Sutras* and Tantras as the *brahmarandra* lotus, resting analogously on the top of the skull. It might also be mentioned that the skull is a frequent symbol in alchemy and other ancient sciences and that it is not by chance that the hill upon which Christ Jesus was crucified is Golgotha, 'place of the skull'. According to the *Yoga-Sutras* and other Hindu texts, this chakra is accessible through the 'void' or 'cavity' of the heart lotus, concealed within the heart (*anahatha*). The latter is also called the Gate of Brahma for this reason. The central canal for the fire of Kundalini Shakti's ascent has its continuance beyond the human realm to that which is beyond, the supra-human domain. It is worth noting that such symbolism refers to the microcosm or realm of man, which nonetheless by upward transposition is identified with the cosmic or celestial domain.

The signs of the Zodiac are best understood in pairs of complementary opposites. At the base of the spine is the tail, in which in the human being is a small hard bone; this is adequately symbolised by the Lion, not raging but sleeping under the Moon.[70]

---

[69] The usual correspondence of the Zodiac signs to the parts of the human body is thought to be generally influenced by Platonic ideas, although this refers more to Hermetic thought than Plato as such. Aquarius is given to the ankles and the blood circulation, thus support to movement and life—one should bear in mind also that the ancient ruler of Aquarius is Saturn.

[70] Regarding the bone, see 'I Am That', *Way of Knowledge*, where the Hebraic *luz* is an analogous symbolism.

51

The analogy will be explained. Although it may seem a digression in the present context, one may think of the famous painting by Henri Rousseau, *Sleeping Gypsy* (1897).[71] A woman dressed in rainbow-coloured oriental clothing is asleep in the desert under the full Moon, with her mandolin beside her, and a pot that closely resembles those depicted in the alchemical text. A lion with a flowing, luminescent mane lingers over her. According to Rousseau, the lion is attracted by the scent of the sleeping woman but he does not devour her. It should be pointed out for those not well familiar with such symbolism that Kundalini Shakti, the animating, magnetic force, is said to be sleeping or coiled up (she is also imaged as a serpent) at the base of the spine or *muladhara* chakra, the support, 'root' or foundation. By the following of certain practices she is able to rise upward to meet her Lord, which is essentially the union (yoga) of knowledge (*jnana*), symbolised by the frontal eye, by which the crown lotus or *brahmarandra* comes into being or realisation. Thus the Tantras, which utilise this kind of imagery, are comparable to a form of inner alchemy and indeed the *Yoga-Sutras* include alchemical allusions. It is unlikely that Rousseau was thinking of this when he made his painting, but the symbolism is nonetheless there, and it no doubt helps the allure of the work.

The title of *Aurora Consurgens* is rather subtle; the literal meaning is 'Morning Rising', and this alludes to several things according to the book, including the dawn that represents an intermediary realm between night and day.[72] The intermediary realm corresponds to *taijasa* in the Hindu doctrines, which is the subtle realm and also the dreaming state as opposed to the waking state. The symbolic language of alchemy seems to speak directly to the subtle realm and contemplation of the texts can precipitate for some persons a certain kind of *dhyana*. Although rarely reaching to *samadhi* in the full sense, this can amount to a lesser *samadhi* (*sa'asmita*) where there is at first an experience of 'melting', where the symbolism being contemplated flows continually, undergoing a rapid kind of transmutation or change of state, yet without ceasing to be 'what it is' in essence.[73]

---

[71] Also called 'Sleeping Bohemian'. Artists at that time thought that gypsies or 'bohemians' were of Egyptian origin.

[72] *Aurora Consurgens* Book I.iv.

[73] See 'Transmutation'.

At the same time, the meditator realises that what is being seen and the Seer (or Witness) are not separate either. Thus he passes beyond the level of the mere concentration (*dharana*) or 'fixing of the volatile' as it is put in alchemical terms and, as it would be put in those same terms, there is a certain kind of production, which can be symbolised in various ways: for example, a child, a bird, an egg or a stone that will pass through further stages. The one that knows this will understand how it is that the alchemical tincture, often used as a term for the final outcome of the Great Work as quintessence, is a sort of wonder or marvel as it goes on reproducing itself as according to the capacity of the yogin or practitioner. To the subtlety of the yogin, this will be be seen as indefinite or even a permanent change of state in the being. To the lesser *sadhaka* it will give off a kind of 'scent' that is very attractive but is not long lasting as it will be devoured by his strong attachments to worldly objects or pursuits. That devouring principle is the Lion when symbolising the untamed or undisciplined nature, while the sublimation of such desire is the Eagle, when it is associated with the whitening or purification stage.

According to the book of Revelation seven stars or angels are sent to give teaching to men before the end of time. In the context of Revelation, the seven stars are the light of the seven churches, and are in a sense the direct apostles of Christ. The symbolism is in perfect agreement with that of other traditions, for example in the Hebraic there are seven palaces of Malkuth the Kingdom that must be cleansed of the influence of the evil Qliphoth ('shells') so that the earth may be restored. In the Tantras the seventh chakra or lotus of the crown only comes about when the other six are brought into a state of perfect equilibrium. These seven stars, angels, spirits or holy abodes of the upper waters of heaven, the firmament, have their reflection in the lower waters of man's humours or mental states. The angels speak forth, but who can hear them? He who would search them out by practice of the Eight Limbs of Yoga 'gives seven to the seven stars' and by this, as according to the alchemical text *Aurora Consurgens*, the nine are made pure, which is called the whitening of the stone, or Albedo.[74] In that way Nuit is exalted in heaven and the Lion is given a golden crown.

---

[74] Nine is the Qabalistic number of Yesod, the Foundation, the equivalent of the root chakra *muladhara* of the *Yoga-Shastra*. In the Hindu doctrines there are nine doorways that can symbolise the nine openings in the body of a man. See *The Way of Knowledge*, p. 58.

The fool will think we speak in riddles, for the light shineth in darkness but the darkness comprehendeth it not, as it is written.[75] Having made use of the same kind of symbolic language, it is in keeping with the spirit of the *Aurora* to represent the warnings given in most alchemical texts. In the *Aurora* it is also put thus:

> For the scorning of knowledge is always at the root of ignorance.[76]

Anyone that has followed this writing thus far, even not understanding it at all, is not necessarily the kind of fool referred to here, for a golden light may yet dawn in due course. The real fool is the ignorant person that, in not knowing, is the enemy of the truth, and that works to shut it out even from the ears and eyes of others. That kind of fool will never grasp this wisdom Sophia, and neither shall she ever minister to his needs, for he has defiled and sought to abuse her in every way. Hell awaits him.

To conclude: in spite of the bizarre nature of the illuminations and the sometimes corrupt Latin, compounded by translation errors in places, the *Aurora Consurgens* contains a wealth of knowledge not communicable in terms other than a symbolic language. As it is put in Book Two,

> Those who wish to master this Science therefore need to sharpen their wits most subtly and ingeniously; to ponder and deliberate as much as possible upon both the inner and the outer meanings of the words of the Sages; and to show a willingness to examine them from various points of view. For the Wise are not acting stupidly when they speak out in this manner, since the sense of their words is flatly contradicted by the sound of the letters. For a person who merely listens to the sounds of the words but does not have the necessary inward understanding of them will derive little benefit from them.

---

[75] Book of John 1: 5. Also, according to the book of John 1: 4: 'In him was life; and the life was the light of men.'
[76] *Aurora Consurgens* Book I.111.

Tradition and Universal Gnosis

There is a primordial root language, which it would not be wrong to call 'universal'. The Egyptian AUR, 'intelligence of the heart', is identical to the Sanskrit OM or AUM, especially when the hieroglyph of the 'heart vessel' (*ab*) is looked at in detail, for it has three parts and a hidden fourth *turiya*. At least one of the names of Ra includes exactly the seed syllable AUM. For a further example, one might use the Sanskrit *Om Tat Sat* as part of discrimination. In Vedic ritual, if there was a mistake made then the leader would repair it by saying *Om Tat Sat*, 'everything (in reality) is Brahma'. This and other Vedic mantras formed from the primal roots of language are identical to ancient Egyptian words. *Om Tat Sat* in Egyptian is phonetically identical and carries the same meaning:[77]

In the West, Christianity is our tradition but the initiatic elements were destroyed centuries ago. Christianity, however, was born in Egypt, not Palestine. The Hermetic tradition was a small part of the Egyptian doctrines that went out to the world before that civilisation vanished, finding its way to India, Persia, and even the Greeks and Romans. The Hermetic tradition is not separate, in the West, from Christianity. The earliest forms of Christianity utilised the Egyptian symbol of the *ankh* or *crux ansata*. According to René Guénon:

> It is noteworthy that the cross, in its ordinary form, is found in Egyptian hieroglyphs where it has the meaning of 'health' (for instance in the name of the Ptolemy *Soter*). This sign is quite distinct from the *crux ansata* or the 'looped cross' (*ankh*), which for its part expresses the idea of 'life', and which was frequently used as a symbol by the Christians of the first two centuries. It is a question whether the first of these two hieroglyphics has not a certain connection with the representation of the Tree of Life, and this would link together these two different forms of the cross, since their meaning would thus be partly identical; in any case, there is an obvious connection between the ideas of 'life' and 'health'.[78]

---

[77] See Budge, *An Egyptian Hieroglyphic Dictionary*: Om (Am) 'to know' Vol. 1 p. 6; Tat ('that'), Vol. 2 865–866; for a further example *ta em ab*, 'to put that in mind (heart)'; Sat ('wisdom'; a name of Tahuti), Vol. 2 p. 640.
[78] *The Symbolism of the Cross*, pp. 56–57, footnote 13.

Among the sayings of Jesus is this, from Matthew 16: 24,

> Then said Jesus unto his disciples, If any man will come after me, let him deny himself, and take up his cross, and follow me.

Firstly, the *ankh* is a symbol of Universal Being as well as the integral or whole being of any individual. It should be noted that in using the term 'universal' there is no allusion to anything of a collective order. It is the cosmic order that is implied. The book of Hebrews contains many references to this but most succinct is 6: 20:

> Whither the forerunner is for us entered, even Jesus, made an high priest for ever after the order of Melchizedek.

The order of Melchizedek, the Prince of Peace, is the cosmic order of priesthood, that is, the primordial tradition symbolised by the head of the vertical axis of any cross. The three-dimensional cross or 'Cube of Space' is formed from three lines, the third at right-angles to the first two; the extremities then mark six directions of space: height, depth, north, south, east and west. The last four form the horizontal plane. The same symbolism may also be found in nature, for example the cross that can be drawn from the projected points of the solstices and equinoxes about the ecliptic path of the sun. The symbolism of the four arms of a cross is used in weaving designs, where passing a thread through the centre forms two more. The ancient Egyptians made much use of this so it is not mere ornamentation when it appears on the garments or nemmys of a Neter.[79] By the Hermetic axiom 'As above then so below', each individual being is such a cross. By passing to the centre of the cross it is possible to receive a transmission from the integral Self, and that in turn is a reflection of Universal Man or Pure Being. Thus to 'take up thy cross' and follow the Lord of Life is to tread the path of initiation as that exists in all traditions that carry the current of the primordial gnosis. This is not to propose attachment to Christianity in any shape or form, but is to show how symbolism may be interpreted metaphysically. It is not to deny the relevance of any attached exoteric or historical meaning; it is more the case that metaphysics underpins all true primordial symbolism. Scriptures, including the Vedas and Pyramid Texts, were not intended to convey one meaning alone but were composed so as to convey multiple and quite different levels of interpretation, as according to the degree of knowledge attained.

---

[79] That which we call 'Gods' are named *neteru* in ancient Egyptian, which means 'principles'. The Egyptian sacred science was metaphysical, not theological or even 'religious', as Egyptologists and others insist.

The Deliverance of Horus

T he ancient Egyptian Metternich Stele is perhaps the most well-known *cippi* of Horus, which are a group of magical objects associated with healing and characterised by Hoor-pa-kraat standing upon crocodiles firmly grasping creatures such as snakes, scorpions, lions and antelopes. This motif is typical of amulets and carvings found from the Third Intermediate Period of ancient Egypt until the end of the Ptolemaic dynasty, although it comes from a time much earlier than that.[80] In beautifully engraved hieroglyphs covering the front, back and sides, the Stele describes the journey of Ra through the subtle realms, and recites thirteen spells to cure poisoning or stinging from a variety of creatures. The focus of the stone is the story of Isis, which is also symbolised by a tableau in relief wherein Horus upon the crocodiles is the central figure. The tale relates how Isis went to Teb to bear Horus, to raise him and hide him from his enemy Set. However, one of the creatures of Set found him and in the form of a scorpion stung him to death in the heart. Isis used all her formidable skills and knowledge to resuscitate him, but nothing worked. She was beside herself with grief. On the advice of her sister Nephthys, she appealed to Ra who was travelling with Tahuti in his Sun Boat overhead. The boat stopped dead in its tracks and Tahuti sent her the words of power to revive her son. Thus did Horus live and the poison die. We present here our translation and abridgement of the text of the Stele.

I am Iset, and I came forth from the throne that Set built for me, upon which he placed me; with his own hands he did place me there. And the Messenger of the Eternal said unto me: Come forth Iset! For the spirit giveth life to those who are obedient to the path. Thus it shall be when the Great Day is with us. Beloved one, hide thyself with thy Sa, thy child, who shall be the crowned King of the Earth.

And in the evening I came forth with my seven scorpions: Tefen and Befen and Mestet and Mestef, Petet and Thetet and Maatet showed forth the way. For as a wise man practices obedience, allowing wisdom to enter into him, so disobedience is the mark of the low man who does not bring forth. Thus did my words enter the ears of the seven scorpions: Ye shall bend down your faces on the way! And downward they bent their faces, to make a way to the hidden places of Khebit.

---

[80] The motif is found much earlier in the New Kingdom. These round topped amulets depict a young regal god in a similar pose to Hoor-pa-kraat on the later Horus stele, but in profile, and named in the accompanying hieroglyphic inscription as Shed 'the saviour'.

Metternich Stele (obverse representation)

58

And so it was that when Horus was afflicted by the slayer, Tahuti sent unto me his words of magick. From the sun boat of millions of years he came forth with his words, and the protection of Horus is from the sun boat of Ra. At Teb, near the place of the papyrus swamps, truly I did raise up a child to life by commanding the poison to turn back, by power of Seb the earth, and by power of my words given me by Tahuti, which are magick. Thus did Horus live and the poison die.

The heavens are peaceful and content at the utterance of Iset. Strong is Horus in the belly of his mother, for he is the seed of the Future Time. He is the Bennu, born on the incense trees in the House of the Great Prince in Aunnu, beloved of the cat within the House of Net. Bes protects him, and no poison shall conquer his limbs. Neither earth nor water shall he fear, no reptile or stinging creature, no lion shall he fear— for he has mastery even over the tomb and death. And so have I come, Iset, from the suns of ancient time in the place of yesterday and tomorrow. And as the night cometh so does the light come forth. Thus is Horus made strong for Iset.

And verily I say unto you: these words are true and a million times true! And so are they true for every person that knows them.

Our study of the Metternich Stele was begun when we came upon these words from the ancient Chinese sage Lieh Tzu:[81]

The absolutely simple man sways all beings by his simplicity ... so that nothing opposes him in the six regions of space, nothing is hostile to him, and fire and water do not harm him.[82]

We were struck by how this expresses exactly the same idea as that given in the legend of the Stele:

Bes protects him, and no poison shall conquer his limbs. Neither earth nor water shall he fear, no reptile or stinging creature, no lion shall he fear—for he has mastery even over the tomb and death.

Lieh Tzu gave us an opening to the deeper meaning of this story of Isis and Horus. We find that its nature is essentially metaphysical and concerns spiritual realisation as expressed in other traditions. We do not have the space to look at the whole story in depth here, so the focus will be on how the tale refers to a certain advanced spiritual state figured by 'the absolutely simple man', also known in other traditions as Universal Man, or one who is a Muni of the *sannyasins*. We suggest therefore that the Stele and others like it became disseminators of this knowledge on the cusp of the end of the ancient Egyptian tradition, so that it might not be lost but find new life in different forms for different peoples.

---

[81] See *The Symbolism of the Cross*, René Guénon [Sophia Perennis].
[82] Lieh Tzu, Chapter 2, quoted by Guénon [ibid].

The Metternich Stele dates from the 30th Dynasty, around 360–343 BC, which was during the reign of Nactenebo II, the last native Pharoah of ancient Egypt. Egyptian life, arts and tradition flourished under his rule, whilst he kept the on-coming Persian Empire at bay. Eventually he was betrayed by a former servant, Mentor of Rhodes, which led to his armies being defeated by a combined Greek and Persian offensive at the battle of Pelusium. Nactenebo fled to Upper Egypt. Not much more is known of his life after that although it is said that he remained influential for a while. In the meantime, the Persians had seized control, marking the beginning of the end of ancient Khem.[83]

During the reign of Nactenebo II, the priest Esatum is said to have visited Heliopolis where he was impressed by certain magical inscriptions. He had these copied onto a specially carved block of stone. The Stele was set up in the public part of a temple, so that people could be healed of sickness. Water was poured over it and drunk or rubbed on the body, sometimes accompanied by priests performing rituals to affect a cure. Water consecrated by words of power on a holy stone is not of course exclusive to the Egyptian tradition alone. It has universal application; holy wells for example have been used in this way since time immemorial. One can hardly forget also the importance of baptism in Christianity, which at one time was clearly an initiatic function although this soon became purely exoteric. As we shall see, the Stele is more than a magical talisman for healing on the physical level; it has metaphysical import, and it is that which enables the former. From the spiritual point of view, being cured of sickness is to become Simple Man. To explain this doctrine we will turn once more to the sage Lieh Tzu:

> To him that dwells in the Unmanifest, all beings manifest themselves ... United with the Principle, he is thereby in harmony with all beings. United with the Principle, he knows all through general reasons of a higher order, and consequently no longer uses his various senses to know in particular and in detail. The true reason of things is invisible, ungraspable, undefinable, indeterminable. Only the spirit re-established in the state of perfect simplicity can attain it in profound contemplation.[84]

---

[83] Khem, 'the black land', is the Egyptian name for Egypt and the origin of the word alchemy.

[84] See 'The Resolution of Opposites', *Symbolism of the Cross* [ibid].

Such a supreme state is recognised across traditions as being one of the ideals of spiritual practice. The Simple Man, like Universal Man in Islamic esotericism, Adam Kadmon in Judaeo Christianity and the Muni of the Hindu tradition, is the justified soul who, by abiding in the centre of his being through profound meditation, has realised the Self, the spiritual principle, eternal and immutable. He has thereby overcome all oppositions within himself; he has returned to the primordial state. His 'simplicity' is often symbolised by the child. We will now return to the Metternich story where Isis calls out to the Sun boat of Ra. We have included our comments on the symbolism in parentheses:

> Then Isis sent forth a cry to heaven, and addressed her prayer to the Boat of Millions of Years [eternity]; and the Disc [of the sun, symbol of the immutable Principle] stood still, and moved not from the place where he was. And Thoth [Tahuti] came, and he was provided with magical powers and possessed the great power which made his word to become Ma'at [i.e., the Law or ordinance], and he said 'O Isis, thou goddess, thou glorious one, who hast knowledge how to use thy mouth [i.e., true of speech like Simple Man, and one who knows how to utter words of power], behold, no evil shall come upon the child Horus, for his protection cometh from the Boat of Ra. I have come this day in the Boat of the Disc from the place where it was yesterday. When the night cometh the light shall drive it away for the healing of Horus for the sake of his mother Isis, and every person who is under the knife [threatened by death or sickness] shall be healed also.'[85]

It is important to bear in mind with what follows that metaphysics by its nature cannot be limited, or only in the sense that it deals with truths of a natural (but not naturalistic) and universal order. So whilst our story is sequential the meaning can be symbolic in the same way, for example, that the story of Christ Jesus is linear but also speaks of spiritual knowledge, which is outside of space and time. In the same way that the justified soul is depending from spiritual reality, so Horus as a child is dependent upon his mother Isis, his supreme principle, and in death upon the power of the Word that she invokes.[86] The poisoner of Horus is a scorpion of Set, who is presented as an enemy of Isis and Horus. However, from the metaphysical point of view the spiritually supreme can have no enemies for everything is effaced by it; let us recall again the Simple Man that nothing opposes.

---

[85] Chapter XIII, Isis, *The Gods of the Egyptians Volume 2*, E. A. Wallis Budge.

[86] A deity and her devotee are often referred to as mother and child in traditional doctrine.

The death of Horus is effected by the poison of false cognition or superimposition that totally obscures the immortal consciousness. This is the real enemy of truth. Set was only demonised in the later period of ancient Egypt. Originally, he was Mercurial, a shape shifter. It is worth mentioning again something we said previously concerning the nature of Set:[87]

> He is the most difficult of gods to 'pin down'; his very nature forbids it. He is on the other side of wherever we happen to be in terms of point of view ... The function of Set is dual. Firstly, Set veils the invisible in an almost infinite variety of forms. Secondly, he destroys the illusion of the appearance of things.[88]

From the point of view of unresolved duality Set is the enemy of Horus; but in terms of initiation, all dualities are resolved in their common higher principle: Set destroys the illusion of the world. Only then is Horus, like the initiate of tradition, resurrected by the Real, which is all that remains. This is something that can only be known when one knows it, so to speak.[89] This is why it is Tahuti that sends forth the word to Isis to heal Horus in the legend, for he is spiritual knowledge par excellence. Death is the transition of one state to another. The death and resurrection of Horus can be compared to the opening of the central eye of Shiva, symbolising destruction of the illusion of temporary existence and transition to unity and full spiritual realisation. Tahuti says to Isis, 'I have come from heaven in order to save the child for his mother', and he immediately speaks the words of power which restore Horus to life and protect him ever afterward in heaven, on earth, and in the underworld; his new state of being is permanent.

Tahuti sends forth his words from the central point, that is from the sun boat of Ra that has stopped dead in its tracks in the high heavens above. It is only by abiding in the centre of the individuality that the celestial influence of the divine principle, that which alone can unify the integral being, is received. This central point is symbolised across traditions by the heart, the heart lotus and the cave of the heart. It is the throne of Isis in the Egyptian doctrine and the Brahma-pura (City of Brahma) of Hinduism.[90]

From the *Chandogya Upanishad* VII: 1–3:

---

[87] From *Egyptian Tarot*.

[88] Set XV, *Egyptian Tarot*.

[89] Knowledge and the Seer are one. The seer does not see the eye.

[90] It is interesting to note with reference to the story above that one of Tahuti's names is Het Abtit meaning 'house of the heart'.

OM. There is in this city of Brahma an abode, the small lotus of the heart; within it is a small *akasha*. Now what exists within that small *akasha*, this is to be sought after, that is what one should desire to understand.

If they should say to him: 'Now, with regard to the abode, the small lotus, in this city of Brahma, and the small *akasha* within it—what is there in it that is to be sought after and what is there that one should desire to understand?'[91]

Then he, the guru should say: 'As far as, verily, this great *akasha* extends, so far extends the *akasha* within the heart. Both heaven and earth are contained within it, both fire and air, both sun and moon, both lightning and stars; and whatever belongs to him (i.e., the embodied creature) in this world, and whatever does not, all that is contained within it (i.e., the *akasha* in the heart)'.[92]

We are reminded of another figure of Hoor-pa-kraat where he sits upon a lotus in the mudra of silence—silent that is to the lure of worldly life. It is by dwelling in the centre, the seat of intelligence, further symbolised by the island of Teb where the tale is located, that Horus receives the power to harmonise all the oppositions within himself—oppositions that form a part of ordinary manifested life. Having been restored, he will not dwell thereafter in the world of multiplicity, drawn this way and that by phenomena, but instead partakes of true knowledge. It is called 'Intelligence of the Heart' in ancient Egypt. The senses and ordinary mind cannot comprehend it. In all esoteric traditions it is essential to overcome the limitations and bonds of individual existence—though this does not mean that one ceases to be an individual—which is always the fear of the profane. In fact the truth is quite the reverse for the true individuality is only realised when all accretions of ego are stripped away and the soul laid bare. The means of so doing necessarily involves certain practices, in which the study of sacred scriptures and concentration of the mind is foremost. Further means of support to realisation include ritual, meditation and devotion to God or the Absolute, as well as continual self-observance and the practice of discrimination based on universal principles. In this way it is possible to achieve detachment from the world in the concentration upon the Self as opposed to all manifestations of non-self or objects of mind.

---

[91] This reminds us of the city that the initiate requests entry to in the Swallow Spell in the *Egyptian Book of Coming Forth by Day*.
[92] *The Upanishads Volume Four*, translated by Swami Nikhilananda.

The metaphysical import of the story is further figured in the central image carved in relief on the Metternich Stele (above).[93] Here, Horus is Hoor-pa-kraat. The figure of the youth in traditional symbolism corresponds to the Simple Man of Chinese esotericism, as we have already mentioned, signifying one who has unified all the powers of his being and abides in the primordial state full of bliss and empty of desire for things of the world. This is a definite state of the yogin. In the Hindu tradition it is Balya, the state of childhood. It is worth pointing out here that the 'state of childhood' is a symbolic term that bears no relation whatsoever to the anti-spiritual New Age notion of the 'inner child'. It is the first of three attributes of the *sannyasin* who has achieved perfect realisation.[94] In Balya, the *sannyasin* is a truly integral being wholly concentrated in undifferentiated simplicity; the state is comparable to embryonic potentiality. The second attribute is *panditya*, or learning. As a possessor of knowledge, the yogin becomes a guru or spiritual master with the power to awaken knowledge in others.

---

[93] Photograph courtesy of the Metropolitan Museum of Art, New York.
[94] See Guénon, *Man and His Becoming according to the Vedānta*, Ch. 23.

The third attribute is Mauna, the state of the Muni, the solitary one. The word solitary is meant in terms of non-duality, perfection and the 'void' that is absolute fullness and the only condition in which Union can be truly realised. There is a curious painting of Shiva as a child, lying alone atop a mountain. He is sleeping upon a leopard skin; snakes are in his hand and his hair. He carries the trident, and the drum lies quiet beside him. All duality is forgotten for his two eyes are closed. Only the central eye is open proclaiming Shiva's perfect non-dual state. He is master of all states of existence and transcends them realising perfect totality. The picture is reminiscent of the *sannyasin* and its symbolism corresponds to that of the Hoor-pa-kraat central relief on the Metternich Stele. This is not to say that Shiva *is* Hoor-pa-kraat or visa versa, but rather that the two different traditions are expressing the same truth. There are similar teachings in the Gospel, for example:

> Truly, I say unto you, whoever does not receive the Kingdom of God as a child shall not enter it.[95]

> Thou hast hidden these things from the wise and understanding and have revealed them to babes.[96]

We will mention once again, to avoid all confusion, that the 'child' or 'babes' referred to in Luke and Matthew here has nothing to do with any sentimental notions of infancy, as is made clear by what we have said above concerning the Simple Man of the Far East and Balya of Hinduism. Upon the crown of the head of Hoor-pa-kraat is the face of Bes, who amongst other powers, is the god of childbirth and childhood. Bes as the dwarf symbolises the principial point, Atma— for what is smallest is greatest by inverse analogy.[97] Consider for example the sun, or a star small in our sight but bigger than the earth, or the far away summit of a mountain. Bes is adored on either side by two eyes, for here he is the 'one without a second' wherein Horus has become an integral being.[98]

---

[95] Luke, 18: 17.

[96] Matthew, 11: 25 and Luke, 10: 21.

[97] 'He is my Self within the heart, smaller than a grain of rice, smaller than a grain of barley, smaller than a mustard seed, smaller than a grain of millet; He is my Self within the heart, greater than the earth, greater than the mid-region [the subtle formal domain], greater than heaven [formless domain], greater than all these worlds.' *Chandogya Upanishad* III: 14.3.

[98] See 'Vayus and Integral Being'.

The Hindu doctrine tells us that the living soul, the *jivatma*, is a reflection of Atma, the point, if one likes, replicated, but not ever the same.[99] The Self or Atma only appears to be the creature self, the *jivatma* from the point of view of manifestation. In reality the self is the Self and the individual ego only exists in the way of a reflection in a mirror. Budge says,

> On the Metternich Stele we see the head of the 'Old Man who renews his youth and the Aged One 'who maketh himself once again a boy,' placed above that of Horus, the god of renewed life and of the rising sun, to show that the two heads represent, after all, only phases of one and the same god.[100]

The image symbolises a change of state from individual man to Universal Man.[101] Horus is protected by Bes for opposition no longer exists within him. To quote from Guénon, *Symbolism of the Cross*:

> In the primordial state, these oppositions did not exist. They are derived from the diversification of beings [inherent in manifestation and contingent like it], and from their contacts caused by the universal gyration. They would cease, if the diversity and the movement ceased. They cease forthwith to affect the being who has reduced his distinct ego and his particular movement to almost nothing. Such a being no longer comes into conflict with any other being, because he is established in the infinite, effaced in the indefinite. He has reached the starting point of all transformations, the neutral point at which there are no conflicts, and there he abides. By concentration of his nature, by nourishment of his vital spirit, by reassembly of all his powers, he is united to the principle of all births. His nature being whole [synthetically totalised in the principial unity], his vital spirit being intact, no being can harm him.[102]

---

[99] As if to illustrate this, multiple images of Bes are often found in the temples of ancient Egypt. Even if the image or principle is unchanging, the position and condition are changes of state. There is no repetition in the world. The repetition of gods and other sacred symbols such as the *ankh* can be compared to the power of the number one indefinitely repeating itself to produce multiplicity; and yet the number one remains the same and is unaffected by the repetition. That which is first in the principial order is the least or smallest in the order of manifestation.

[100] Bes, *The Gods of the Egyptians Volume 2*.

[101] This is not the only occasion where the return to youth is figured in ancient Egyptian texts as a transcendent state: 'I am the Great One and the son of the Great One. I am Fire and the son of Fire, and I shall not lose my head in the underworld. I have renewed my youth. I am Horus arising as the phoenix bird of heaven'. See 'Ceremony of the Khu', *The Phoenix and Other Stellar Rites of Initiation*.

[102] Chuang Tzu, chapter 19.

Hoor-pa-kraat, standing upon the crocodiles, walks towards us left foot forward, having become master of the conditions of existence. His left foot forward includes the idea of orientation towards the principle, approaching knowledge with firmness, the union of the self with the Self. He holds in his hands all that could harm him, snakes, scorpions, a lion and an antelope—all of which are creatures of Set. He stands within a reed shelter held on either side by Isis and Tahuti by whose principle Horus is restored to new life and given protection ever afterward. The shelter is cognate with the abode of Shekinah in the Hebraic tradition, and of Brahma-pura in Hinduism reminding us again of the central point mentioned above. To emphasise his spiritual state and what it portends, Horakhty, who is Horus of the horizon, uniter of heaven and earth, and he whom the child becomes, stands by his side. Having reached the primordial state the next step for Horus, implicit in the symbolism, is complete realisation of the supreme and unconditioned state that is beyond even the pure being of Simple Man. In the Hindu tradition it is freedom from the cycle of births altogether and is known as Deliverance.

Having looked briefly at the metaphysical import of the symbolism, we will now turn once again to the story of the Stele itself and its influence upon later traditions. The Stele was named after Prince Metternich to whom it was presented by Muhammad Ali Pasha, the ruler of Egypt in 1828. Curiously, it had been hidden for thousands of years until discovered in a Franciscan monastery in Alexandria. Perhaps the Franciscan monks had recognised the Simple Man in Hoor-pa-kraat—simplicity is synonymous with poverty in the practices of spiritual life. It is notable that Francis of Assisi shed himself of attachment to the worldly in assuming a life of poverty, preaching and contemplation; although religious salvation is not the same as metaphysical realisation, this seems to reflect the path of a *sannyasin* in the Hindu tradition. In any case we cannot say how or why the Stele arrived at the monastery in Alexandria, but what is curious is that it contains many elements that found their way into Christianity and Islam. One might refer amongst others to the Gospel story of Joseph and Mary's flight to Egypt.[103] However, the link most clearly seen is alchemy—it was exactly this single branch of ancient Egyptian sacred science that was assimilated into the above religions, and forms the principle technique of the Hermetic Tradition.

---

[103] See Matthew, 2: 13.

A complete tradition is made up of the Greater Mysteries, the metaphysical, and the Lesser Mysteries, the cosmological. Ancient Egypt had both, and what was later known as the Hermetic wisdom constituted their Lesser Mysteries. These were Hellenised in the Alexandrian period—let us recollect that the Metternich Stele was found in Alexandria—and from there the mysteries were transmitted to the Islamic and Christian worlds. Hermes, the principle god of Hermeticism, was identified by the Greeks with Tahuti, *preserver and transmitter* of tradition, and the sacerdotal authority of the Egyptian Priesthood,

> ... in whose name it formulated and communicated initiatic knowledge.[104]

The story tells us that Isis restores life to Horus by the word of Tahuti and by the power of Seb the earth. These are celestial and terrestrial forces, known across different traditions as essence and substance, *yang* and *yin*, *purusha* and *prakriti* and their dual cosmic force is the alchemical *solve et coagula*, the secret of the Hermetic Great Work. Isis has this power because she is the soul, microcosmic and macrocosmic, and is the foundation, the throne or seat at the heart of all, the principle from which manifestation comes and returns. Here then we have an additional point of view, for the Deliverance of Horus pertains to the Greater Mysteries, but his transmutation, his healing by *solve et coagula*, is of the Lesser Mysteries to which alchemy belongs. As has been explained elsewhere, true alchemy is spiritual, not material; it is inward and not outward. [105] It is comparable with certain branches of yoga where, by the invocation of the double spiral action of the forces of heaven and earth, the being passes through ascending states each of which is marked by the acquisition of spiritual knowledge. The ascent is effected by an inner fire that purifies and consumes the elements as it moves through the various centres or chakras; it is often symbolised by a rising serpent upon a staff, or tree or some other axial image, and by the union of the Sun and Moon. Both Greater and Lesser mysteries are implied here, for they do not invalidate each other—the same symbolism is used in both, and the point of view depends on whether one applies metaphysical or cosmological principles to its meaning. Tahuti as the sacerdotal principle governs initiation in all three worlds, the gross, subtle and formless.

---

[104] See 'The Hermetic Tradition', *Traditional Forms and Cosmic Cycles*, René Guénon.
[105] See 'Magick and Alchemy', *Hermetic Qabalah Foundation*.

Our Stele, like so many stone tablets of ancient Egypt, offers knowledge on these three states. The gross is in the spells for healing the body, the subtle is in the alchemical symbolism of the stories of Isis and Horus, and Ra's journey through the Duat; the formless or universal is attained by way of transposition of that symbolism. The latter would become hidden as Egypt moved further into the Kali Yuga where, for the most part, only the Lesser Mysteries would be understood until finally even they were lost or forgotten, as with the present times.

Hermeticism as it has been understood since the Alexandrian period does not constitute an entire tradition since it is cosmological, not metaphysical. It is all that remains of the Egyptian tradition—yet how did it come to be assimilated so completely into Christianity and Islam? It is said that when a tradition disappears (as Egypt did) it withdraws, but its principial truth takes on new forms in the world. The Metternich Stele was made in the very last days of ancient Egypt, just before that civilisation was lost from the world altogether, and is an example of its knowledge going out in the world.[106] As was pointed out earlier, Tahuti was the *preserver and transmitter* of sacerdotal wisdom; he governs initiation in all three worlds and that which is passed on when the time cycles change.[107]

Alchemy, as with the technique of Hermeticism, is a Royal Art, a method of initiatic realisation that is appropriate for Kshatriyas—kings, nobles and warriors. Throughout its long history Egypt was governed by sacerdotal authority, but in the period following Nactenebo II she was ruled by a succession of kings, empires and armies (*kshatriyas*) as the Persians, the Ptolemies, the Romans and finally Islam occupied her land.

---

[106] That ancient Egypt preserved and transmitted knowledge is related by an Egyptian priest to Solon in Plato's *Timaeus*: 'Now the Nile is our saviour from fire, and as there is little rain in Egypt, we are not harmed by water; whereas in other countries, when a deluge comes, the inhabitants are swept by the rivers into the sea. The memorials which your own and other nations have once had of the famous actions of mankind perish in the waters at certain periods; and the rude survivors in the mountains begin again, knowing nothing of the world before the flood. But in Egypt the traditions of our own and other lands are by us registered forever in our temples.' The priest then invites Solon to hear about these traditions from himself and read them in the temples.

[107] These are the gross, the subtle, and the formless states. The two former correspond to the individual and the latter to the universal.

The Egyptian priesthood did what was necessary to keep their temples and worship alive. They revealed only the Lesser Mysteries from their tradition: oracles, divination and alchemy—for the invaders would only have been interested in that which appealed to their natures and did not threaten their newly acquired power as sacerdotal authority necessarily would. This perhaps goes some way towards explaining the survival of the remnant known as Hermeticism—the Metternich Stele with its magical and alchemical symbolism was surely one of its disseminators.

We have in no way fully explored all the possibilities of symbolism in this study, and indeed we have barely scratched the surface. The difficulty as always with the study of ancient Egypt is that its tradition disappeared from the world thousands of years ago leaving it open to desecration on the one hand and erroneus interpretation on the other. René Guénon suggested that one's understanding would benefit from applying the knowledge of Vedanta to the remnants that are left; we have seen that this does in fact scrub clean a stone often obscured by the materialistic thinking of modern Western minds. It is clear that the Metternich Stele and others like it are extraordinary objects of great magical power formed from traditional sciences. Crucially, their spiritual principles that cure the poisoned at all levels of the being give the keys to exalted supra-human states and ensure the continuance of such knowledge across time and space.[108] Traditional symbolism has universal meaning and application because it is true, and it is true because it comes from a supra-human, that is a principial spiritual source. Our Stele might as well be a stone from heaven.

---

[108] At the end of time all is withdrawn in what Hinduism calls the great dissolution or *mahapralaya*. Tradition and knowledge is preserved across Manvantara Cosmic Cycles, however, as illustrated in such stories as Jonah being swallowed by a whale. He is the seed principle of all knowledge of the previous Manvantara. His disappearance in the belly of the whale, or the ark that sails across the waters of dissolution (*pralaya*) between cycles, is the interval between the ending of one cycle and commencement of the next. The biblical tales of Jonah and Noah have their counterpart in the Arabic tradition and exactly concord with Hinduism, where Vishnu appears to the Lord (Manu) of the next Manvantara in the form of a fish (*nun*, which also means a whale in Arabic).

Alexandrian Gnosticism

I n an earlier work we commented on the Hermetic source text known as the Sethian Gnosis, of which two fragments have survived down the ages from the hands of the historian Flavius Josephus and the early Christian theologian Hippolytus of Rome.[109] Hippolytus condemned all pre-religious 'heresies' in his works, yet while doing so preserved some of them for posterity.[110] He ascribed the earliest form of Christian Gospel writings to the Sethians, whose cults, or at least their scriptures, originated towards the end of the first century, and rapidly spread thoughout the Roman Empire. The Sethians—they were really the classical Gnostics, for 'Sethians' was an invention of Hippolytus—produced the very exceptional scripture, 'Thunder Perfect Mind'.[111] There are three other Gnostic texts that can be related in some ways, and it is worthwhile providing them here with a commentary. The first is from Philo of Alexandria, writing on an early Gnostic cult called the Therapeuts, or Servants of God, thought by some to be very early Christians, or in fact precursers to Christianity:[112]

> Now they who betake themselves to this service of God, do so not because of any custom, or on someone's advice and appeal, but carried away with heavenly love, like those initiated into the Bacchic or Corybantic Mysteries, they are a-fire with God until they see the object of their love. Nor because thou hast a tongue and mouth and organ of speech, shouldst thou tell forth all, even things that may not be spoken. Wherefore I think that all those who are not utterly without proper instruction, would prefer to be made blind than to see things not proper to be seen, to be made deaf than to hear harmful words, and to have their tongue cut out, to prevent them divulging aught of the ineffable Mysteries. Nay, it is even better to make oneself eunuch than to rush madly into unlawful unions.[113]

---

[109] See *Nu Hermetica*, 'Sons of Gods'.

[110] Flavius Josephus is thought to have lived from 37–100 AD and Hippolytus from 170–235 AD. The latter was the first Antipope.

[111] We produced a lengthy commentary on 'Thunder Perfect Mind' for our book, *Thunder Perfect Gnosis*.

[112] Philo of Alexandria is thought to have lived in the very troubled times between the end of the first century BC and the middle of the first century AD.

[113] See Volume I *Thrice Greatest Hermes* translated by G.R.S. Mead.

Philo describes an intensely inspired, devotional cult. The Romans slandered the Bacchic rites for political reasons, making them out to be no more than orgies of drunkenness and debauchery. Philo, on the other hand, makes favourable comparison with fervour for union with God. He frequently refers in his writings to an oath of silence, by which one should not divulge the 'ineffable Mysteries', and as is very clear from his language, this was meant to be taken with utmost seriousness. Philo defended the orthodox Jewish religion and yet at the same time, as an Alexandrian, saw no difficulty in combining this with the Gnosticism that flourished at the time. It took a few centuries before the emergent 'proto-orthodox' Christian religion succeeded in almost entirely suppressing it. The Gnostic cults were almost certainly the antecedents of later Christianity but differed greatly. Gnosticism was not in any way a religion but was initiatic, for an elect. Christianity was not in any sense at all initiatic, and was dedicated to religious law 'for all'.

In Philo's account of Gnosticism the soul is clearly the 'Virgin' of the mysteries, who must become wedded to God. In the higher or cosmological sense, the Virgin is Intelligence and the Son of God is Logos, the Word. The equation with the sephirotic Tree of Life where Chokmah and Binah are exactly Logos and what is sometimes called the Intelligible Light is obvious to anyone that has studied the subject. It is the Great Work for the Son of God—who is not always named 'Jesus' in Gnostic texts—to rescue the soul fallen into the evil of the world. The soul, likewise, is not always called 'Mary'. Some of the Gnostics that were later singled out for utmost condemnation characterised their holy man, whether he was called Jesus or by some other name, as eschewing religion and scriptural authorities, preferring the company of social outcasts and taking as a consort a harlot named Mary Magdalene. This 'Jesus' was not Jewish, even if he is referred to as 'Rabbi' in the Gospels, first written in Greek not Hebrew, and neither was he a Christian priest—as the religion was not yet invented. When Hippolytus conceded that the earliest form of Christian writings belonged to the Sethians, he perhaps inadvertently gave away the secret of the original and authentic Christianity. Soon, all traces of it were to be obliterated, with deliberate intent it seems. The second Gnostic source work is from Macrobius, and is called 'The Descent of the Soul from the Height of Cosmos to the Depth of Earth'.[114]

---

[114] This is from the Roman Neoplatonist Ambrosius Theodosius Macrobius, from his commentary on Cicero's 'Dream of Scipio', which is essentially a reworking of the 'Vision of Er' from Plato's *Republic*.

According to Pythagoras, when the Soul descends from the Boundary where the Zodiac and Milky Way meet, from a spherical form, which is the only divine one, it is elongated into a conical one by its downward tendency [that is, an egg-shaped or elliptical form resembling that of a pine cone]. Just as the line is born from the point and proceeds into length out of the indivisible, so the soul from its point, that is 'monad', comes into 'dyad'—its first production or lengthening. And this is the essence that Plato in the *Timaeus,* speaking about the construction of the World Soul, describes as indivisible yet at the same time divisible. The Soul of the World as well as the soul of an individual man is in one respect incapable of divorce if it is regarded from the standpoint of the simplicity of its divine nature. In another sense [that is from the point of view of manifestation] it is capable of division, since the former is diffused through the members of the world and the latter through those of a man.

The pinecone is one of the primary symbols of Bacchus or of Dionysus. The cone is related to the egg of cosmos, the Orphic Egg that is related in the Microcosm to the individual soul. This is no different from Hiranyagarbha of the Hindu doctrines, the world egg that divides into two halves, heaven and earth. Later this was assimilated to Ishvara, the Lord of the Universe, which most nearly matches the God of religions, though as such he does not create anything *ex nihilo*. It is rather that the universe is ontological, not composed of some vague 'matter'. Hiranyagarbha is Pure Being, not a symbol of the cosmos but the principle by which the cosmos is able to manifest. 'Monad' and 'dyad' are analogous terms as the principle is not 'self-contained' as a unit in manifestation but is Infinite.

When then the soul is drawn to body—in this first production of it—it begins to experience a material agitation, matter flowing into it. And this is remarked by Plato in the *Phaedo* when he says that the soul is drawn to body staggering with recent intoxication—meaning us to understand by this a new draught of matter's superfluity, by which it becomes defiled and gravid and so is brought down.

The word 'matter' used in the Mead translation is from the Greek *hylē*, which is much better understood as 'substance' or 'form'. The soul's 'recent intoxication' refers to previous states of existence. The transmigration of souls, as with metempsychosis, must not in any way be confused with modern reincarnationism.[115] The word 'gravid' indicates a sort of mould, into which something is poured. Latent impressions from other states of being persist and desire draws the soul to rebirth, for more temporary pleasures and suffering.

---

[115] See 'Reincarnationism'.

A symbol of this mystic secret is that Starry Cup (*Crater*) of Father Bacchus placed in the space between Cancer and Leo—meaning that intoxication is there first experienced by souls in their descent by the influx of matter into them. From which cause also forgetfulness, the companion of intoxication, then begins to secretly creep into souls. For if souls brought to body memory of the divine things of which they were conscious in heaven, there would be no difference of opinion among men concerning the divine state.

But all, indeed, in their descent drink of forgetfulness—some more, some less. And of this cause on earth, though the truth is not clear to all, they nevertheless all have some opinion about it; for opinion rises where memory sinks. Those, however, are greater discoverers of truth who have drunk less of forgetfulness, because they remember more easily what they have known before in that state.

The Starry Cup or Crater of Father Bacchus is 'placed in the space between Cancer and Leo'. The Crater refers to the constellation of the same name, but is symbolically the true centre of the Zodiac. It is the point of conjunction of the Sun and the Moon—the latter being the star of Cancer and the former that of Leo the Lion. For the word 'descent' we could almost substitute *nescience*, for the consequence is the same. It is the mistaking of the Self for the objects of desire created by the mind and senses that leads to the endless chain of rebirth into further states of being. The forgetfulness is thus not knowing the Real, the Self as Infinite, Absolute, Indestructible, Eternal. It is interesting to learn there are degrees of forgetfulness. Some souls remember more than others, quickly recovering what they knew of the celestial worlds, for example. Of the profane, these are the utterly forgetful, 'for opinion rises where memory sinks'.

Hence it is that which the Latins call a 'lecture' (*lectio*) the Greeks call a 're-knowing' (*repetita cognito*), because when we give utterance to true things we recognise the things which we knew by nature before the influence of matter intoxicated our souls in their descent into body. Now it is this matter (*hylē*), which, after being impressed by the divine ideas, fashioned every body in the cosmos that we see. Its highest and purest nature, by means of which the divinities are either sustained or consist, is called Nectar, and is believed to be the drink of the gods, while its lower and more turbid nature is the drink of souls. The latter is what the Ancients called the River of Lethe or Forgetfulness. Orphic initiates, however, suppose that Dionysus himself is to be understood as *Hylic Nous*—that Mind which, after its birth from the Indivisible Mind, is divided into individual minds.

And it is for this reason that in their mystery tradition, Dionysus is represented as being torn limb from limb by the fury of the Titans, and, after the pieces have been buried, as coming together again whole and one; for Nous—which, as we have said, is their term for Mind—by offering itself for division from its undivided state, and by returning to the undivided from the divided, both fulfils the duties of the cosmos and at the same time performs the mysteries of its own nature.

What the Greeks called *ambrosia* or nectar is called *soma* in the Vedas. It is the sum total of all knowledge of that which makes up the integral being, whether that is understood on the macrocosmic or microcosmic level. Souls who drink from the waters of Lethe, however, become intoxicated and forget, or fall asleep. The reference to the Orphic mysteries is interesting, because it is clear that Dionysus, later called Bacchus by the Romans, is an intermediary that is born from what Christians would call the Father or Spirit into an individual human state of being. Essentially, the human individuality is in the domain of subtle form, and is linked to a body made in the gross form. But more than that, Dionysus is the principle by which individual minds are realised as such, and separated by this knowledge from the principial state. Thus the being torn limb from limb, as with Osiris, is to be born human so as to recover full knowledge and re-ascend, and which is obedient to the laws of the cosmos while at the same time fulfilling a divine destiny.

The soul, therefore, having by means of this first weight of matter fallen down from the Zodiac and Galaxy into the series of spheres that lie below them, in continuing its descent through them, is not only enwrapped in the envelope of a luminous body, but also develops the separate motions which it is to exercise: In the sphere of Saturn it develops the powers of reasoning and of theorising [or of contemplative reason, synthesis as opposed to analysis]; in that of Jupiter, the power of putting into practice; in that of Mars, the power of ardent vehemence; in that of the Sun, the nature of sensing and imagining; in that of Venus, the motion of desire; in the sphere of Mercury, the power of giving expression to and interpretation of feelings; on its entrance into the sphere of the Moon it brings all into activity through following its nature of making bodies grow and of moving them. And this soul, though the last thing in the divine series, is nevertheless the first thing in us and in all terrestrial beings; just as this body of ours, though the dregs of things divine, is still the first substance of the animal world.

And this is the difference between terrene bodies and supernal—I mean those of the heaven and stars and of the other elements [apart from those of earth]—that the latter are summoned upwards to the abode of the soul, and are worthy of immunity from death [that is immortality] from the very nature of the space in which they are and their imitation of sublimity. The soul, however, is drawn down to these terrene bodies; so it is thought to die when it is imprisoned in the region of things fallen and in the abode of death. Nor should it cause distress that we have so often spoken of death in connection with the soul that we have declared to be superior to death. For the soul is not annihilated by what is called its death, but is only buried for a time; nor is the blessing of its perpetuity taken from it by its submersion for a time, since when it shall have made it worthy to be cleansed clean utterly of all contagion of its vice, it shall once more return from body to the light of Everlasting Life *restored* and whole.

The Dionysian cult and Orphic mysteries are essentially positive, as is the Hindu doctrine when properly understood, in that the integral Self is not in any way affected by the separated souls that fall into forgetfulness, or their pleasures and sorrows. The way of the Initiate is to return, through what is called an 'imitation of sublimity', which is the higher intellect or Sanskrit *boddhi*, that has its abode at the formless level, upwards through the degrees of supra-human states of being, to the True Self, or Atma. The final source work we shall look at here is 'The Vision of Aridaeus', as related by Plutarch.[116] The vision begins in the following manner:

When his consciousness passed out of the body, he experienced from the change the same sort of sensation that a sailor would who had been swept overboard into deep water. Then, coming up a little, he seemed to breathe in every part of him, and to see on every side at once, as though the soul—the 'single eye'—had been opened.

Of objects with which he had been previously familiar, he saw none save the stars; they were, however, of stupendous size and at enormous distances from one another, and poured forth a marvellous radiance of colour and sound, so that the soul riding smoothly in the light, as a ship in calm weather, sailed easily and swiftly in every direction.

---

[116] Plutarch of Caeroneia, in Boeotia, flourished from about the middle of the first to the last quarter of the second century AD. See *Thrice Greatest Hermes* [ibid]. It is curious to learn from the latter that some have supposed Plutarch to have derived certain ideas from Christianity, whereas what we are including here from his work vastly predates the Christian era. It would be as though monotheism, which is only meaningful when understood as an expression of one supreme principial Absolute, is an 'invention' of recent times!

He then passes through the region of Hades where souls, some in a state of great confusion, pass up and down as 'flame-like bubbles', or spindles bobbing up and down. Others are joyful and occupy a place at the top of the 'envelope' or surround, which suggests that the regions are enclosed to a certain extent. Here, Aridaeus encounters a man that he thinks died when he was a boy, but of this he is not completely sure. In any case, he is to all intents and purposes a hermit that plays the role of psychopomp for Aridaeus. He gives Aridaeus the name Thespesius, which means 'Sent by the Gods', "for indeed, thou art not dead!" After visiting the regions of Justice, where souls suffer greatly for their iniquity, the mysterious guide conducts Aridaeus across a Chasm or Crater:

> He was conducted by his kinsman [the afore-mentioned hermit] at great speed across an immense space, as it seemed, nevertheless easily and directly as though supported by wings of light-rays; until having arrived at a vast vortex extending downwards, he was abandoned by the power that supported him.

What is being described here is really no different than that which was explained by the Neoplatonist Macrobius previously. The difference is that here we have a 'vision' that might easily be mistaken for a dream or even mere fantasy but is more likely the resultant of a man coming into contact with an initiatic organisation—though without yet having undergone the necesssary preparations for initiation. The travelling at great speed across immense space is described in almost exactly the same terms in the *Yoga-Sutras*, regarding certain of the Supernormal Powers.[117] Such powers are sometimes latent within the person from birth, owing to what was gained in previous states of the being, or otherwise they spontaneously appear if Samyama Yoga is persisted in for a long time. The Greeks called the Logos the Heavenly Horn of Men, the Cup in which is mingled the elements of life. A horn becomes a vessel, cone or cup when inverted.[118] When the horn or cone is travelled upwards to its principial point, then comparison can be made with the *sutratma* and *sushumna* in the *Yoga-Sutras* and Tantras. This is also likened to a light-ray that can be followed to its source and also equates to the *boddhi* or higher intellect, belonging to the formless realms.

---

[117] See Part Two, 'Divine Hearing and Light-travelling'.
[118] The horn is also spelled *qorn*, from whence 'unicorn', for example—the point being that it is a single horn, an upward path that can also be inverted.

He observed also that the same thing happened to the rest of the souls there, for checking their flight, like birds, and sinking down, they fluttered round the vortex in a circle, not daring to go straight through it. Inside it seemed to be decked like Bacchic caves with trees and verdure and every kind of foliage, while out of it came a soft and gentle air, laden with marvellous sweet scents, making a blend like wine for topers, so that the souls feasting on the fragrance were melted with delight in mutual embraces, while the whole place was wrapt in revelry and laughter and the spirit of sport and pleasure. Thespesius' kinsman told him that this was the Way by which Dionysus ascended to the Gods and afterwards took up Semele. However, since it was the Place of Lethe (Oblivion), he would not suffer Thespesius to stay there, as much as he wished to do so, but forcibly dragged him away, explaining that the rational part of the soul was melted and moistened by pleasure, while the irrational part, and that which is of a corporeal nature, being moistened and made fleshly, awakens the memory of the body, and from this memory comes a yearning and a desire which drag down the soul into generation. The soul is, as it were, being weighed down with moisture.

Comparison might be made with Dante's *Divine Comedy*, where a descent is made into hell before ascending.[119] This is understood by first positing a sphere: to reach its centre one must travel downwards in a spiralic manner. The circles are ever-decreasing until one arrives at the centre but after that, if the direction is continued, the spiralic path widens again until the other side of the sphere is arrived at. Through going down and continuing, one has arrived back at the top but on the opposite side of the two hemispheres. Thus Dionysus was able to ascend to the Gods and rescue Semele from the Place of Lethe. The memory of having a body is awakened in this place, for the soul is here to be considered as discarnate. The promise of sensual pleasures cannot therefore be fulfilled until the soul suffers rebirth. This blend of scents like 'wine for topers' is the inverse form of the nectar of the Gods, alluded to in 'Descent of the Soul'.

Next Thespesius, after travelling another great distance, seemed to be looking at a huge Cup, with streams flowing into it; one whiter than the foam of the sea or snow, another like the purple which the rainbow sends forth, while from a distance the others were tinged with other colours, each having its own shade. But when he came closer, the Cup itself (into which they flowed)—the surroundings disappearing, and the colours growing fainter—lost its varied colouring and only retained a white brilliance. And he saw three beings (daimones) seated together, forming a triangle one with the other, mixing the streams in definite proportions.

---

[119] See 'Knights of the Cross', *The Way of Knowledge*.

There is now a second cup, similar with its streams or rivers to the paradise or Garden of Eden in other traditions, which usually posit four of these. The journey of descent has culminated in ascent to the surface of the sphere or world, from where it is possible to pass upward through the Gate of the Gods. The Gate of Men (*pitriyani*) is entered by way of the summer cup or solstice, symbolised by Cancer and Leo, while the Gate of Gods (*devayani*) is entered by way of the winter cup or solstice, as figured by Capricorn and Aquarius. At the beginning of 'Descent of the Soul' the boundary was marked by the crossing of the Zodiac with the Milky Way. In likewise fashion, it is the crossing made by the ecliptic circle with the celestial pole that forms this greater sphere, and which may be likened to the Cube of Space or three-dimensional cross, called Chi-Rho by early Christians and still depicted on priestly garments as the monogram of Christ. Notably, the colours of the rainbow resolve into pure whiteness or effulgence once Thespesius reaches the outer limits of the sublunary worlds. The three daimones ('angels') that mix the streams in definite proportions remind us, though no exact correspondence should be assumed, of the three Gunas of Hinduism, and from which their weaving together produces all the multitudinous worlds and beings of manifestation out of the undifferentiated ground.

The hermit instructs that here the true is mixed with the fictitious, in the way of dreams, by which can be inferred all the various modifications that are made in the realm of the soul as individuality, the cogniser of things. The three angels in fact form a kind of tripod, and though Thespesius wants to see into it, he is unable to as the light is too blinding. He has reached his limit at the sphere of the Moon, where he hears the oracles of the Sibyl, and various omens corresponding to the lesser magical powers. From there he sinks to the lowest of the hell regions, and witnesses souls in awful torment. At the last Aridaeus very nearly succumbs to a devil in the form of a vast woman, that would have tortured him horribly, but by the intervention of another woman he escapes, and returns to his normal consciousness.

> Then, as though he were suddenly sucked through a tube by a terribly strong and violent in-breath, he lit in his body, and woke up just as they were on the point of burying him.

Clearly, Aridaeus was not able to get further, to the pure light and the supra-formal regions, owing to his own earthly limitations. For this reason he was only able to hear the voice of the Sibyl—in some ways the personification of the face of the Moon as the limit to the sublunary or intermediate realm—foretelling mundane events.

After this, the vision becomes frightful, and the hermit leaves Aridaeus in his terror, for he has descended to the worst of the infernal realms. Plutarch is essentially giving us an idea of the vision of the sublunary regions such as might be experienced by one not prepared. The hermit has already warned Aridaeus, before trying to show him the tripod:

> As for the Oracle of Apollo, you have not seen it, nor will you be able to do so, for the stern cable of your soul does not give or slacken further upwards, but drags it down through being made fast to the body.

Thus initiation, preceded by the necessary training and preparations, will be needed before Aridaeus is able to advance beyond the terrors of Hades. It is the same vortex or Crater—which to the mortal man signifies the descent of the soul into forgetfulness and generation—that is the means of raising the soul upward towards heaven. For this reason the hermit tells Aridaeus that this, "was the Way by which Dionysus ascended to the Gods and afterwards took up Semele"—yet at the same time it was called the Place of Lethe, or Oblivion. As according to the Greek legend, when Semele saw Zeus in his true form she was killed instantly by his light and power. She was subsequently restored to a new life with the Gods through the power of her son, Dionysus that was fathered by Zeus. Thus Dionysus has frequently been compared with Christ Jesus—not without some justification although there is no reason to assume that anything has been 'borrowed' from one tradition into another; it should not be surprising that the same truth is expressed in all traditions, which when realised perfectly are all expressions of the one primordial tradition. The 'second birth', which is a reconstitution of the psychic elements and is the necessary preparation for real or true initiation, cannot take place without a sort of 'second death'.[120]

The Guardian Angel or Intelligible Light is effectively, and to all intents and purposes from the corporeal point of view, the saviour of his own soul by uniting with her and raising both to a higher state. In the Tantras, the Shakti power resides in her subtle body, and that body is animated at the beginning by ritual and other practices, though it should be emphasised that nothing is possible without concentration of the mind as she is also the intellectual power.

---

[120] The doctrine of the second birth is revealed in the Gospel of St. John, in the meeting between Jesus and Nicodemus, who visited him 'by night'. In other words, he became aware of the Master first on the subtle plane (see the book of John, 3).

It is evident that for long ages of time these ancient mysteries were preserved and practised by various cults. It is recounted in the Gnostic *Pistis Sophia* that karmic agencies administer a draught of poison or Oblivion that is made out of the Seed of Iniquity, itself composed of every kind of desire and forgetfulness. This is no different from the yogic science of the *karmasayas* or latent impressions of past deeds and actions that are able to become active and regenerate afflictions and woes, and which, as according to that doctrine, is without beginning or end but Knowledge (*jnana*), or Gnosis, in the special sense of the word, alone destroys ignorance forever.

This 'draught of poison' or Oblivion causes the soul to forget all the regions she has passed through, all the spaces she has travelled in countless births in other states of being, therefore suffering the great misfortune of forgetting all she has learned. The deadly draught then becomes an external body, a double or counterfeit. Likewise, the evil demiurge that the Gnostics considered as no different from Satan is the 'Creator God' of religions that have become separated from true knowledge of the symbolism they carry. When a soul has undergone purification through the sacred rites, or yogic training, it is a different matter—for then the Cup that is brought to the soul is not the Cup of Forgetfulness, but as recounted in *Pistis Sophia*, 'a Cup full of intuition and wisdom, and also prudence'. When this happens, the soul is cast into a body that does not fall asleep and forget but goes on 'seeking after the Mysteries of Light, until it hath found them, by order of the Virgin of Light, in order that it may inherit the Light for ever.' The Virgin is the pure soul, Sophia, conceiving of itself the form of a child of light so the Guardian Angel or principial being may be known, and born forth in consciousness.

Although it has not been the main purpose of writing this article, the question of the real origins of Christianity has been touched upon and there might be some advantage in adding something further in respect of that. René Guénon went as far as he wanted to go with it in the first two chapters of his posthumously published work, *Insights into Christian Esoterism*. He attempted to explain to his readers, some of whom were Catholic, that Christianity in its present form has no initiatic elements whatsoever. What he said was met with as much incomprehension as it would no doubt be met with today, although possibly for different reasons. In essence he was saying that there must have been 'two Christianities' in the very earliest beginnings. One was initiatic and exclusive, as is always necessary with initiatic organisations, and the other, which came about later, was purely exoteric.

Christianity today is not in any way initiatic, and has not been for very many centuries, certainly not in the Western Roman Church let alone Protestantism. 'Traditionalist' Catholics were fairly upset and shocked to hear this and angrily responded by saying that the Holy Ghost is present at the Mass. Guénon went on to politely explain that the Holy Ghost does not initiate anyone in itself, initiation is carried by the initiatic chain. So it makes no difference in that respect if the Holy Ghost is present or not, it can only be effective on an exoteric level in this case. Initiation is esoteric, not exoteric. The Eucharist is not a rite of initiation, though it might once have been a rite reserved for those who were already initiates. Without the initiatic rites, the work and preparation that is necessary, no initiation can take place. Baptism was at one time an initiatic rite, but as babies are routinely baptised, no matter what their latent qualifications, clearly this has no effect at all. A baby can hardly be prepared for initiation.

Without an extension or 'bridge' formed between the realm of the human individuality and the formless essence, no true knowledge of an initiatic order can be gained.[121] The bridge or means is then no different really than the Logos of the Alexandrian Gnostics and early Christians, or pre-Christians. This brings us to the rare exceptions to the rule, one of those being *heysachasm*, which is part of the Eastern Church or Orthodox Church. Although it was not mentioned by Guénon, there must almost certainly be an initatic core remaining in the Egyptian Coptic Church, which still survives to this day in spite of relentless persecution, and which owes its origins to the very earliest Alexandrian Christianity.

Guénon also wished to draw attention to the curious fact that Christianity does not have a sacred language, as do other traditions. The New Testament was first written in Greek, and it is from Greek that translations into all other languages were made. The question then, considering it must have been orally transmitted at the first, is how is it that the teachings of Jesus were not first written in the language he spoke, that language itself being unknown? It is indeed 'hard to answer', as he wrote. When explaining why it was that he needed to return to the very question of the character of Christianity, which owed in fact to the perplexity of some of his readers, Guénon stated unequivocally the following:

---

[121] The answer to the obvious question that then arises with certain of the saints, is that they got their initiation from somewhere other than the Church itself, which is purely exoteric. And that there were initiatic links until the Middle Ages. After that, there was only 'mysticism' as a possibility within the exoteric Christian religion.

There are several reasons for this, the first being the almost impenetrable obscurity that surrounds everything relating to the origins and early stages of Christianity, an obscurity so profound that, upon reflection, it seems impossible that it should simply have been accidental, but more likely was expressly intended.

Earlier he had said that there must have been initiatic rites, but they are lost or were never written down. At the time of his writing, what existed of the Gnostic source texts was scanty and fragmentary, like the texts we have commented on here, some from those that were vehemently opposed to the doctrine, as is the case with Hippolytus. The Dead Sea Scrolls were not pieced together and translated until decades after Guénon passed on and so although it is speculative, it is hard not to think that if he had been able to access them he might well have found in them the proof of what he had already intuited in regard to the real character of early Christianity.

It is interesting to note in this respect that many branches of Christianity, East and West, still incorporate the bishop's crozier, which in some cases is identical to the *hekat* of Egyptian gods and kings, and in other cases is in the form of a tau-cross or is even headed by two serpents, somewhat like the Hermetic Caduceus. We will explain this further in the following chapter.

Coptic Iesus Christos Monogram

Sophia: Gnosis and Syneses

I n a previous work we gave a synthetic overview of the Gnostic schema.[122] There was not the space to explore the subject very thoroughly. Indeed, to explore the Gnostic cosmology in depth would take an entire volume but it is worthwhile looking more closely at one detail concerning the divine Sophia. Sophia, the feminine 'wisdom' or Intelligible Light plays a central rôle in the Gnostic Cosmograph. Syneses and Gnosis are best understood as complementary and not opposed. While there is no comparison between the pure and direct knowledge of Gnosis and Syneses, which might be called a simulacrum of knowledge, it can be seen here that the two are in a sense interlocked, and not separate; one can reach into the other and Sophia is the means of so doing.

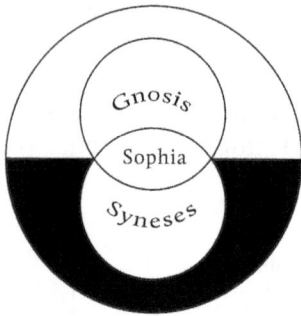

Gnosis

Sophia

Syneses

The diagram is a detail from the Gnostic Cosmograph, more or less equivalent, by comparison with the Qabalistic model, to an expansion of Binah, inclusive of the Garden of Eden and Da'ath (Knowledge) as hidden within her. This is not inclusive of the supernal trinity, in which she is enclosed, or the lower worlds consisting of the planetary spheres, and which we may posit as being below her feet in the usual order commencing from Saturn and culminating in the Moon.[123] It is also possible to equate the central position of Sophia with the ancient Egyptian Throne of Isis, especially as the throne hieroglyph, Iset, which is her name, always includes a rectangular enclosure where the the base and the back of the seat form a right angle. The inset is expressive of the *phi* ratio in mathematics; by extension it forms a spiral wave, symbolising all the possibilities for the multitudinous 'worlds' of the cosmological sphere. Looked at another way, it is the Brahma-pura, the 'city of the God', or heart lotus in which yoga meditation is done. It is full of *akasha* or ether, permeating all of space.[124]

---

[122] *Thunder Perfect Gnosis*, 'Gnosis of the Thirty Aeons'.

[123] In the Gnostic Cosmograph the terrestrial sphere is placed in the exact centre of concentric circles, and within that the most inferior region of Tartarus, or hell.

[124] It is not the *anahatha* chakra but the 'shrine within the heart', the seat of deity.

Gnosis is the special kind of knowledge, and the direct equivalent of the Sanskrit *jnana*, not separate from supreme reality, while Sophia is the world soul or feminine personification of Universal Being. The latter, it should be well noted, has nothing to do with the human collectivity and is descriptive of that which transcends the human individual state entirely—a collection of individual states is no different in this sense than any particular individual being. Syneses, 'Insight', is relatively a state of unknowing compared to the pure knowledge, yet so long as it is inclusive of Sophia—which is a matter of faith, not reason—there is a possibility of gaining Gnosis.

There is a relation between Syneses and the Sanskrit *manas* (mind) and its adjunct mental faculties, which perceives upon the basis of the sensory perception of objects. Syneses literally means 'to put things together', which is to form reasoned mental concepts. Gnosis is not about forming mental perceptions; it is direct knowledge, which is the etymological meaning of metaphysics. When the mind is fully clear of its own perceptions, as in yoga meditation, then it may be informed by the ray of the higher intellect or Sanskrit *boddhi*, which is almost the exact equivalent of Binah, or Da'ath in its superior aspect as opposed to the Abyss, its inferior aspect. Concerning the latter, it will suffice to say here that the collapse of the mind into the Abyss is the resultant of total ignorance of Sophia, a wilful shutting out of the divine presence in all things, so there is no relation between things, no *sutra* or 'golden thread' to follow the way that leads out of hell.[125]

What is really important to grasp is that divine Sophia is placed exactly between the direct knowledge or Gnosis and the reflected knowledge called Syneses.[126] She is situated between the light and the darkness at the junction of the two spheres, thus forming the sacred symbolism of the *vesica piscis*.

---

[125] A great deal of overblown nonsense has been made in certain areas of the Western Mystery Tradition over the so-called 'crossing of the Abyss', as though it were the achievement of an 'adept', whereas it only refers to the inferior aspect of Da'ath—ordinary knowledge. The grades in neo-spiritual or occult organisations count to nothing much at all spiritually—or in terms of a genuinely initiatic tradition, where such a 'crossing' would only qualify the veriest beginner.

[126] There is a further comparison where Gnosis has a relation with Sanskrit *shruti*, direct or 'received' knowledge that forms the basis of the written Vedas, and *smrti* or reflected knowledge of commentaries and other derived or secondary teaching.

The Shakti—a term that is the direct equivalent of the Shekinah or feminine Holy Spirit in the Hebraic tradition—has differing functions, including that of intermediary between Heaven and Earth, Spirit and Mind. As Spirit, she is the 'fragrance' that permeates both light and darkness, as is recounted in the Gnostic source work, 'Sethian Gnosis'.[127] Sophia, as with the Egyptian Isis and the various forms of Mahamaya Shakti in Hinduism, is a personification of Pure Being, which is the principle of manifestation and all 'life' or existence in manifest worlds. What is rarely understood, however, is that Eve of the biblical book of Genesis, who is tempted by the Serpent in the Garden of Eden and precipitates the 'fall' of Adam, is no less than the same principle, but as operative on different levels, higher and lower. And it is precisely this dual position that is represented by Sophia on our Gnostic Cosmograph. As we have pointed out previously, in the book of Genesis, Eve (or Sophia) was supposed to have eaten the apple of the fruit of knowledge, or otherwise is said to have 'stooped down' towards the Kingdom of Shells or Matter, thus precipitating the fateful Fall of Adam. In fact, the true Knowledge or Gnosis is the crown of Sophia; however, if we follow the other circles below Sophia indicative of cosmic manifestation the possibility of 'falling' becomes easier to understand: immediately below the Realm of Sophia as depicted above is placed the Garden of Eden, in which is the Tree of Life and Tree of Death. The inner abode of the Garden is protected by the flaming sword that turns every way, to keep man from desecrating Eden.

It is not really divine Sophia or Eve who 'falls', or is tempted by ordinary knowledge; it is man's consciousness that becomes degraded as the Cosmic Cycles move him (spatially) further and further away from the supreme principle as we near the end of time. While the rôle of Christ as both son and consort of Sophia is more readily understood in that he is the saviour who descends in order to re-ascend, the function of Sophia, which is integral, is rarely comprehended owing to inability to 'put things together' beyond a moral interpretation. No matter what side it falls on, whether it is favourable to the Woman, something that usually comes about through fashionable political idealism, or unfavourable, which comes about through ignorance of the importance of the sacred feminine, such interpretation is fated to utterly miss the mark. And that is to say, it 'falls' into sin or error, and even begets and multiples further sin or ignorance.

---

[127] See 'Sons of Gods', *Nu Hermetica*.

It will help to recollect that Adam and Eve are not separate in Eden, and neither are they really human—for the human state implies separation where the mind and body dwell within the confines of time and space, and are then subject to death. In several ancient languages, the words that declare 'the woman' share a common etymological root: Asha (Hebrew), Isa or Isis (Egyptian) and Isani (Sanskrit). The same words also have the meaning of 'being', 'existence' and 'life'. In Egyptian, Isa has the meaning of 'fragrance', which is a reference to the essential nature of the Tree of Life, which is a universal symbol for all worlds of being. If we return for a moment to the Throne of Isis, which is also her name, we can then recollect that all worlds of being and their possibilities are contained in the one symbol of the rectangle.[128] All moralistic notions, which arise from the exoteric telling of the 'story' of Eve and the Serpent, are destroyed when it is realised that Sophia is Life Itself. If one would run in blind panic and crash into a tree, not seeing it, one could hardly blame the tree. Likewise, if one does not perceive Life, its real meaning and import, one can hardly then blame Life for the resultant state of affairs, which includes subjection to separation and death and all illusions and afflictions arising therefrom.

There is a subtler error made by some who study Eastern doctrines, especially those whose scriptures have been 'Westernised' or otherwise badly translated, or even made up or re-invented by modern day charlatans (however sincere they may be); this is to repeat, after the manner of a parrot, 'all is illusion'. The productions of Maya, and Maya as the mysterious cause, without beginning, of all such phenomena, are illusionary from the point of view of the supreme Atma but there are degrees of reality. Furthermore, imagining that Nature is a 'void' or emptiness, and so nothing at all, is exactly that— an imagining that has no root in reality at all. It is better to say the mantra Om Tat Sat—'All of that (everything) is Brahma (in reality)'. The working of Shaktimaya, Isis, Sophia or in whatever name we know her, is sublime and most wonderful to behold—indeed, he that truly does behold it is very much blessed. Returning to the Cosmograph again, Sophia is seated between the light and the dark hemisphere of the circle. She is not that light or that darkness but she permeates all of it, and all, thanks to this mystery, are able to partake of the Intelligible when they know Sophia within them.

---

[128] The rectangle is also a symbol of Set, whose name only differs from Iset, 'Throne' or 'Foundation', by one letter. Set is particularly the builder and layer of foundations, also the 'measurer' or Geometer, as the Greeks put it.

To know Sophia is to be known by her. It is for this reason that Christ Jesus said to his disciples, of those who did not know him, that *he never knew them*. It is worthwhile quoting Matthew 7: 21–27 in full:

Not every one that saith unto me, Lord, Lord, shall enter into the kingdom of heaven; but he that doeth the will of my Father which is in heaven.

Many will say to me in that day, Lord, Lord, have we not prophesied in thy name? and in thy name have cast out devils? and in thy name done many wonderful works?

And then will I profess unto them, *I never knew you*: depart from me, ye that work iniquity.

Therefore whosoever heareth these sayings of mine, and doeth them, I will liken him unto a wise man, which built his house upon a rock:

And the rain descended, and the floods came, and the winds blew, and beat upon that house; and it fell not: for it was founded upon a rock.

And every one that heareth these sayings of mine, and doeth them not, shall be likened unto a foolish man, which built his house upon the sand:

And the rain descended, and the floods came, and the winds blew, and beat upon that house; and it fell: and great was the fall of it.

The original Greek rendition of 7: 23 uses a form of the word *gnosis* (placed in italics above).[129] Here it is made very clear that 'wise sayings' are certainly not enough, and that many apparent miracles mean nothing and indeed, may well be the tricks of Antichrist. All are as a house built upon sand unless founded on the rock, the Seat or Throne, which is faith, from which comes strength, and which is the special domain of Sophia.[130] He that knows it is Sophia who has descended through worlds of existence, from the height to the depth, knows also that she will arise, for she loves truth more than anything else in this world. All this is portrayed in the story of Magdalene's love for Christ Jesus, or Emmanuel.[131]

---

[129] Matthew 7: 23 gives γινωσκω (*ginosko*) from εγνων (*egnon*), 'knew'. 'I never knew them': *oudepote ginosko hymas*.

[130] It needs to be said that the true meaning of 'faith' has nothing to do with the conventional notion of 'belief', yet even the latter has been degraded as the real and etymological sense of it is 'of the heart', which has nothing to do with emotions. As for faith, it is inseparable from innate knowledge, from which comes certainty.

[131] Matthew I: 23: 'Behold, a virgin shall be with child, and shall bring forth a son, and they shall call his name Emmanuel [Εμμανουηλ], which being interpreted is, God with us.'

Now, as it is said of the law of *apurva* within Hinduism, Sophia is the cause and the effect and at the same time that which transcends this *karma*, since she is wholly outside of time and space, and yet she is the relation between the act, as perceived in time, and its outcome, for the cause and the effect cannot be separate or neither could exist.[132] Likewise the symbolism of sacred texts involves complex relationships at times, involving supra-human deities in ancient civilisations, or the human personifications of principles that came about in more recent times. All these differences between deities or divine personalities, as the case may be, are to convey different aspects and functions of the primordial unity, as it finds its expression in our hearts and minds. Mary the mother of Christ, Mary Magdalene and Mary of Cleophas, who mourned at the foot of the cross, become merged in various tellings.[133] The identities of Jesus and his initiator, John the Baptist, seem clear enough, yet the relationship involves universal symbolism. John the Baptist said, in answer to a question from one of his disciples, 'He must increase, but I must decrease'.[134] This may be construed in various ways, but John the Baptist was born at the summer solstice, which is the beginning of the decrease of light, while Jesus was born at the winter solstice, after which time the light increases. Also, summer solstice equates to the Pitriyana, 'Gate of Men', and the winter solstice to Devayana, the 'Gate of Gods'.[135]

In the ancient Egyptian tradition many gods find their ultimate in the Sphinx or Hormaku—known variously as Herakhuti, Hu, or Mentu. Both Horus and his mother Hathoor are at times identified with the enigmatic Sphinx, which has a lion's body and human head, and which points the way to the vernal equinox where the Sun rises in differing zodiacal signs as according to the precession of the equinox.

---

[132] See *Way of Knowledge*, 'Key of Magick' and 'I am That'.

[133] There is some ambiguity over exactly who are the three Marys at the foot of the cross and also later, at the tomb. According to John 19: 25: Now there stood by the cross of Jesus his mother, and his mother's sister, Mary the wife of Cleophas, and Mary Magdalene.

[134] John 30: 28–50.

[135] Also called Uttarayana and the Dakshinayana, or the Northern way and Southern way. Pitriyana is also the 'realm of darkness', or ancestors, and Devayana the 'realm of light', or helpful spiritual beings (angels or gods).

The Sphinx embodies all, and yet is specific to each and every particular expression of the Absolute in time and space. She is the marker of time, where all identities are defined until once more they fall back into the great unmanifest.[136] Owing to her unique position among the stars, and at the same time beyond them, Sophia is able to lift us out of the darkness. She is the Guru, a word that means all of that, and that is much more than is conveyed by the word 'teacher'. The Way of Return, the ascension and transfiguration of the soul, is in the realisation of all symbolism as total unity and beyond—to the realisation of 'that' which is nameless to eternity, and which nonetheless contains all possibilities, both manifest and unmanifest. '*That* thou art':

AUM: Tat tvam asi

---

[136] See 'The Sphinx: Symbol of Love and Will', and 'The Sphinx: Time and Alchemy', *The Law of Thelema—Hidden Alchemy.*

Hekat and Nekhak

I n a previous work we briefly mentioned the Egyptian symbols of the *hekat* and the *nekhak*, which were the primary attributes of Egyptian gods and kings.[137] The *nekhak*, usually thought to be a flail, symbolises the triple flow of resistance imminent in action, and is 'substance' in its triple nature.[138]

This is easily comparable to the three Gunas of Hinduism, which include resistance (*tamas*), action (*rajas*) and the peaceful nature of the upward tending spiritual force (*sattvas*). 'Substance' is a word directly applicable to the Sanskrit *prakriti*, in which the Gunas are in a state of perfect equilibrium until manifestation takes place through mutation. By forming an upward analogy or transposition, *prakriti* is no different from Maya, the Shakti that weaves the universe out of her own essence. Hekat, 'the hook', understood simply, is the magick power; *nekhak* is the triune Sophia or Shakti power. The *hekat* is a symbol of gathering all about the seed principle, which is not shown in the symbol except by implication of the curvature of the sceptre, which is enclosing. As with a circle, the principial point in the centre must exist.

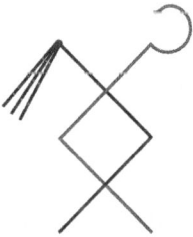

The crossing of the two sceptres in the hieroglyph and in the mudra of the Egyptian kings and gods sometimes shows a double-cross, when the arms of the pharaoh are crossed over below the sceptres. The linear form made by the two crossing points happens to be identical to the Anglo-Saxon rune called Ing (*ng*). Ing is the brother of Eostre, the maiden of Easter or the 'crossing' of the year at the lunar fulmination of the spring equinox (marked by Easter in the Christian festivities). Ing is the god that 'crosses the water', returning to bring new life or resurrection, and the Lord of the South. His sister Eostre is the goddess of flowers (*prakriti*), and is Lady of the North.

---

[137] *Babalon Unveiled* in the First Edition (p. 299). This was a development of what R.A. Schwaller de Lubicz had said in *Symbol and the Symbolic*.

[138] We have adopted this spelling of *nekhak* for convenience. The word is sometimes spelled *nekhakha*, owing to a doubling up of hieroglyphs—though that might have indicated a certain kind of emphasis to the Egyptians. It is impossible to be certain.

The emphasis on action is no doubt due to the kingly function, which is to preserve peace through the application of justice where needed. The ideal, nonetheless, is not action but peace, involving the 'activity of non-action', which is descriptive of the supreme principle, Brahma of Hinduism and the Way of Tao to the ancient and classical Chinese. In Egypt, this was typified as the Law of Ma'at, perfect truth and equilibrium. We are looking at a dual action: one effective in the world and one in heaven, which is to say that 'right action' or the expression of the Law of Ma'at has its continuance in other states of being, most particularly, the supra-human states.

It is by maintenance of this link between the worlds that true law and order is maintained; once the sacerdotal authority is lost, as in today's world, there is nothing to prevent ever-changing rules with no basis but chaos and disorder. The *nekhak* 'flail' is that which gives life and restores nature, the south or 'below', and is held in the right hand. The *hekat* 'crook' is that which receives, the north or 'above', and is held in the left hand. Here is the dual action and function of consciousness, with the trinity latent: when body, form, quantity, determination is made, the King is dead. The flow of perception ceases when the object is formed. That is the first crossing, and it marks an end or failure unless a second crossing is achieved. With the second crossing of the sceptres, the complement is realised and appearance ceases. When appearance ceases the principial power or seed is fully realised and there is change in the state of the being, which then permanently occupies the higher ground, as it were. The resurrection takes place as the individual self has known form and is able to transcend it altogether. The crossed sceptres are therefore to symbolise not only governance on earth but total transformation of the being through all worlds and that which is beyond them. In this may also be seen the symbolism of the 'second birth' and the 'third birth', the two phases of effective initiation, of which the former is really but a preparation for the latter.

The *hekat* (*heq-t*) is a symbol comparable to the Arabic letter *nun*, which is the 'fish' or 'whale'. This is also immediately recognisable as the same symbol that forms the crescent and seed-point or *bindu* of the Sanskrit OM. According to Hindu tradition, Vishnu took the form of a fish when he initiated the Manvantara, for each Cosmic Cycle must flow from the principle itself. The shape of *nun* embraces the seed or principle, and also has every appearance of an ark or vessel. So while *hekat* is 'action, seed and ferment', it is not the principle itself but embraces the principle as an ark or vessel, carrying it through to manifestation or 'ferment'.

92

The meaning of the *hekat* is then to 'gather the light that was scattered', which is to bring together the dismembered limbs of Osiris, so removing the illusion of separate existence in a world of self-created objects. There is a strong association with the Egyptian god Menu, who is also the fisher or fisher king, the *hekat* forming an integral part of his name in most cases. He is also the sceptre-bearer, and by that is meant the *nekhak*, when carried in the 'uplifted arm', which is an Egyptian symbol for the constellation of Orion, itself identified with the Sahu or resurrection body of a king or Initiate. So Menu has both attributes, and is governance (*hekat*) and substance and continuance—especially as he is an ithyphallic God. Clearly, there is no difference at all between Menu and Manu of the Hindu doctrine of the Cosmic Cycles. The king's attributes are of governance and continuation of the primordial tradition itself. These belong to Menu, and King Menes otherwise known as King Narmer was 'Menu on earth', as sovereign.[139] The king, in the purest and original sense, is a type of the Holy Guardian Angel or the 'Personal God' (Ishvara) as intermediary between the higher and lower worlds.

The threefold nature of the *nekhak* links the unmanifested parts of the being with the king or Prince of the World, also called Universal Man. While all manifestation is dual, the ternary indicates the principle that transcends any two things. Manifestation can also be formless. The Arabic and Hebrew *barach* is the 'fire from heaven'.[140] By the addition of one letter in Arabic, this then become *barzach*, 'the bridge' between the upper and lower worlds. Formless manifestation includes the Hindu *boddhi*, the principle of intellect itself as first production of *prakriti*. The *boddhi* is such a bridge, and is the means of apprehending the formless, as it is itself formless, as must be. This is all the more so when the *boddhi* is personified as the Shakti, who is ultimately no different than the *shakta*, or the soul of the *sadhaka* (practitioner). The Guardian Angel is also properly of the realm of formless manifestation, as is Nama, 'the name'. The Nama is able to produce the individuality on the human scale in the same way that in the higher worlds Manu or Menu produces the worlds of Being or of a particular Cosmic Cycle. According to René Guénon:

---

139 See *Nu Hermetica*, 'King Scorpion and the Royal Way'.
140 Also called Zelbarachith, which has the Qabalistic value of 657, a number that has special properties: 6 x 5 x 7 = 210 = NOX or 'night', the great unmanifest.

Boddhi, like everything that proceeds from the potentialities of *Prakriti,* participates in the three gunas; that explains why, when viewed from the standpoint of distinctive knowledge (*vijñāna*), it is regarded as ternary, and in the sphere of universal Existence, it is identified with the divine *Trimurti.*[141]

The Hindu *Mahat* is conceived distinctively as three Gods, being three aspects of the Intelligible Light and also the Logos as it is termed in Alexandrian Gnosticism. This comes about through the influence of the three Gunas, being one single manifestation (*mūrti*) of the Gods Brahma, Vishnu and Shiva—Ishvara as the personified and manifested aspects of the one principle.[142]

---

[141] *Man and His Becoming according to the Vedānta* p. 58 [Sophia Perennis].
[142] It is interesting to note that Murti is an Egyptian Goddess of the Nile, the 'one single manifestation' that the Nile symbolises. Her crown of lotus flowers is *prakriti,* by which all life is formed, but she does not in herself partake of formal manifestation.

PART TWO
YOGA POWER

We continue here from where Part Two of *Thunder Perfect Gnosis* left off. The reader is referred to that work in order to gain familiarity with the terms and concepts used in what is necessarily a highly technical subject. The ten chapters cover the essential knowledge for yoga practice, including the cosmological basis, importance of devotion, discrimination and the concentration of mind, without which nothing can be achieved.

O Neïth, Lady of Sáis
Thou art the weaver of worlds
Thou are maker of the pathways of light
Thy love is enduring, boundless
Thy house is the abode of the everlasting
Thy lamp of fire is imperishable
It shineth forever on
Through countless days and nights
AUM

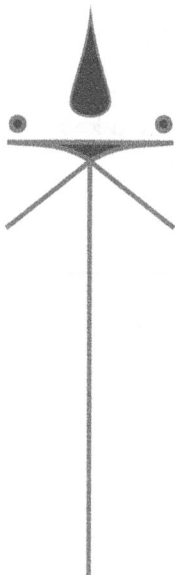

The Way of Self-Realisation

The Way of Self-Realisation involves spiritual enquiry into the nature of the Self. The four qualifications for the path are derived from standard teaching within Advaita Vedanta, but the requirements really apply to any serious spiritual path aimed at direct knowledge as opposed to religious belief.

1. *Viveka*: Ability to discriminate between the real and the seeming or apparent.

2. *Vairagya*: Dispassion. Freedom from the attachment or binding to desires, including likes and dislikes.

3. *Shadsampatti*: Literally 'Six Treasures', which we gave previously, but here they are presented as within Advaita Vedanta:

Shama—Mastery of the mind. Calmness; tranquility.

Dama—Self-control; mastery of senses (worldly pleasures).

Uparati—Mastery of the mind and senses to the extent of being able to concentrate in yoga, or otherwise achieve meditation.

Titiksha—Forbearance; being able to withstand the ups and downs of life and everything that life throws at you, whether good or bad.

Saradha—Trust (faith) in Vedantic Knowledge; trust in the Preceptor and God. From *saradha* comes *virya*, strength of a special sort.

Samadhana—The mind fully concentrated in spiritual Self-enquiry.

4. *Mumukshutvam*: Strong desire for freedom from dependence on the world for happiness—which is understood to involve temporary happiness and endless suffering.

Viveka discrimination is the first qualification required for the path of Self-Realisation. It is knowing the difference between what is real and what is not real—all the things that are passing and seeming, that only appear but are of the nature of the impermanent. Advaita Vedanta rejects the world or universe, Jagat, its very nature, as ultimately unreal; in reality it is all imagined, whether by you or us or by God (Ishvara) makes no difference. The technicalities of the discrimination practice in the *Yoga-Sutras* are only there to support the real *viveka*, which means knowing the true from what seems to be true so long as we do not know our Self, which is Brahma:

If we think someone has made us angry the first mistake we make is to think, 'I am angry', or even 'You made me angry'. That is the first point of misidentification. In reality, the Self, the Witness—the pure consciousness—is the light by which we perceive anger as an object and we are allowing our mind and emotions to put us under the delusion that we are that object. One must think of the mind and emotions in the same way one thinks of any external object—a book, a computer keyboard or a cup of coffee. While we will not think 'I am that cup of coffee' we are always very ready to believe, 'I am angry!' We jump straight in without even thinking and we are lost in the delusion. The path of Self-Realisation requires that we reflect and are continually vigilant. In most cases the discrimination comes after the event but that is how it is. Practice of patience, perseverance and *virya* self-resolve is the key.

Meditations on elements, *tanmatras* and so forth, involve discrimination. In that case the aim is to acquire discriminative knowledge. Viveka-khyati is the highest form of discriminative knowledge—knowing the difference between *prakriti* and *purusha*. According to the commentaries on the *Yoga-Sutras*, that is very advanced and even the Buddhists cannot do it so long as they reject all the principles including even Atma and Brahma and only posit a 'void'. The refutal of the void theory would take us far from our topic, however, and Shankaracharya has done that more than adequately. Let us consider the difference between the knower and the Witness:

Above and beyond the sphere of the magician, which is the mind, the great illusionist, is the I-sense *ahankara*, which is the knower, the enjoyer, sufferer and doer of things: the sense of 'I'. You are reading this and you know something because you are the knower. But that is false from the point of view of Advaita Vedanta and the *Yoga-Sutras*. It is false so long as we think we know something as the knower. It is false so long as we think we are the one who knows things, 'this' (thing here my body) which we imagine to be our self with all the attributes, identifications and other things pinned on. In dreamless Deep Sleep where is my body? I am not aware of it at all. What of my name? It is not there. Where was my body born—am I English or Irish or American?—it is not there. I live in such and such a place, in a state, country or nation—not there. I am older than I was twenty years ago—it is not there. I like this; I hate that—none of that is the Self. The body is not there, the mind is not there. So long as we think 'I am this body', 'I am this mind', we are in ignorance of the real Self.

98

How is all this illumined then? How can we know anything? What is the light that shines on it all, whether it is something perceived as real, or unreal, or a dream or even dreamless where there seems to be nothing existing or a void? That is the Witness or Seer, which does not take part in actions but is always there as consciousness, or maybe better, the provider of consciousness, which we use to know things. The Witness is not in our body, not in our head or our thoughts. It is not in books we write or read, or things we do, whether good or bad or indifferent. It is not in our idea of ourselves or your idea of us. It is none of that. Ultimately the Self is that which is sometimes called a pure light, the Atma—unconditioned, without birth or death, endless, infinite, eternal and without suffering. All thought and sensation including even the sense of 'I myself' as 'this here' is a covering or superimposition upon that real Self, and Atma as personal Real is one with Brahma, the impersonal or universal Real. The goal is to realise it in the fullest measure, constantly, always and forever.

Vairagya, 'dispassion', means freedom from all that binds us to internal and external objects. We have dealt with the intellective process of Ashtanga Yoga at length in our previous works so let it suffice to say here that we may regard that which we like and that which we dislike with equal indifference. From the Advaitan point of view, the purpose of this is to know that none of these attachments has anything to do with Atma, the real Self. This arises naturally from *viveka*, the previous qualification.

Shadsampatti, literally, Six Treasures or virtues, has also been explained as an essential practice in our previous works and the first five should be self-explanatory by now. Raja Yoga, whether that of Ashtanga Yoga or of Advaitan Raja Yoga, is not possible without these, otherwise we do not have the conditions conducive to meditation. The last, *samadhana*, has nothing to do with sceptical enquiry, 'free enquiry' or psychological interest in the self—or non-self as it is termed. It is placed last here but it is really where the path begins and where it ends, as the goal itself is to return to the Self-in-Itself, which is the ultimate goal of both yoga and Advaita Vedanta as total knowledge and freedom (*moksha*). As we have said, all this involves spiritual enquiry into the real nature of the Self. It is the beginning and the end of the path.

Mumukshutvam is the powerful desire for freedom from all that binds us to the world, so we can realise the final goal of *moksha*. A word here about *moksha* or *kaivalya* as it is termed in yoga, usually translated as 'liberation', which is the ultimate goal in both yoga and Advaitan Self-Realisation.

This is often linked to other things such as incarnation, past or future births. This can become complex, leading to endless fruitless speculation, but we can summarise the whole matter of 'incarnation', which is perplexing for so many persons. What follows is the doctrinal view: Incarnation or birth into many states of being comes about through *kama*, 'desire', and *karma*, 'actions' in previous births born of desire. This is *maya*, having no beginning or end. Maya is the Shakti power of God or Ishvara, so it could be said that God incarnates things, though even Ishvara does not act directly on the universe.

We could then say that the power is with God. We desire things so thanks to the power of God we are born into multitudes of states of being, experiencing birth, temporary happiness, suffering and death as a consequence. However, when we desire liberation, God gives us that too. Praise be to God! That is the general Advaitan point of view, and is also inclusive of, and certainly not in disagreement with, the view of the *Yoga-Sutras* and their commentaries.

It is all too easy to become trapped into endless considerations of the details of such things as have been described. So many questions arise that are no more than contingent and of a philosophical or speculative nature. 'Can I achieve liberation in this life or do I have to wait until the posthumous state, or live for countless more lives?' 'What is an avatar and why does he delay the final liberation so as to help others?' 'Is there even such a thing as avatars or *bodhisattvas* and if so can they really help us?' All these questions are well and good for the person who does not wish to leave their comfortable armchair or change anything at all about the way they live what they call their 'life', their thoughts, deeds and actions. While there is nothing wrong in asking the kind of questions we have mentioned here sometimes, it can become what amounts to a delaying tactic, a means of avoidance of the real spiritual enquiry into the Self that is the whole subject under discussion—and the work to be done, which is not inconsiderable. None of it has anything to do with the means and the goal of Self-Realisation.

The subject of all the *Upanishads* and the Advaitan texts is the Self—infinite, eternal, deathless and unchanged by anything. Make no mistake, the fact you are even reading this when you could be doing other things means you are much blessed by God. The fact you may understand it is no less than a miracle.

Fiery Aspiration

Blessed be thou, o creature of fire! Such are the words said when igniting the sacrificial flame. The nature of 'sacrifice' has become greatly misunderstood today, which owes in part to the lurid and ever-popular stories about the slaying of animals and even human beings as part of ancient rites and practice. The evidence supplied by profane historians is not trustworthy; however, when such practices are done they form a part of exoteric, public duties. From the Advaitan point of view, which is a view supported by the *Upanishads*, all that pertains to ignorance. In fact the prototype of all sacrifice as given in the Vedas does not involve killing anything at all, but is about fire or incense that symbolises the prayer or aspiration going upward to heaven. The Hindu doctrine of Vaishvānara, the principle of Cosmic Being or universal manifestation, is likened to the head, arms, body, legs and feet of a man. Thus there are seven members of Universal Man, the integral individuality at both the macrocosmic and the microcosmic level. Across all traditions the seven members are symbolised in various ways, as a star or flower, for example. The earliest Egyptian kings had the seven-petalled flower design as part of their royal attributes. The seven members are as follows:[143]

1. The head, symbolising the 'luminous spheres' or higher states.

2. The sun and moon (as principles) or two eyes.

3. The mouth is the igneous (fire) principle.

4. The ears are the directions of space.

5. The chest is the cosmic environment or 'breath' (*prana*).

6. The middle is the intermediary between heavens and earth.

7. The feet are the earth or entire corporeal manifestation.

It is important to understand that Atma, the supreme principle, only appears this way from the corporeal point of view; in reality, Atma is one with Vaishvānara from this point of view or perspective. For the present purposes it is only needful to be aware that the sacrifice of fire symbolises, and in some ways even actualises, the rising up of consciousness from earth, where the fire is made, through the various faculties and inward sense (*manas*), through the celestial or luminous abode to higher states of consciousness.

---

[143] For a complete explanation of this cosmology see René Guénon, *Man and His Becoming according to the Vedānta*, chapter 12 [Sophia Perennis].

This is not separate or different in any way to the ascension of cosmic Shiva and Shakti in the Tantras, or in Laya Yoga, for example. The Hebraic Kabbalah also includes the same principle, where God is envisioned in exactly this way, and as forming a Tree of Life or 'emanations' that can be ascended from earth to heaven, and where the leaves of the tree are the sacred letters of the alphabet. In Hinduism, the chakras of the subtle body have petals and upon each is inscribed one of the Sanskrit letters. The words or letters proceed from the mouth of Universal Being or Cosmic Man, and this can variously be seen as fiery or airy breath.

It can then be seen that fiery aspiration, which is how one of the *niyamas* of the Patañjali Eight Limbs of Yoga is interpreted, is far more than a moral or mental attitude and extends into the operative level. The fire comes about through Sanskrit *tapas*, which is the 'austerity' that strengthens or firms up the self through the discipline. As with sacrifice, austerity is misunderstood by the same mentality that also condemns asceticism, to which it can only ascribe negative values—even though the real meaning of the word, from *ascesis*, has nothing to do with any harm done to the body. In fact asceticism is a more exact interpretation of *tapas* than 'austerity'. Tapas is mentioned in the Patañjali *Yoga-Sutra* II: 1, which concerns how a devotee that is in the Distracted mental state can nonetheless attain yoga. The five mental states have been explained so it will suffice here to mention that Distracted means a practitioner that is habitually in a non-yogic state, pursuing objects of attachment, while at the same time is able to concentrate in their practice to the level of *dhyana* meditation or even *samadhi* sometimes.[144] Sutra II: 1:

> Tapas (austerity of sturdy self discipline—mental and physical), *svadhaya* (repetition of sacred mantras or study of sacred literature) and Ishvara Pranidhāna (complete surrender to God) are Kriya Yoga (yoga in the form of action).

Yoga requires rigorous self-discipline, for otherwise the snares and dross arising from attachment to worldly objects, which are the retained mental impressions without beginning or end, cannot ever be eliminated or even weakened and dissipated. According to Advaita Vedanta, *maya*, as the dream of existence, only appears because of ignorance. It is thus without beginning or end. Only knowledge destroys ignorance; the dream ends when we awaken. Towards this end and no other, the discipline involves *tapas* practice of austerities.

---

[144] See *Thunder Perfect Gnosis*, Part Two on Yoga.

Yogins must undergo self-purification in their thoughts and deeds, as there is no other way of obtaining the state of mind that is necessary for the goal of yoga to be realised.[145] Tapas or fiery aspiration is practiced alongside the other methods mentioned, for example repetition of mantras and the study of sacred literature, especially Ishvara Pranidhāna, which will be described in detail later.[146] Thus Kriya Yoga, which means 'actions supporting yoga', is to bring about stability and calmness of mind, for without this there can be no *samadhi* or even concentration (*dharana*). The actions are not yoga as such but can lead to yoga, i.e., the goal of union. The modern mentality is particularly hostile to any suggestion that one should renounce sensuous pleasure, but to do so is also to renounce pain, once it is realised that the one leads to the other and that all such pleasures are momentary. Abstinence is therefore helpful to the practice of yoga so long as it does not involve either attachment or aversion—which might only come about for example if abstinence is taken as a goal in itself, which becomes pathological. It must be emphasised that asceticism does not require any kind of injury to the body or mind, penance, or deprivation of that which is needed for sustenance. Any pathological disturbance arising from imbalance is clearly anti-yogic; it cannot possibly act as support to realisation. The actions to be avoided are all those which lead to attachment or its counterpart, aversion, and are therefore harmful to the practice.

Kriya Yoga is to bring about, in the long term, *samadhi*, and this (*samadhi*) is able to weaken and attenuate the *kléshas* or harmful mental impressions. Such impurities are likened to mud on a stone, for it is only when the dirt is cleaned away that the stone sparkles. And further, the natural but harmful actions (*rajasic*) and the inertia (*tamasic*) that also comes about through lack of self-control bring about restlessness in the one case and dullness of the senses in the other. Kriya Yoga destroys these tendencies and frees the mind (*chitta*) to turn towards *samadhi*.

Tapas involves control of the actions of the mind and the body, to the aim of purifying the character so that one is in a fit state to do yoga. There is no use in practicing control of the breath or assuming special postures or even in saying mantras unless this essential self-discipline is practiced and constantly brought to mind, along with the thoughts of the deity.

---

[145] We here paraphrase the commentary of Vyasa.
[146] See 'Ishvara Pranidhāna', p. 127.

The control of emotions is as central as is the control of mind, for the turbulent emotions will drive the mind until they are harnessed. It must be confirmed that *tapas* or 'austerity' is a positive practice not a negative one. As indicated at the beginning of this chapter, the first meaning of *tapas* is 'heat', which in this context is the interior fire that consumes impurities or what is called Qliphoth in Qabalah. The impurities comprise all that opposes spiritual realisation and as a sum total, is referred to as the Evil Genius in Western writing, of which we have spoken. There is a very close relationship between the special kind of interior fire and that igneous principle of Sulphur ♄ of alchemy and Hermeticism. Methods of purification as a preparation for initiation or spiritual realisation form part of the methods in most if not all traditions. A mirror covered in mud or painted with black ink will not possibly reflect the rays of the sun, for example, which here serves as analogy for the spirit. There is rather much made of 'trials and ordeals', especially in the Western Mystery Tradition so-called, and to which are attached sentimental values, but any real trials amount to the practice of the austerities, which is of course difficult at the outset until greater pleasures are known than the ones afforded by the mind and senses

And so, to return to where we began with sacrifice, the *tapas* or ascesis must be seen not only as sacrifice but also the supreme ritual, and a very necessary one otherwise there is no possible way we can detach ourselves from the worldly chains that bind us. One might consider the Gospel parable of the rich man that has less chance of passing through the eye of a needle or the Narrow Gate of heaven than does a camel.[147] To put this in the simplest terms, the man who spends all his time fixed upon acquisition of goods and then the need to protect what he has acquired will not concentrate his mind upon a metaphysical grain or a mustard seed that yields no material reward. The desire of this man is turned wholly towards the world and he will not hear it if he is told of the shortcomings of that. As in John 3: 12:

> If I have told you earthly things, and ye believe not, how shall ye believe, if I tell you of heavenly things?

Since there is a need for detachment from worldly chains, the ritual of sacrifice sums up all rituals and this is why the Vedas begin with the fire sacrifice. This is continued in the *Katha Upanishad*, for example, where Nachiketa asks the God of Death for the Fire Ritual that leads to heaven.[148]

---

[147] Matthew, 19: 23–26.
[148] See the verses I.1.13–19.

As with the practice of yoga, all this must be seen as a long, gradual process over time; there is nothing 'mystical' about it, for it rests on very exact ancient science. The mere performance of a rite as such cannot ever accomplish all that is necessary for the attainment of higher states of the being. Ritual, as with meditation, is only effective when it is used as a means to absorb and to thoroughly assimilate what has been learned from study, and the answers to questions given by the guru or Preceptor. On this last point, it is very important to understand that the competent teacher will not give the same answer to the same question asked by different people and at different times. What he says will be carefully considered, and is to be of benefit to the student at the particular stage they have reached, and as according to their individual *karma*. The student must be prepared to put time in to consideration and prolonged thought over all that is learned and taught to them in this way.

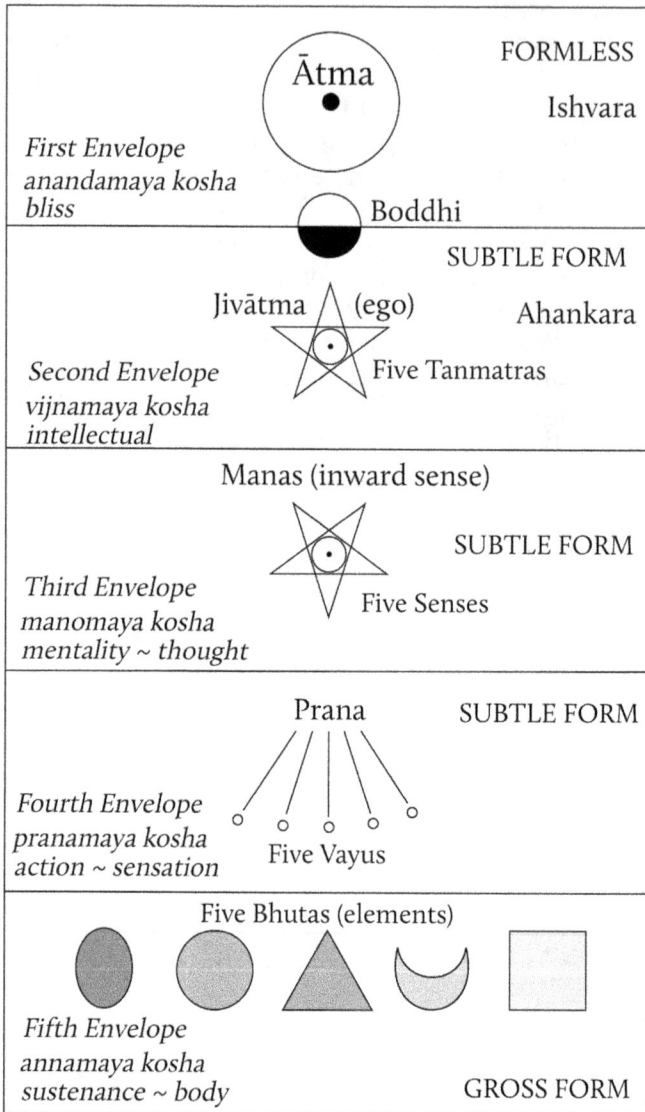

The Five Envelopes of Being

Note that in the Second Envelope, Ātma shines as a reflection in a clear mirror—he does not shine in the lower states but is obscured. The *boddhi* is comparable with the Gnostic Realm of Sophia. Cf. 'Sophia: Gnosis and Syneses', p. 70. It will be seen that the translation of *ahankara* with 'ego' is correct (I-sense) but does not accord with the conventional Western ideas of what the ego is, which is more to do with the modifications of the I-sense in the lower states.

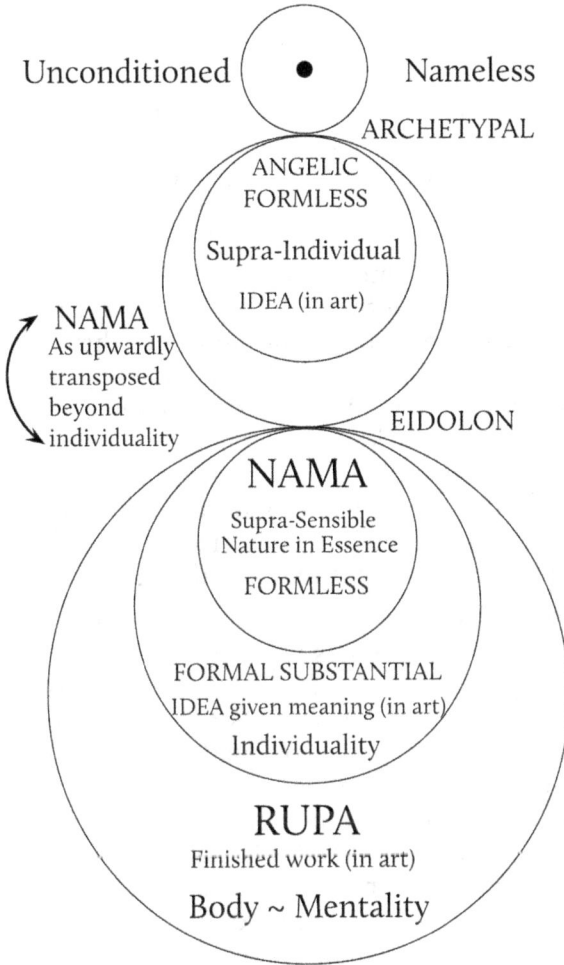

Unconditioned $\bullet$ Nameless

ARCHETYPAL

ANGELIC
FORMLESS

Supra-Individual

IDEA (in art)

NAMA
As upwardly
transposed
beyond
individuality

EIDOLON

NAMA

Supra-Sensible
Nature in Essence

FORMLESS

FORMAL SUBSTANTIAL
IDEA given meaning (in art)

Individuality

RUPA
Finished work (in art)

Body ~ Mentality

Nama and Rupa: Name and Form

Cf. 'Name and Form: Nama Rupa', *Way of Knowledge*. That which is 'Nameless' is with Eternity as it is not subject to any determination. The angelic realm (*Deva-Loka*) is formless manifestation and is beyond any individual state. Note that the *Nama*, 'Name', which properly belongs to the formless realm, and which defines individuality, is capable of upward transposition so that it can enter the supra-individual or angelic worlds and yet still retain a Nama. This is important as it provides the means by which a being may regain its integrity. The individuality as such belongs to the realm of subtle form and substantiality. While this is usually regarded as *Rupa*, the Form that complements the Name, and for obvious reasons, sometimes the individuality is called *Nama*, in which case the body and mentality is *Rupa*.

107

The Vayus and Integral Being

Our intention here is to explain more of the five *vayus*, for very little has been said of these. The *vayus* are of supreme importance to the human being as they are intermediate between the gross or physical body and the mentality that forms objects based on the senses, and which the *ahankara* is easily prone to mistaking for reality. Thus it is said in the Oracles attributed to Zoroaster, 'Stoop not down to the darkly splendid world', which was a meditation instruction given to initiates, that they would continue their journey of the soul without being detained by 'astral glamours' or phantasms of the senses. Likewise, the Judaeo Christian notion of the fall of Adam, by now widely misunderstood and despised by the ignorant, refers to the 'sin', which only means 'error', of mistaking sensorial objects for reality. There is no real difference between the error of sin as it is put in the biblical scriptures and the ignorance or *avidya* of unknowing as it is put in the Vedanta.

The word *va-yu* implies 'going forth', and so action within the realm of sensation. Vayu also has the meaning of 'air'; the same word is used for the gross element of air as movement is one principal characteristic of air. As *prana*, Vayu is not to be confused with the gross element. Comparison may be made with the Hebrew *ruach*, which is sometimes interpreted as 'spirit', at other times 'breath' or 'mind'. The *vayus*, as modifications of *prana*, the vital sustenance of existence, are at the heart of the Vedic sacrifice. The *agnihotra* fire sacrifice is the beginning and end of all. What is offered is taken upward and that which is taken upward descends in a new form then moves outward again. This will be explained, but first there is a need to summarise the five envelopes of being, of which *prana* and its five modifications called the *vayus* forms the fourth.

The elements of the Shankhya *darshana* have become relatively well known to the West but are always wrested from their context and then gone to work on so practical applications can be developed without doctrinal knowledge.[149] The Hindu doctrine of five envelopes of being, as adjunct to the supreme *paramatma* principle, is not limited to the Shankhya *darshana* in fact but is suffused throughout the Vedanta.

---

[149] The Golden Dawn included in their knowledge a book by the Theosophist Rama Prasad, *The Science of Breath*. This was mainly about the *tattva bhutas* (see p. 106), which were made to 'fit' the Golden Dawn's syncretic system, thus rendering the knowledge ineffective.

The gross elements form the fifth envelope of being (*kosha*); their immediate higher principle is *prana*, belonging to the subtle fourth envelope. Prana has five modifications called *vayus*. The higher principle of the *vayus* is found in the third envelope, which broadly speaking includes the mentality as that is commonly understood, and which is able to perceive through the five senses of hearing, touch, vision, taste and smell. The mentality is itself a modification, through the intermediary inward sense (*manas*), of the second envelope of being called 'intellectual'. By this is not meant what is commonly understood as reason, logic and so on, for that belongs to the third envelope. This realm of subtler form than the mentality includes the *ahankara*, which is rather incorrectly translated as 'ego', for we have already pointed out that the intellect is above the reason and sense perceptions.[150] It includes the centre of the individual being called *jivatma* (the 'creature self') and this has five rays or subtle elemental roots, called *tanmatras*. Comparison can be made with the five-rayed star of Egypt that is frequently depicted on the walls of temples, sarcophagi, or on the clothing of divine *neteru* ('principles').

While the translation 'ego' is always misleading owing to the common ideas associated with it, the *ahankara* is nonetheless the first appearance of the individual self, as direct reflection of the light of *atma*. The centre of this self, the *jivatma*, is sometimes referred to as the I-sense and when it is known without the modifications of sense-objects created by the mind then it is called the pure I-sense. Practitioners and others frequently assume that they know this I-sense, because of its association with ego, and after all we all have one of those do we not? It is not as simple as that and in fact few persons have direct knowledge of the I-sense let alone *paramatma*, of which the I-sense is the third veil of reflection. Beyond the second envelope is an intermediary called the *boddhi*, or higher intellect, and the first envelope called 'bliss', which is the realm of Ishvara the Lord of the Universe, abiding in the formless state. The first envelope is adjunct to Atma Itself, which is not an envelope, and the five *kosha* envelopes are not really bodies as such because they exist on the subtle level, and neither do they 'enclose' Atma, for Atma cannot be contained or limited in any way.[151]

---

150 See 'The True Self', *Way of Knowledge*.
151 In the *Yoga-Sutras* 'Purusha' is the term generally used for Atma, as Purusha relates to the world of Being. See 'Immaculate Faculty of Knowing', where the subject of the five *vayus* is resumed. Cf. also René Guénon, *Man and His Becoming according to the Vedānta*, 'The Five Envelopes of Being'.

The *vayus* are faculties of action and sensation, which is the characteristic of the fourth envelope of being. In some translations of Hindu texts these faculties are sometimes called 'organs', which can unfortunately make it seem as if the physical body is being referred to but the *pranamaya* envelope ('made of *prana*') is on the level of subtle form. The five *vayus* are linked with actions of the body that are vital to organic life, and are the subtle principles of these: aspiration, inspiration, expiration, circulating blood and digesting food. The *vayus* are nonetheless to be understood in the widest possible sense, and an example will serve to illustrate this: one person reads a book and gets nothing from it. They do not assimilate the knowledge so that it becomes a part of their individuality, in the same way that assimilation of food builds up the physical body. Another person reads the same book and the knowledge becomes part of him. The language informs and changes him so he is able to perceive things differently.

Digestion then can apply as much to knowledge of subtle things as it can to food and gross things. This is why it is said in the *Upanishads* 'everything (in this world) is *prana*' sometimes. As the body is really made out of *prana*, and food is *prana*, then it is said that '*prana* eats *prana*'. A further key to understanding the *vayus* is that actions are divided into two broad categories: receiving or taking in from the cosmic environment and projecting or putting outward into the cosmic environment. Here then is the wider understanding of the respiration: aspiration is conceived as upward movement, inspiration is conceived as downward, and expiration as 'going out'. The aspiration attracts elements from the cosmic environment that are not yet individualised. Through assimilation, which is the function of the inspiration, they become part of the individuality of the being. There is an intermediary phase between these, which involves actions and reactions that come about through the being contacting the cosmic elements. The vital movements that come about as a consequence relate analogously to the circulation of blood. The being is thereby nourished in every part by what has been received. Expiration is now to be understood in this sense as far more than merely the expulsion of a waste product: the 'breath' is projected outwards beyond the limitations of the ordinary human being, the limits which in many ways define that being as such. This is projecting into what is termed the 'extended individuality' and its possibilities, which is called the integrality or integral Self. This in fact constitutes a change of state in the being that is permanent. Finally, for the digestion, this is put very clearly by Guénon:[152]

---

[152] P. 70 [*ibid*].

(v) digestion, or inner substantial assimilation (*samāna*), by which the elements absorbed become an integral part of the individuality.

He goes on to say that it is clearly stated in the *Upanishads* and elsewhere that this is not about bodily organs and their functions and must be taken as assimilation in the 'widest possible sense'. Chapters 19–23 of the *Chandogya Upanishad* concern the *agnihotra* fire sacrifice, which is analogous with this functioning of the five *vayus*, understood in the special way that we have here indicated. The five oblations are thrown into the fire and an equal amount eaten or consumed by the sacrificer, and thus '*prana* is satisfied'. By feeding himself he feeds Vaishvānara, which is the integral Self composed of seven limbs.[153] That is the true sacrifice. It is in *Chandogya* 24 that this is explicitly stated, to the effect that unless the sacrifice is done with this knowledge of the Self, then it is nothing. However,

> But if, knowing this, one offers the Agnihotra oblation, it is like an oblation offered in all the worlds, in all beings, and in all ātmans.[154]

The difference between the ordinary individuality and the integral Self needs to be clearly understood as the difference is vast, which is no exaggeration. We have to take it as more or less known what an individuality is like, even if a person has never known the I-sense directly, which takes prolonged meditation over a lengthy period of time in most cases. The integrality on the other hand is not even limited to the human state, which is in itself a strict limitation and a fractional degree of the Being in its entirety. The integrality includes all creatures and life, not only men, and it is not limited to the terrestrial world, which is a particular set of conditions. For this reason we can speak of a cosmic environment—otherwise we would automatically think in terms of earth or even the human world.

The expiration *vayu* is compared in the *Upanishads* with death, or the soul leaving the body after death, and this is precisely the change of state in the being as already alluded to. The meaning by now should be clear, and it also becomes clear to those who have well understood it that some aspects of this impinge directly upon the domain of magick, though this knowledge is not in any way limited to that domain.

---

[153] See 'Fiery Aspiration' for the description of the seven limbs.
[154] The plural 'ātmans' is used to indicate multitudinous individualities in all worlds and states of being, for *paramatma* is not in any way plurality. *The Upanishads Volume Four*, Swami Nikhilananda [Advaita Ashrama].

To take a simple practical example, we can consider the ritual called the Cube of Space, which involves the formulation of a three-dimensional cross, where the centre point of that, where all lines meet, is the heart lotus. In some ways this is the most important of all rituals. Here we symbolise individuality as centred amidst the six directions of space: Above, Below, East, West, South and North. Aspiration, inspiration and expiration are included in the gestures typified by the standing Tau, Horus the Enterer and Horus of Silence. The greater significance of the fire, water, perfume and anointing oil should never be forgotten by the magician, for these are *prana* and form an essential part of the oblations for the sacrifice. Usually, in the practice, we want to concentrate inwards to that centre, which is called the Seat of Brahma, or the Throne of Ra in the Egyptian schema. Each of the three primary lines has a polar axis, however, even if it is posited on the horizontal plane. The lines are of course theoretical, not actual. It is closer to reality, though still an analogy, to imagine that a line is actually composed of an indefinite series of infinitesimal 'points' occupying space. Each point, of which there are an indefinite number, is a reflection of the first or the point that is central to the axis, yet it is separate or better, not identical, as it is defined by space. This is sometimes alluded to in writing as 'space-marks'. Each infinitesimal point is itself the centre of its own 'star' or cross-mark in the woven tapestry of *maya*, of which all things are 'made'. The individualities are then indefinite, countless in number though not infinite, which applies only to *paramatma*. Here we are looking only at one projected line from the centre. Other radii are not only as close together as the points on a line but are also situated above and below.[155] When all the points are made luminous from the centre, then that centre is realised as the centre of the centres, which is the integrality.

The resultant effect has elsewhere been described as the Arabic *Al-braq*, or the Hebrew *barakah* or the more particular Zelbarachith, which means 'transmission' and also lightning, as well as a bridge, crossing or intermediary.[156] It is the type of all real initiation, or of initiatic *transmission*. Thus the idea of projecting the *prana* outward to the as yet unindividuated possibilities is to act as support to the possibility of total realisation.

---

[155] Cf. The geometrical representation of the universe is given by Guénon in *Symbolism of the Cross*.

[156] Zelbarachith (ZLBRChITh) counts to 657, which has special properties. It has factors of 3 and 219, and the multiplication of its integers results in 210, which is itself an expression of the triune perfection of zero as 3 x 70.

That Thou Art: Rainbow Bridge

Even Sa'asmita Samadhi retains dualism, which is necessary in any case. The union (yoga) of *sa'asmita* implies 'with ego', which is by its nature separative, in the sense of the knower as the doer and enjoyer of things. All traces of dualism cannot be removed until an extremely high level is reached and sustained. Before that, but quite a long jump away from ordinary *samadhi*, Nirvikalpa Samadhi dualism is negligible, and might be thought of as subliminal. Nirvikalpa is, by implication, without error, or without any mental modifications, which here means without separation of *That*, the Infinite, and *thou*, the self as doer and enjoyer of things.

It is argued by some and refuted by others that final liberation *moksha* or *kaivalya* cannot be entered while still living in a human body. On the side of the refutation, we could say that denies the undisputed avatars such as Shankaracharya, who is recognised within tradition as an incarnation of the Lord of the Manvantara. In such cases there is ascent, descent and re-ascent.[157] In the descent, nothing of the already accomplished ascension is lost. The Lord of the Manvantara gave to men the latent impression of Himself (as God), which can be acquired by rational means under certain conditions, though knowing it, in the technical sense of direct knowledge (*jnana* or *gnosis*), is only acquired through devotion, Raja Yoga, or the total self-renunciation as taught by Advaita Vedanta. If it were not for this act of divine grace, however, the Real could not be known at all in this Dark Age of Kali Yuga. In that case, even taking into account the acceleration of the ending of time, the end would have come about so prematurely as to contradict the ordinance, which is impossible.[158] Thus, it is divinely woven into the fabric of things, to use a manner of speaking.

Many of the terms used in the above paragraph are what is technically called *vikalpa* in the *Yoga-Sutras*, 'with the use of words as support', and this is also described as 'false cognition', as the words themselves are not an actual thing such as a tree, a star, a stone or a creature. All the same, we cannot speak or write without *vikalpa*, for language and symbolism is necessary for spoken and written communication.

---

[157] An avatar is born into the earthly existence with knowledge already gained from countless births in other states of being than the human state.

[158] As we near the end of a Manvantara, there appears to be an acceleration of time as we are further removed from the primordial and principial origin.

Vikalpa is necessary for concentration (*dharana*) and meditation *dhyana* up to the point where words are no longer needed as a support. In yoga meditation practice, Samyama, both the mind and language are needed for a long time. In Nirvikalpa Samadhi, as mentioned above, all mental activity or modification ceases and only pure consciousness remains. Only knowledge can destroy ignorance, which stands in the way of knowledge. Only the mind can command the mind to be still. Furthermore, as we shall set out to show here, the mental faculties, in particular the memory, can retain knowledge that is beyond the mind to grasp. As much as this sounds like impossibility, we shall attempt to explain how it works in so far as that can be done with the use of discursive language.

The *Siddhāntabindu of Srimat Madhusūdana Sarasvati* is a rare, old book.[159] The author is a highly revered classical writer on Advaita Vedanta, though little known outside of India. This book, with an excellent translation from one who clearly knows the meaning of the text, comprises a commentary on Sri Shankaracharya's *Dasa Sloki*, 'ten verses'.[160] *Siddhāntabindu* is very advanced and requires a great deal of thought. Our purpose here is to examine one aspect of the teaching that has vital import for those who practice Raja Yoga. In *Siddhāntabindu*, there is mention of 'non-attributive memory'. This means memory that is not based on any object. A latent impression (*samskara*) or retained memory that leaves a deep imprint can be formed of knowledge that is beyond the knowledge of objects, and so can be recollected in Samyama Yoga practice. Suppose we experience Nirvikalpa Samadhi, which is sometimes called the highest *samadhi*. We cannot turn it on like a tap whenever we want. We can recollect the *smrti* latent impression though, and go into *samadhi* as a result.

Verse 6 begins with a comment on the scriptural *That thou art*. It is very important here which way round the words go as this section of the book, the first part, is going deeply into the meaning of words and what is implied by them. There are three levels of meaning with scriptural texts:

1. Literal or spoken.
2. Metaphorical or symbolic sense.
3. Implied meaning by way of the context.

---

[159] Translated by Achalānanda, University of Mysore 1981.
[160] Understanding is helped by familiarity with some of the six *darshanas* or schools of thought, and our own works on yoga.

The last in the list, 'implied meaning', is what perplexes students the most. Terms can have very different meanings according to context. Akasha usually means only the fifth element, as in the *bhuta tattvas*. But in some *Upanishads* it can refer to no less than Brahma. It is all about context and comparison with other texts, from which a whole meaning is implied.

That is the Infinite; *thou* is the individual, the doer and enjoyer or the reflected light. Art (are) is the verb, the 'doing word', to be. I am, you are, she is, we are (etc). It expresses the identity that otherwise is not found in *That* and *thou* if taken separately or in the usual sense. This is, we must remember, about non-dual reality. In verse 7, it is stated that the expressed meanings of both words are not understood through repetition. The two words *That* and *thou* are not the same thing replicated. Nothing is replicated or identical in metaphysics because the Infinite cannot include two things the same, otherwise it would not be Infinite. Repetition does not convey the understanding of the meaning intended. And yet these two things are united by the verb, which states the identity of both. This is non-dual reality. There is difference but no separation (or replication) in the Infinite.

To return to verse 6, *That thou art* 'is known reasonably as a non-attributive memory.' What then is a non-attributive memory? It is a latent impression (*samskara*) that does not rest on any object. There is such a thing as meditation without an object. This knowledge, though non-sensorial, and without an object, can nonetheless be retained and recollected, as follows:

The latent impression (*samskara*) of the whole meaning implied by *That thou art*, which is non-dual reality, can be recollected by one that already knows it, or that has inferred the meaning from the use of the words. The very fact that statements such as *That thou art* have been used for many centuries to convey non-dual knowledge means they are proven to carry this possibility. The Infinite contains all possibilities and is not limited in any way. The whole thrust of this section is that, although the mind is arrested in *samadhi* such as Nirvikalpa, the mind is absolutely needed. Only the mind can destroy the ignorance that alone stands in the way of the Self. Also, words from sacred texts carry an ineffable value for those that have the knowledge latent. As stated earlier, 'art' is the verb here, and verbs always carry the sense of going forth. It is the identity of *That* and *thou*, which is only known through their relation, and their relation with the whole context of non-dual Vedanta, which is implication.

The verb is thus the arc or arch, for example, which connects two extremities, defining them and giving them vital meaning. In similar fashion, there is something in the Hindu doctrines called the *law of apurva*, of which we have written and shall here quote:[161]

> As an action cannot be separate from its consequence in time, removed from it as it were by a line or measure of space, *apurva* is the line, or 'that', which is the relation between stars or points in space and time. However, *apurva* necessarily exists both inside and outside of space and time. As related to the microcosm, *apurva* has a correspondence with the *pinda* or embryonic latency. The Shakti Herself is thus able to produce *apurva*, and she is in truth the *apurva* itself. This means that Nuit or Mahadevi Shakti is not only the 'cause' that is in itself causeless, and unaffected by anything, but is also present in the resultant. This has considerable import and is something that can only be fully understood by way of thought and profound meditation.

This returns us to the consideration of the Lord of the Manvantara, who is not really in any way separate from the Shakti power. Love is not cognition (*vritti*) but when regarded as only the opposite of hate, then it is a *klésha* affliction, because it is unreal attachment. But beyond that simple delusion, love is born from the relation of two things that is yet neither of those two things; it is the 'distance' between them measured in the way of *apurva*. As such, love extends to the metaphysical by this unknown factor, which is outside of time and space and yet partakes of the two subjects, or subject and object. This mystery of love forms a major part of *bhakti* devotion. In the first veil of the Infinite, *sat-chit-ananda*, Being knows Itself by Itself. In the second veil of the spiritual or higher intellect, this is known by reflection, which is love. In the mind of man, this is retained as the footprint of the eternal.

---

[161] See p. 109, *The Way of Knowledge*, 'I Am That'.

On the Practice of Knowledge

Vikalpa, 'the use of words as support (to yoga)', is needed in savitarka and savichara, meditation on the gross and subtle objects, but not in nirvitarka and nirvichara, respectively 'without words' and 'without following', which means passing to the subtle qualities of the meditation object—for these concepts still require language, images or verbal support. It is a careful weighing in the balance in meditation practice to determine when to completely reject all images and when to go with them because they can be helpful as latent impressions that destroy (or become stronger than) the unwanted impressions. The use of 'luminosity' or 'effulgence' is that it can lead on to the apprehension of the Seer or Witness without determinations. Experience teaches that some things are proven to work even if they are *vikalpa*.

Everyone knows there can be lazy or tired days, when we simply cannot be bothered and so we let thoughts wander from one object to another. And yet that is in truth a self-contradiction, as will be here explained: Once the art of discrimination is really learned and well understood, it is not actually possible to take a day off, so to speak. We can still let the thoughts go where they will but we will be aware of exactly what they are and where they are leading us. Once learned it cannot be dispensed with in reality. It is crossing a bridge that vanishes away behind us; there is no return and no return is wanted. The bridge leads out of one world and into another, yet that in itself is no more than a support, for in reality even ordinary thought has no spatial location, though it is within the limits of time.

There is a difference regarding what happens in the meditation practice and what happens in our 'normal life'—for discrimination is an ongoing vigilance, not something done for one hour in the day. In meditation, the seated posture, the *pranayama*, the concentration of mind, everything is set up to establish meditation *dhyana*, so it is even possible. In 'normal life' we engage with exterior and interior objects as needed. We can still practice vigilance and discrimination but we are not in *samadhi* if we are engrossed in painting a door, digging the garden, reading a book, cooking a meal or playing with the cat. The *sannyasins* that Shankaracharya wrote his most absolute teaching for did not do jobs of work; they literally were in meditation all day and night. They were not householders and did not do yoga. The great sage Sri Ramakrishna, who is relatively modern, having lived only a century ago, said he had to come down three steps from *samadhi* in order to speak to other people.

Only the practice of yoga discrimination can weaken the harmful latent impression *kléshas* and strengthen the helpful *samskara* impressions. And this is done not by destruction or negation of the impressions, which is temporary, but through the willed recollection of helpful impressions. So the helpful impressions, even if they are ultimately *vikalpa*, cannot be dispensed with. Karmasayas, however, which are the 'ongoing' effects of the original cognition subsisting in memory, subsist latently until all the *karma* is totally exhausted, and this is so even with the most super-advanced yogin living a monastic life. The only difference is that the super-adept is not moved at all by them and is hardly aware of them, as they are by then very tenuous subliminal transmutations.

The danger of the *karmasayas* is that when they are activated they are more than mere memories, but may enter life in new forms, and through this transmutation in appearance they may easily deceive the unwary. Fully succumbing to such thoughts, or events, means that further actions are taken that strengthen still further the afflictive power, and produce more or less complex new *karmasayas*, prolonging the suffering indefinitely. So long as we do not act on the affliction, we are nonetheless stuck with the *karmasayas* at least until all the effects of *karma* are totally exhausted, which means it has reached the limit of its cycle across time. None of it is the Self, which does not participate in pleasures or pains, even though the Self is eternally present, ceaselessly and infinitely, without beginning and without end.

AUM

Elements of Discrimination

The practice of discriminative knowledge is not about pinning labels on things, saying it is a *viparyaya* or *samskara* or something like that, as if simply throwing a word at it would dispel the illusion. For this practice, while made as simple as could be with its three, five or ten classifications of everything, has no similitude at all with anything in our cultural or educational domain. We must make clear it is no mere game of psychology, for example; the practice does not rest on invented psychological theories but principial knowledge. As operative principles are ultimately adjuncts to the metaphysical ones, and can only be truly understood thereby, psychology and other theoretical modern sciences can never reach this knowledge. Raja Yoga involves an exact science of consciousness itself; it is not limited to examining thoughts and feelings as though they were something important in themselves.

We cannot separate discrimination from concentration of the mind as the whole purpose of discrimination is to make real yoga possible in the first place. Yoga, or even magick come to that, is actually harmful to the being unless the knowledge of discrimination is practiced and understood. Firstly, then, a word about *pratyahara*, which is mentioned in the Patañjali Eight Limbs of Yoga and means 'withdrawal of the senses'. This is listed after *pranayama* regulated breathing and before the *dharana* concentration but effectively, the senses follow the mind, not the mind following the senses. At least, in yoga, the senses follow the mind. In the ordinary case the mind does follow the senses, upon which all objects are created by the mind, *manas* or the 'inward sense'. When the senses follow the mind, in concentration and so withdrawal of senses, then it is yoga. If the mind is following the senses it is not yoga; for example, the mistaken belief that if the body is still, the mind will be still also, so it is a matter of waiting until the body is relaxed. No, that is wrong. The mind commands the body to be still and then the mind wills that the mind will be still also. So concentration (of mind) is necessary for *pratyahara*, even though it is listed before *dharana*. According to Vyasa,

> Just as bees follow the course of the queen bee and rest when the latter rests, so whenever the mind stops the senses also stop their activities.[162]

---

[162] Vyasa comment on *Yoga-Sutra* II: 54.

The practice of concentration involves the use of a variety of Sanskrit terms, and in our writing we have reduced these to the minimum needed. In most cases when we use a Sanskrit term we put the usual translated meaning next to it, to the extent that it is repetitious, and this is intentional. One must first establish clearly the meaning of the term: For example a *samskara* is a 'latent (retained) impression', something that has made a deep almost indelible impression from a past deed or thought. It subsists and can become active again and again. Karmasayas on the other hand are the ongoing effects of the original cognition and can owe even to a deed or action done in a previous birth in a different state of being; a *karmasaya* will seem to replicate itself in other 'events' or experiences, though these can never be exactly identical. These are generally harmful.

Samskaras, 'latent impressions', on the other hand, can be either harmful or helpful. These are deeply retained, like footprints baked into clay or a stamp made on a metal plate. Even the experience of a non-sensorial state, such as Nirvikalpa Samadhi, can be recollected as it makes a *samskara* impression. Such a recollection can even lead to further *samadhi*.

Five Mental States

We have explained the five mental states previously.[163] These are firstly *Arrested*, which only refers to a very advanced yogin and means stoppage of the mind. In practice, we might experience this but as a mental state it really means the habitual state, not only something acquired in one hour of the day.

One-pointed is the concentraton needed for true meditation. As mental state, once again it does not refer to something only achieved in one hour of the day so few can attain this in the sense usually meant in the *Yoga-Sutras*.

Distracted is typical of most practitioners today. It is anti-yogic in so far as the mind pursues objects, following the senses a great deal of the time. Nonetheless, Samyama Yoga can replace the Distracted state, with great effort, so that one-pointed yoga is even possible.

Stupefied typifies the habitual state of mind of most people today. It is encouraged through television, films, media, 'entertainment', computers and cell phones. It is encouraged by much of modern working and living conditions. In this state, the person is continually engrossed in objects created by the mind, of which, especially in today's modern world, almost all of them are totally unreal things.

---

[163] *Thunder Perfect Gnosis*, Part Two.

Restless is the lowest of all the mental states as it impinges on the demonic—for attachment and aversion, and the resulting anger, hatred, frustration and all other other afflictions are controlled by the demons (*asuras*). Anger, for example, is taking pleasure in misery and mistaking it for happiness.

Five Cognitions

There are five cognitions (*vrittis*):

Pramaña is valid cognition of a real thing like cat, tree, bird, pot, creature or thing whatsoever.

Vikalpa means 'words, language', and in particular a word that is not a real thing but is still needed for the purpose of communicating something. For example, 'void' denotes an absence or emptiness, it is not a real thing. Nonetheless, language is needed to indicate or otherwise provide analogies for non-sensorial things.

Viparyaya is totally false cognition. Once we looked in the porch of our house and were surprised to see a cat. A moment later we saw that it was a bag, but for a moment we really thought it was a cat. Only for a moment; but that is an example of *viparyaya* totally false cognition.

Smrti is recollection, of which the memory is a mental faculty but a remembered thing can be cognised so it is a special case. Recollection can be based on *pramaña*, true cognition, or a totally false cognition for example. In reality there is often a mixture but we have to limit this to make it workable.

Nidrā is called 'deep sleep' but it is not the same as *prajna*, which is the Dreamless Sleep that is one of the three states of AUM. Nidrā is more about vacuity of mind and absence of cognition. A person does not have to be literally asleep to be in the non-cognition state of *nidrā*. Sometimes people will even think they meditate but they are really in *nidrā*. It is characterised by not remembering anything about where one has been.

Five Kléshas

There are five *kléshas*. We know that a *klésha* is a 'harmful cognition' but there are five kinds of *kléshas* and identifying which one is a vital part of intellective process:

Avidya, nescience or ignorance is the *klésha* (affliction) from which all other *kléshas* arise. Essentially it is mistaken identification of the Self with the doer, the enjoyer of pleasure or pain through sense objects. The Self does not participate in doing and enjoying but is Witness to all.

Egoism arises from the *klésha* of ignorance, through the possessions of 'mine', 'this belongs to me', or 'that does not belong to me'.

Attachment (to an object) also give rise to the affliction of *Egoism*. This is usually through remembered pleasure.

Aversion is related to *Attachment*, and is usually remembered pain or hurt. From this arises anger, and hatred.

Fear of Death is the root of all fear, and fear itself is the affliction of the ignorance of not knowing the True Self and mistaking it for the body, mind or other object.

We can now discuss the Intellective Process, which is necessary for the gaining of discriminative knowledge; it is needed in order that real yoga can be done at all.

Intellective Process

From Intellective Process arises discriminative knowledge. The use of this, which must be understood as vital and not a mere psychological game, is that knowledge is involved. It is about the destruction of ignorance that alone stands in the way of knowing the Self, which is Knowledge.

Firstly, identify accurately the cognition. If it is harmful, identify which kind of *klésha*. If it is attachment, for example, identify the nature of the attachment. Is this pleasure? If so, then what kind of pleasure? For example, is it emotional or physical? If it is aversion or anger then one is 'mistaking misery for happiness', which is another kind of *klésha*. One or two specific examples of discrimination are now needed. To qualify, it is not all that easy to find examples that apply to 'everyone'. One person is sentimental and worries about stray cats, another one gets angry with his work colleagues. Or the same person might suffer both at different times and even at the same time. Everyone has the same classes of cognitions and *kléshas* but what torments one person, or gives them mistaken pleasure, differs from one person to the next as according to disposition, temperament and so forth.

1. A cat follows us home to our doorstep and rolls on it, wanting to be adopted. Do we adopt the cat there and then or do we close the door on it and let it find a home somewhere else? We quickly decide that we are not prepared to be looking after an animal for the rest of its life and go inside. But later when we try and concentrate our mind we find our thoughts keep going back to worrying about the cat.

Intellective Process follows: what kind of cognition? It is memory (*smrti*) based on valid *pramaña* cognition of the cat, which is a real thing as such. Clearly the cognition is harmful (*klésha*) because we cannot concentrate the mind. What kind of *klésha*? Attachment to the object (cat), and which brings pain or perhaps a thwarted sense of pleasure that might have been taken with enjoyment of the cat. This is egoism through self-identification. This leads to desire for possession of the cat. Possibly also concern about the cat's safety, which is fear of death superimposed on an object other than the self as the doer and enjoyer—but which amounts to the same thing. Fear of death is one of the three great afflictions and gives rise to many other afflictions. How does this amount to the same thing? In both cases one mistakes the Self for the doer and enjoyer of pleasure and pain.

The self as the doer and enjoyer is a superimposition upon the Real, the Infinite. The Self is Witness (Seer) to all but it does not cause anything and neither does it participate in the actions or the pleasure and pain. We recollect the Eight Limbs of Yoga and the Six Treasures.[164] *Om Tat Sat.*

2. A work colleague or boss does not rate the work we did very highly and sends us an email or calls us, expressing displeasure, and which might even extend to some personal remark, indicating anger and frustration. Later, thoughts of this keep returning and we are completely unable to concentrate our mind.

Intellective Process follows: what kind of cognition? It is memory based on valid *pramaña* cognition so long as we take it that the person was really angry and insulting, as opposed to us not reading him correctly. If we did not read (or hear) him correctly then it is *viparyaya* false cognition. The cognition is clearly harmful (*klésha*) as we are unable to concentrate and our practice is destroyed. What kind of *klésha*? It is multiple: firstly, our attachment to work as an object, and then egoism owing to wanting others to think it is good or bad—which is the same as wanting them to think that 'I' am good or bad. Wanting others to think our work is bad? Yes, because it is no different than wanting them to think it is good. All is the enjoyment of pleasure and pain of the doer and enjoyer of things, which is not the Self. This also gives rise to aversion as we now loathe that person, which arises from attachment to the object in the first place. Egoism and attachment is giving rise to aversion. Anger is one of the three great afflictions and impinges on the level of Demons or Asuras. From anger arises countless other afflictions and endless suffering and torment. We then recollect the Eight Limbs of Yoga, especially practice of self-control (Yamas) and not having harmful thoughts, and the Six Treasures. *Om Tat Sat.*

The practice of discrimination will not instantly eliminate attachment to pleasure or pain and so forth, and there is no need to fear that we will never enjoy these things again, for we will enjoy and suffer these things over and over until we have had enough of them! But discrimination weakens their power to affect us over time, while strengthening the will and faith to practice the path of love, devotion and knowledge, which is Samyama Yoga.

---

[164] See 'The Way of Self-Realisation', p. 97. See also *Thunder Perfect Gnosis*, Part Two, for the Six Treasures as found in Patañjali Yoga.

There is only one other thing to add, which is that students tend to focus on *kléshas* and sometimes are led to think that every kind of cognition is harmful, which is not at all the case. Recollection is used in devotion, in the prayers and oracles, songs or stories, and in the *bhakti* images of deity. Vikalpa is needed as language is needed to communicate. Even if the word is not a real thing in itself a *vikalpa* is needed to convey something *non-sensorial*. Of these cognitions, only two are always harmful: *nidrā* is always harmful, as it is no cognition at all but vacuousness. Viparyaya is always harmful because it is a totally false cognition.

Avidya as explained in the Yoga-Sutras

Those who regard animate and inanimate objects as part of their own self and rejoice at their prosperity and bemoan their decay are all victims of delusion.[165] Avidya has four divisions. It is the source from which all *kléshas* flow as corresponding latent impressions are produced. It is neither right cognition nor the mere absence of cognition but cognition that is contrary to correct cognition.

1. Sense of permanence in transient things is the chief factor in fear of death.

2. Sense of purity in impure things is found in attachment.

3. Feeling pleasure in affliction predominates with hatred; although hatred is a form of misery, it appears to be pleasant or desirable when engrossed in aversion.

4. Considering animate or inanimate objects as part of oneself, or belonging to oneself, is egoism.

Avidya is false knowledge without any beginning; it is its own cause as modification and latent impression thereby. All living beings have correct *vidya* and incorrect *avidya* knowledge. Normally there is a preponderance of wrong cognitions and a paucity of true cognitions, whereas in discrimination true cognition predominates and wrong cognition is negligible. There is no separate thing called *avidya* over and above the modifications of the mind. Thus when it is said that *avidya* is eternal, that is to say, without beginning or end, it means that the flow of such modifications of the mind is ceaseless.

---

[165] Achārya.

Summary

Avidya is misapprehension about the real nature of things, and is the breeding ground for all other *kléshas*. This includes:

Regarding a transient object as everlasting.
Regarding an impure object as pure.
Mistaking misery for happiness.
Mistaking or imagining the not-self for Self.

Egoism (*asmita*) is tantamount to mistakenly identifying absolute awareness with the cognitive principle as instrument of knowing.

Attachment is the mental modification that follows remembrance of pleasure, also regarding evil as good.

Aversion is the modification that results from misery, hurt or anger and its recollection. It is mistaking misery for happiness.

Fear of death is the inborn fear of annihilation; it is the desire for self-preservation afflicting both learned and foolish men alike—for all have the same *vasana* 'field for culture of *kléshas*' arising out of the experience of pain and death.

Ishvara Pranidhāna

All needs are unfulfilled except the need to know God, for God is unlimited, endless, infinite and eternal. All other desires lead to temporary pleasure and pain, and endless rebirth into other states of being where more suffering is perpetuated. Kriya yoga involves 'actions'. One must replace the harmful mental impressions with the helpful ones. Recollection, prayer, mantras, all these things reinforce the helpful mental impressions, forming an important part of the Samyama practice. Also, when *dhyana* 'true meditation' or even *dharana* concentration is achieved with certainty in practice, we must remember it at other times. The recollection is brought back to mind constantly, that is, not only in the meditation time as such. We must remember the feeling, the sense of it—what was it like? This strengthens the helpful mental impression and weakens the harmful *klésha* impressions over time.

There is also Ishvara Pranidhāna, a special kind of devotion. This has been described in many different aspects previously but it will be helpful to place it in concise terms.[166] Ishvara Pranidhāna is a term translated as 'Surrender to God', and is part of the Eight Limbs of Yoga. The deity is kept in the heart lotus at all times. In practice, the sense of 'myself' or ego is removed to this heart lotus so the deity replaces it. In this way, all is given up to Mahadevi Shakti whether it is perceived as good or ill; every phenomenon is understood as proceeding from her *maya*, which is a veil upon her and the true Self. Although it is not meant to be taken literally, everything is then seen as coming from God and by this discipline all is returned to God; the ego self is replaced by the sense of the divinity as within the heart.

One feels the existence of Shakti in the innermost heart; in giving all up to Shakti, peace is gained. One feels that all one's actions are prompted by her, even unknowingly, and the fruits of those actions whatever they may be, whether they bring happiness or misery, are given back to her. In that way we affirm that we do not want either happiness or sorrow and will not be moved by either. This devotional practice brings about indifference to phenomena. It also, at length, destroys all egotism and strengthens faith in Shaktimaya.[167]

---

[166] See *Thunder Perfect Gnosis*, 'Love, Devotion and Surrender'.

[167] This paragraph paraphrases Sutra 1: 23, commentary of Hariharānanda Āraña, p. 56 *Yoga Philosophy of Patañjali with Bhasvati* [University of Calcutta 2012].

Samyama

There are three distinct states of the yoga practice, and yet these are not truly separate in reality: *dharana, dhyana* and *samadhi,* taken together as one practice is called Samyama. At the beginning of the yoga practice and perhaps for a long time there is fluctuation, even if almost imperceptible, between the three yoga states. By sustaining this three-fold Samyama, *samadhi* is purer and deeper in quality. Sometimes practitioners forget that these three parts of meditation are 'states' in themselves and they are not really separate. There is seeming fluctuation or rapid passing between them, at least until *samadhi* of a high level can be gained. So in practice, and for the most part, *samadhi* really consists of all three states and these have their own qualities. Ultimately the goal is that of pure *samadhi* of deepening levels and yet *samadhi* will not be gained unless the practitioner understands well the three states, and the differences that are involved. This is the practice of Samyama.

The more that is understood about the intellective process and the modifications of the mind, the better the chance of getting some satisfactory results even in the beginning stages. The mind is fixed in the lotus of the heart.[168] Part of the concentration is keeping it there until it becomes habitual in meditation. This use of the heart lotus as a 'location', even while we know that the consciousness is not located in the body or anywhere else as such, is the most ancient method. It is not the only way to do it but generally speaking it greatly helps in most cases to shift the I-sense to the heart lotus, or at least to begin that way.

It is important to know clear distinction between the three parts of meditation at the very beginning: *dharana*, concentration of mind, *dhyana*, meditation, and *samadhi*, union—the goal of yoga, although there are many degrees and stages of *samadhi*. At the beginning, the concentration of mind does not equate to true *dhyana* meditation. Even when the mind is made to be still and fixed on the object, it is really more like contemplation in effect. It is only with prolonged concentration and deep meditation that true *dhyana* can come about. This will be explained further:

---

[168] It is worth mentioning again that the heart lotus is not exactly the same thing as the *anahatha* chakra; it is posited as somewhat below or within the latter, and is the gateway to the higher states, summed up as the 'seat of Brahma' (Brahma Loka).

Only when flow of knowledge of the object itself is continuous, without interruption, does the real *dhyana* meditation come about. It is the difference between a succession of mental modifications and one continuous stream. According to the ancient commentary of Vyasa, *dharana* is like drops of water while *dhyana* is more like oil or honey flowing continuously, in one stream without a break. Continuous knowledge (*dhyana*) then is not a succession; it is as though only one idea is held in the mind. This is what is meant by 'continuous flow of knowledge'. It is not having thoughts about the object, or indeed having any thoughts at all as such. It is non-reflective in that way.

Now *dhyana* meditation involves a powerful effort of will, while *samadhi* does not. However it is much easier when the devotional element, the sense of God, of yearning to know God, in turn inspiring love, reverence and so forth, is at all times present. The purpose of yoga is to know God directly. It is not a small deal, obviously. Let us suppose then that we begin with a devotional invocation of the Egyptian Neïth, a name of God as the unmanifest ground or sub-strata. It is from there that her 'lamp of fire' is removed to the heart lotus, placing the particular deity in the shrine of the heart and our self awareness. As the sub-strata, Neïth will not appear to any man, but there are other Egyptian gods that might be willing to bless us with their real influence. When the name of the tutelary deity is known, then this is the deity in the shrine of the heart.[169]

As we pass from the gross to the subtle, the idea is to get closer to what the deity really is—it is not 'abstraction'. When reverence and heart-felt devotion is at all times present—not just in the meditation hour but at all times, as one never forgets that one is a devotee—then one may also be helped by divine grace. We need all the help we can get with such a monumental and once-only Great Work.[170] When sustained, this *dhyana* can lead to *samadhi*, 'union of subject and object'. Samadhi is when deep meditation consists only of the object, without reflective thought. In *samadhi*, all process is lost. There is no sense of 'I am meditating'. All difference between the knower and the known, or the knowable, disappears in *samadhi*. True realisation of the Self is only gained by *samadhi*, and no other kind of knowledge. In repeated Samyama is the key to what is called Supernormal Powers in the yoga aphorisms of Patañjali.

---

[169] Following the particular example used here, the tutelary deity does not replace Neïth as unmanifest ground; therefore the preliminary invocation to the Lady of Sáis is retained. See 'Can God be Plural?'

[170] We visit the human state once and once only.

Transmutation

The word 'transmutation' is indicative of changing from one form to another, especially in the ordinary sense of the word. The term is sometimes used in alchemy, as in the changing of a base metal into gold, but this is symbolic analogy, whereas we will find in our dictionary, written by profane and uncomprehending linguistic experts, 'the supposed alchemical process of changing base metals into gold'. That is to say, 'supposed' because the writers of dictionaries think that all terms used in ancient languages can only be understood literally. They do not have a passing acquaintance with even the most superficial aspects of the traditional science of alchemy and yet will confidently assert that the changing of base metal into gold must rest on some kind of 'belief', as in the dictionary sense of that word, which means believing in something that is not true. The reverse is true; conventional science knows nothing of any reality; all it knows and all it can ever know is suppositions based on 'facts' produced by theories that are constantly being replaced, which is as much a superstition as any other.

What we are really concerned with here is change; change in the state of the mind, which passes through continuous and countless modifications, and change in the state of internal and external objects. ARARITA is a formulaic expression of the unity of the three-fold divine principle in seven Hebrew words:[171]

One is his beginning! One is his spirit! One is his permutation!

This requires a commentary: properly speaking the Lord, whatever the tradition, has no beginning or end; the unity of such a beginning implies that it is without end, making a positive statement possible—otherwise one could only use a figure of speech (Sanskrit *vikalpa*) that is pure negation, such as endless, or deathless, or 'bornless'.[172] Spirit has both a divine and an elemental sense; as 'essence' (Sanskrit *purusha*) it is all permeating while at the same time not being subject to any changes or modification. Permutation (*temurah*), on the other hand, is a definite change of modality, even if only a rearrangement of elements; so as in the case of 'beginning', the intercession of unity analogously resolves the difficulty.

---

[171] AChD RASh AChDVThV RASh IChVDVThV ThMVRThV AChD.

[172] The use of 'bornless' as descriptive of Hiranyagarbha in a Coptic fragment has led to the absurdity of the literal translation as 'headless one', or 'the one without a head'. See *Thunder Perfect Gnosis*, 'The Bornless One'.

We previously spoke of five mental states in yoga, of which the most advanced is called Arrested; this is so because it represents an almost indefinite prolongation and further advancement of the 'One-pointed' state.[173] Owing to the impossibility of entering the advanced yoga states permanently while still retaining any involvement with 'ordinary life', we said very little about the Arrested state; our readers are unlikely to be recluses living in caves, forests, mountains, or monasteries. However that may be, the Arrested state, if regarded in respect of the mutative conditions of the mind, is the best way of explaining exactly how yoga practice or Samyama is involved with assisting transmutation to further the goal of yoga.

The yogin attains the Arrested state through the cessation of all cognitive fluctuations. These fluctuations shape the mind through the continuous appearance and disappearance of *latent impressions*. All images, thoughts, things heard or felt, seen, tasted or smelled, support the mind in forming an impression of objects, mistaking them for the real. The objects of the mind and senses are really what constitute 'mind'—consisting of impressions resting on sense objects combined with recollection of previous impressions. With Samyama yoga practice, however, there is change or mutation in the mind as there is a mutation in the character of the impressions, which is resulting from the practice itself and discriminative knowledge.[174]

One must first know that the three Gunas are the essential conditioning of all existence; they are as the woven rope upon which the fabric of the worlds is spun. The mind is made up of the Gunas, and is their product. As such, the mind is constantly subjected to modifications that owe to the subtle transmutations effected by the Gunas. In the Arrested state, the *sattva* element of the mind is freed from all variations (called *prakhya*) caused by the other two Gunas. It is through *sattva*, unaffected by *rajas* and *tamas*, that the higher states are known. Thus the *rajas*, 'activity' and *tamas*, 'retention' or 'inertia', are supressed by the yogin in favour of the wisdom of *sattvas*, which is tranquil and upwardly tending.

The Arrested state is the only state that can lead on to the final liberation or *moksha*, yet even this is subject to fluctuations of the mind until liberation is completely gained. The difference is that the mental fluctuations of the yogin that has reached thus far take place on what can best be termed the 'subliminal' level, forming a kind of background to the continuous knowledge being enjoyed.

---

[173] See *Thunder Perfect Gnosis*, Part Two, pp. 108 and 113 in particular.
[174] See 'Concentration', commencing p. 138 [*ibid*].

The latent impressions of the fluctuations are not cognitions as such.[175] They are characteristics of the mind, not mental states, and do not cease to exist when the thoughts are stopped by single-point concentration, or even 'seedless' concentration, where there is no meditation object at all. In the Arrested state, as we have said, the ceaseless appearance and disappearance of the latent impressions taking place every moment in the mind of the yogin is subliminal. The mutation comes about through passing into and out of the single-pointed concentration. In reality, there are 'gradations' even in the mind of the yogin, in the same way that there are gradations of yoga samadhi, which is generally speaking descriptive of the goal.[176]

In the Arrested state, the mind of the yogin does not perceive the latent impressions, even though they subsist—the change is not perceptible or manifested. When the mind transmutes from the state called One-pointed to the more advanced state called Arrested, the latent impressions of knowledge gained in the former state—while needed to help the one-pointedness—decrease. Latent impressions of the state called Arrested then *increase*. In that state, while such changes still take place, they are not perceptible as 'sequence', for once the fluctuations diminish there is also a cessation of time in the mind of the yogin. One must understand that only with liberation (*moksha*) does the mind return to its constituent cause or higher principle (unmanifest). Only then do all mutations cease.

This is the real meaning of changing base metal into gold, as in the symbolism of alchemy. The analogy is that burning lead with gold results in the dross in the gold being destroyed along with the lead. What remains is pure gold.[177]

With latent impressions, suppressing anger, for example, does not remove anger for all of time, even in one individual. The latent impressions are eliminated by being replaced with those of a higher state. This is known, for example, by the continuance of tranquility when the power of the yogin is strong. If it weakens, there is a return to the ordinary states of mind. The usual characteristic of the mind is to want to place attention on all and sundry—every object, as it appears, is attended to. In the extreme case this is the state of the mind called Stupefaction.

---

[175] See the five *vrittis*, p. 144 [*ibid*].
[176] See 'Way to Samadhi', *Thunder Perfect Gnosis*; also see 'Gradations of Samadhi', *Way of Knowledge*.
[177] Swami Hariharānanda, *Yoga Philosophy of Patañjali* p. 260.

Stupefaction is the state most encouraged and even preferred by the bias of the modern world, be it the place of work or the permitted and approved recreational activities, which include physical pastimes such as sport and what is called 'fitness' as well as the endless distractions afforded by media technologies such as social networks, television, films and so forth. All of that is the exact and complete opposite of the one-pointed goal of yoga as it necessarily means attending to all and every contingency. The whole weight of today's techno-industrial society is, as is quite obvious, anti-intellectual. By that is not meant 'intellectual' by today's standards, which refers to pundits that have no metaphysical knowledge; it is the latter that the post-modern world is in every way opposed to.

We can now begin to approach the question of time. Latent impressions, leading to mental modifications, are retained from past impressions, and are dormant or latent until they become active again and through their magnetic qualities lure the practitioner into following them and so losing yoga power. When in *samadhi*, there is no difference between a past or latent impression and one that has freshly arisen. That is to say, there is uniformity in the flow of knowledge. To understand this we need to consider what happens in the One-pointed state, which in the present context means more than ordinary *samadhi* (*sa'asmita*). In this state there is a flow of the same idea appearing and disappearing. When the one-pointedness becomes a matter of habit, and not only for the prescribed time allocated for practice, then the mind rests or settles on one object and the habit of following all and sundry is destroyed. This is true engrossment (*samapatti*).

It should be noted that the further state of Arrested is only possible for those practicing supreme renunciation, with the goal of final and total liberation for all of time. Transmutation in the real or purest sense would then mean the cessation of all mutations and modifications upon reaching the goal of final liberation. Otherwise, mutation is seen to occur between the states of concentration, one-pointedness, and even the Arrested. Mutation goes on in every concentration and throughout Samyama; it is a matter of sending it in the right direction, which involves discriminative knowledge leading to the predominance of *sattvas*, which is called *sattvika*.

Phenomena

The mind, as with any object, passes through three changes involving the temporal conditions of past, present and future. Of these, only the present is manifest; the past has returned to the unmanifest ground; the future has not yet emerged. The present was once the future and is now manifest. The past was once the present, when it manifested, and before it manifested it was the future. Thus only the present is manifesting or emerging from *prakriti*, the unmanifest. Such emergence takes place through a change in characteristic but not in the 'essence' of a thing, which remains with the root or ground unmanifest sub-strata.

Although we speak of passing through changes, it is important to note that this transition owes to our particular perception from the point of view of the ever-changing present moment. In reality, when the mind is engaged with the present, the past and future, though unmanifest, nonetheless subsist at all times without appearing. An object and its attributes are really one and the same; there is a difference between a change of characteristic and a change of state. If something is made of gold and at some point is melted down then made into another object, the gold has not changed; it is only that there has been a change in its character, which in this case is its shape. The term 'state', as always used in these writings on yoga, is technical (Sanskrit *avasthā*) and does not refer to the ordinary or conventional meaning. A clay pot, for example can be the same pot but with the passing of time it becomes an old pot, in which case it has undergone a change of state.

All objects are an aggregate of perceptible characteristics; they emerge from the imperceptible unmanifest (*prakriti*), and this takes place in the present. Objects become quiescent in the past, for they have returned to the unmanifest. The sequence of the change of state only takes place in the present and future for this reason. For example, a pot was once a clod of clay and in the future will be potshards. The knowledge of objects must include all three states. However, the present does not follow the past even though it might appear that way. It is not retrospective. Everything always emerges from the unmanifest. The *present follows the future* and it becomes the past when it is quiescent. At the same time that which is anterior is the unmanifest, principial and the first.[178]

---

[178] The last shall be first and the first shall be last—one meaning of the words of Jesus, Matthew 20: 16, though rarely construed as such.

An object is only manifested, through its characteristic, in its active phenomenal state. The past and future are unmanifest and therefore not subject to determination; thus, our usual idea of a past that is somehow fixed, as it has taken place in our recollection, is imaginary. What has been said requires a good deal of thought especially as we are conditioned through education to habitually think in ways that are foreign and even the complete reverse of ancient sciences. It will be useful therefore to summarise the above as well as add some further considerations: There are three kinds of mutation, comprising characteristic, temporal character and state or *avasthā*. All external objects and circumstances are continually undergoing mutation through a number of modifications. A clay pot is made of earth and that substance can appear to have gone through a change of characteristic along the way. So earth changes character from dust to the character of clay. Someone makes a pot from the clay. Later, the pot is broken and becomes a pile of potshards. All this amounts to a change of characteristic. The pot nonetheless remains as earth, which is its principle (*bhuta*).[179] The essential substance or ground, the substratum of the pot is of the nature of earth. That is substratum, potential within *prakriti* or the unmanifest until a change in character allows emergence.

A change of state (*avasthā*) can owe for example to time or location. The pot can still be of the character of a pot but over time it becomes an old pot. That is a change of state. When a thing moves to a new location or place, there is a change of state even though the thing appears the same. This is why the careful placing of objects, or their moving to a new location, can be an important element in certain kinds of operative fields. A clod of clay or earth cannot be used to carry water from one place to another. When it is made into a pot, which is a change of character though not a change in essential substance, it can carry water. Also, a pot that is full of holes will not carry water because the water will leak out. It might be possible to smash the pot, which is a further change of character, and then re-mould it into a new pot that is capable of carrying water. This analogy is used in the Hebraic tradition with the tale of the heretic, Rabbi Acher:

---

[179] The *bhutas* are called 'gross elements' but owing to the fact that the modern theoretical conception of 'matter' as inert physical substance does not exist in any ancient tradition, we generally speak of them as subtle principles to avoid confusion with matter. The word 'matter' is often used in translation but it is quite wrong; as a technical term, 'substance' means something quite different, as does the 'essence' of a thing.

But all was not lost. Later he said, after going astray, Even as golden vessels and glass vessels have a remedy when they have broken, as they can be melted down and made into new vessels, so too a Torah scholar, although he has transgressed, has a remedy. And the Rabbi Meir said to him: If so, you too, can return from your ways.[180]

There is a point being made in the above quotation that the heretic was nonetheless unable to know the difference between gold and glass in that while the character of both can change, gold and glass are not at all the same; gold is a metal that is symbolically and literally of celestial origin, while glass is artificial, a man-made product. The flaw was in the nature of the Rabbi Acher, who lacked the ability to discriminate.

The mind, as has been said, is composed of the three Gunas, and is their product. So it is with all things in manifestation. Time, involving the past, present and future, comes about through the action (*rajas*) of the Gunas, which owes to movement across space and the appearance of sequence. The Gunas mutate constantly and by this what is called the Wheel of the Gunas incessantly revolves. It has been shown that while this is how things appear to our mind and senses, in reality the past, present and future subsist at all times in the present 'moment', though only one can manifest as the present— a present that appears to be continually passing from one moment to the next. Furthermore, each moment is in fact immeasurable in time. While we can mark out time with seconds, minutes and hours, following the rotation of the earth and its revolution about the sun, for example, time is continuous whereas numbers are discontinuous.

We tend to measure man by his span of life, commencing with birth and ending at death; in reality however, any individual, as with any object, comes about through modifications or determinations reaching backwards and forwards in time to an indefinite (though not infinite) degree. Nothing can exist that did not exist from the beginning. This is not to say that either objects or men are eternal as such, for they rise and fall, they appear and disappear back into the unmanifest *prakriti*. No phenomenon is eternal as it is, by definition, subject to mutation. All the same, the unmanifest *prakriti* is effectively without a beginning or an end. While objects nonetheless can be said to exist within the unmanifest, they do not truly exist until emergence. In the unmanifest, 'everything is everything else'. The points made here are important to grasp before the matter of Supernormal Powers can in any way be comprehended.

---

[180] See 'The Hebraic Tradition', *Thirty-two paths of Wisdom*.

136

Knowledge of the Past and Future

The Supernormal Powers or *siddhis* can come about through yoga practice, most specifically, repeated Samyama over a long period of time. While generally disapproved of, they tend to arise spontaneously when certain kinds of practice are followed; the yoga aphorisms thus go into some detail about them. At the same time the knowledge is presented in a way that is perhaps deliberately obscure or otherwise incomplete. Once deciphered, there is far more to construe than with the degraded form of them called the 'Western magical powers'. In this and the following chapters we intend to elucidate on a subject almost completely unknown, or otherwise not comprehended or misprepresented, in the modern world.

The *siddhis* are useful either in measuring progress or to assist a teacher in the transmission of a spiritual influence. A person may be born with some of the *siddhis*, whether latent or active, and which involves no spiritual realisation in itself. It is also possible for some of the powers to be gained temporarily through psychotropic plant extracts, which is the most dangerous means of acquiring them, especially as this precludes any real knowledge.[181] Of these it is said that all powers gained thereby are in the abode of the demons.

There are three kinds of changes or mutations in phenomena: change of characteristic, temporal character (or modality) and change of state. The knowledge of the past and future can thus be acquired by the yogin who practices Samyama on an object.[182] The yoga powers of concentration and meditation are then applied to the object for this purpose, which involves the sequence of temporal changes. We are really dealing here with cause and effect; while ordinary intelligence can acquire some idea of this, to the yogin whose mind is purified by yoga power, nothing is hidden. Once the immediate cause is known in detail then the effects are known also, and such effects become further causes.

---

[181] This is all the more so when sociologists and others conduct community experiments involving such plant substances. These do not even know that *siddhis* exist as they lack the most rudimentary knowledge of traditional doctrine or sciences and are not interested in acquiring such knowledge. They do not seek the *siddhis* but follow spiritually blind social and political agendas. The resulting destruction of the traditional lives of the rain forest tribes that host the experiments owing to the technologies and milieu of the sociologists is not seen or is overlooked by the latter 'in the name of science'.

[182] See 'Samyama' (p. 128) for an explanation of what this practice involves.

While such knowledge may be total as regards any object, at the same time it must be admitted that it is very limited if regarded as pertaining only to the causal relations between things. Nonetheless, the knowledge of the past and future is first of the Supernormal Powers as Patañjali and his commentators give these. While it is true that the causal relations of things can be deduced by ordinary means, the implication of prophetic dreams, for example is that the mind has the ability, latently at least, to know the future, though the future is as yet unmanifested.

A further consideration is that the ordinary means of perception, the senses and cognitive faculties, are not the only means of perceiving things, as proved by telepathy.[183] While thought takes place in time, it does not require spatial dimension and is therefore not limited by place, distance, size, proportion and so forth. The thrust of the yoga aphorism is that as the mind has the ability to know the future then there is no reason why such power cannot be developed through yoga practice, all the while bearing in mind that the *siddhis*, or magical powers as they are known in the West, are not considered to be in any way worthwhile pursuing for their own sake. However, if an external object can be meditated upon and knowledge gained of that object then the knowledge should properly include that of the threefold mutable nature of all phenomena; acquiring the knowledge of the past and the future cannot be ruled out and must be admitted as possibility.

This inevitably raises the important distinction that must be made regarding the means described here, which involves the full development of concentration, meditation and engrossment, and the ordinary notion of divination, as well as that of clairvoyance. The use of the term 'clairvoyance' in traditional knowledge has nothing to do with psychism; it is only that in modern times all such terms have been blurred, owing to the lack of comprehension of commentators and even occultists, let alone the mediums and spiritists—these last two being one and the same save for the fact that spiritists will often seek mediums to confirm their theories. The exact meaning of the word clairvoyance is 'clear seeing'; we must bear in mind that in all ancient languages words for sight, seeing, or seer indicate a special kind of knowledge over and above the ordinary cognition implied by the same word.

---

[183] Vyasa did not see any need to prove telepathy itself; to the Hindu sages telepathy is self-evident.

Divination, on the other hand, is nearly always placed under the umbrella of magical arts, though it is really a traditional science like astrology that consists of very specialised rules and applications. Keeping in mind what was said about the past, present and future as not being separate in reality but appearing in sequence owing to the determination of time that binds us to the Wheel of the Gunas, then divination takes place in the present otherwise it could not take place at all. Divination usually requires symbolic means of representing universal possibilities; the tarot cards serve as a fine example of such a device. If three sets of cards are drawn, one for the past, one for the present and one for the future, then the relations (by rules of dignity) between them can be examined with ordinary intelligence and, as according to the skill and knowledge of the operator, causes and effects worked out and projected. Further, if one card is drawn at the beginning to represent a question or the questioner, the subject of enquiry, then it could be said that this is no different in effect than meditation Samyama upon an object. The difference is that while divination has been sold as something anyone can do, as with most things that have been taken up by the neo-spiritualists, Samyama yoga is decidedly not and never will be something that anyone can do. Therefore Supernormal Powers rarely if ever enter the domain of those who seek knowledge through such devices as the tarot, and if they do, it will be quite by accident. The yogin, on the other hand, has no need for such trifles. While there is nothing wrong with divination if it is not separated from all higher principles, and is not sought as an end in itself, the danger is always that ignorant use of it leads to deepening delusion and indeed, stupefaction.

Divination is the nearest equivalent to this *siddhi* in terms of the Western magical powers. It corresponds, as according to the Golden Dawn system, to the eleventh path and the tarot trump called the Fool, which is called Spirit of Aethyr. This is curiously apt, given this knowledge is about that of the past and future, and yet at the same time limiting.[184] However, *akasha* (spirit or ether) in its elemental aspect is identified closely with *prakriti* as unmanifest ground, and that is precisely the area that the yogin must have knowledge of before anything can be known about the past and future. This raises the most interesting consideration that true divination, as opposed to either reasoning or psychism, involves a type of evocation.

---

[184] The systematic attributions so highly regarded by occultists were arrived at through quite arbitrary means. In the Golden Dawn, HRU (Horus) was the 'Great Angel of the Tarot', and identified with the eleventh path as first transmission of the lightning flash or order of sephiroth.

Knowledge of the Language of all Beings

This yoga power has an equivalence with one of the magical powers known to the West and placed in Key Scale tables of correspondences. It is most often called the 'power of taming wild beasts', a definition that is so narrow as to inevitably lead to quite absurd notions. While we have redefined and improved this as the 'intelligence of birds and animals', this requires the understanding of symbolism as analogy, which few persons possess today.[185] To quote the Patañjali aphorism directly:

> Knowledge of the meaning of the sounds produced by all Beings.

One must gain knowledge, through higher intellectual intuition, of the language, sounds or vibrations that are produced by all beings. By 'all beings' is really meant exactly that, so we must understand that 'birds and animals' is symbolic analogy; all beings in all worlds and not only that strictly limited world known to the human being, inextricably linked with the terrestrial sphere. Birds, for one example alone, are used in ancient languages to symbolise what is otherwise called the angelic or celestial world; we are concerned then here with non-human and supra-human intelligence.

This aphorism, far from being about some vague psychism or 'intuition' by which the language and thoughts of animals can be understood, is all about *the* Word (Logos) in its most sublime and exact sense. As with all the Supernormal Powers, it is concerned not with divination, magic, astrology or other sciences, but with the yoga practice of Samyama, which, to recapitulate, consists of the three elements of concentration, meditation and *samadhi*, to the various levels as available to the practitioner. It should be noted, however, that the reason why the Arrested state was used previously as an introduction to the whole matter of the Supernormal Powers, is that to acquire the kind of total knowledge the sages had in mind requires a considerable advancement in terms of yoga power.[186] Far from being something 'anyone' can do, or achieve by means of some magical formula or short cut, it is an exacting science that takes great effort and dedication of the whole self over many years to gain even an inkling of the vast possibilities contained within it.

---

[185] See the appendices, *The Enterer of the Threshold*, for example.
[186] See 'Transmutation'.

Language may be broken down into three things: the word itself, or sound, the object implied by the word, and the knowledge of that object. The letters of an alphabet, or sounds, are formed into words conveying a single idea by the power of the intellect. Each letter of a word thus formed, especially in Sanskrit or any ancient language, can convey innumerable associations, as does the arrangement of the letters and their internal relations. Conventional usage associates a word with an object, by inference. For example the noun *owl* has three letters (in English) and when taken all together the word thus formed indicates a species of bird with particular characteristics. Such a word, with its implied object such as 'owl', conveys the idea instantly to anyone who hears the word; that is to say, it is non-sequential, as are the individual letters, and as such is an aggregate. Thus the word 'owl' is associated with the nocturnal avian, so that the word is identical, through the idea, with its object.

Thus the man who understands the distinction between word, object and idea or knowledge of the object, knows the meaning of all uttered or articulated words; so it is written. When 'owl' is uttered or articulated it simultaneously affirms that the creature actually exists as a real thing. Furthermore, one word may convey a whole sentence in terms of its idea, the implied meaning; one only requires another word for specific detail. For example, the Sanskrit word *jiva* means 'life' or 'living', as does the Hebraic *nephesch*. In both languages, the one word also conveys the meaning 'he who has living breath'.[187] How then are the word, the object and its knowledge, known as separate and distinct? The intellectual 'word' does not consist of letters; it is one idea formed in the mind. It is only in the expression of the idea that we need words, spoken or written language, as support. Humans use human languages; other beings use other languages. The word, the object and its knowledge or idea is merged into one through convention. The yogin, through the power of concentration and by the yoga of *nirvitarka* (without verbal support) is able to know these separately; he is thus able to know the idea referred to by any word or sound. There are some meanings of words only comprehended through the special knowledge of yoga.

There are some things that the commentators on this aphorism have implied but have not referred to directly. In Sanskrit the word *vak* means 'uttered speech' while the extension *paravak* means 'beyond speech', literally, though the usual interpretation is 'without words'.

---

[187] Such may ordinarily be known through the etymology of a word.

Para-vak is the primordial utterance, alluded to in the text of the commentaries as the 'intellectual word', described as a word that does not have letters. It is by this same power that words are formed and translated into sounds and written with alphabets. We are really looking at the 'soundless vibration' here, of which the AUM is the foremost and the most universal as it contains the possibilities of all sounds, ideas and language within it. That vibration without sound is also related to the *akasha* or 'ether', which doubles as a fifth element (technically *tattva-bhuta*) and the principle of vibration that is made possible through spatial limitation, within a virtually unlimited field. The *akasha* in its higher sense abides in the heart lotus, also called the seat of Brahma, and which is the centre of all Being as well as any individual being (*jiv-atma*), by transposition. It is no exaggeration on the part of the author (of the aphorism) to have stated that this power is that of knowing the meaning of the sounds produced by all Beings. Again, while it is not disclosed in the textual translation, the implication in context of the Hindu doctrine is not only creatures of earth but all beings in *all worlds*; and these 'worlds' are indefinite, that is to say that while they are not 'eternal' because they are manifest and so subject to determination, causality and so forth, they are quite literally numberless, uncountable or measureless. And so 'all Beings' is inclusive of a totality, of which the human being is but one minute proportion, occupying as it were a fraction of a degree of all manifest possibilities.

From there it is a simple matter for a yogin able to realise and apply this knowledge to hear the 'words' spoken by angels or deities. And likewise, there is the infernal world of *asuras* or demons, which are often symbolised by beasts, serpents or other animals, in the same way that angels or celestial intelligences are symbolised by birds or winged creatures of some sort.

Two things remain to be said. Firstly, it was mentioned at the beginning of this article that the direct Western equivalent of this *siddhi* is placed in Key Scale correspondence tables. This power is there referred to the nineteenth path, the letter *teth* 'a serpent' and the zodiacal sign of Leo the Lion. The associated Tarot trump depicts a woman either closing or opening the mouth of a lion or some other beast (Fortitude VIII or XI). It is strange then to see what turn of mind the occultists have in attributing the meanings to this that they do, for the oldest printed Tarot seems to correspond quite exactly. Finally, it must also be mentioned that 'speaking in tongues' is no doubt derived from a symbolic allusion to this same power, which as usual has been understood only in the grossest terms imaginable.

Knowledge of Previous States of Existence

The translation of the Patañjali aphorisms gives 'knowledge of previous births', which is not wrong but we anticipate that this will doubtless give rise to confusion in the minds of some that have assumed 'reincarnation' to be fundamental to Hindu doctrine, whereas it is in fact a purely modern invention. This has been dealt with in a previous chapter so there is no need to repeat what was said there.[188] According to the aphorism, by the realisation of latent impressions, knowledge of previous births is acquired. The two kinds of latent impressions are firstly those caused by memory of past actions, thoughts or speech, and thereby giving rise to afflictions in an indirect way. In the second case they are the working out, fruition or completion of virtuous or evil deeds done in previous states. Both kinds require *vāsanās* for their emergence, which are best described as the latent or subliminal 'field' as suitable for continuation of the retained impression. The *vāsanā* may be likened to a mould, into which is poured the molten metal of virtuous and vicious deeds.[189]

Of the second kind, 'previous birth' is a broad term because in addition to actual previous states of being, which can extend to other cosmic cycles, there are hereditary and environmental factors that can form a *vāsanā* field for a latent impression to ripen. In the same way that physical characteristics are passed on across generations (heredity), psychic elements are continued.[190] Among environmental impressions are also the 'wandering influences' or dissociated psychic remnants of former (i.e. deceased) humans. The social and other milieu of a time, or collective traits, if allowed to strongly dominate an individual, give rise to a fertile ground for all associated afflictions to emerge. This explains how, most particularly in modern times where psychic disequilibrium is at a maximum, perplexing and even bizarre behaviours of an afflicted kind can seem to spread, in the way that influenza is theoretically supposed to be transmitted from person to person. This takes place particularly through a group that seeks a social self-identity in clothing, music and mannerisms, marks made upon the body and so forth, in an attempt to offset the void that comes about when all tradition has been suppressed, if not erased.

---

[188] See Part One, 'Reincarnationism'.

[189] The word 'vicious' is used especially for its relation to 'vice', which itself is derived from Latin *vitium*, 'failing or defect'.

[190] Similar but not the same as metempsychosis—see 'Reincarnationism'.

All these impressions are understood to form the characteristics of the 'mind stuff' or *chitta*, and they are hidden or invisible until an activation or emergence takes place. The idea is that when Samyama is practiced on latent impressions, they are fully realised, and this naturally includes knowledge of place, time and causality. The yogin that can do this can also know the previous births (or other latency) of other persons.

Previous births, as meaning past states of being, can include the existence of a *deva* or demi-god, or of an *asura* or demon. When birth as a man is referred to, this does not mean reincarnation as that is supposed. 'Man' is a symbol in all ancient traditions for a centre position on the world axis, that is, central (in a macrocosmic sense) to indefinite multitudes of worlds or states of being, both inside and outside of time. One should bear in mind also that past and future are unmanifest, and only the present and future are sequential; the cosmic cycles, for example, are simultaneously occurring in reality.[191]

The real purpose of realising previous births is to understand that all birth comes about through desire of pleasure, which is equally tempered by pain throughout existence. Even contentment is a temporary arrangement of the Gunas. The only real and lasting peace and tranquility is the supreme renunciation and *moksha* liberation, which is freedom from all births, never to return again to manifest existence. It is to know and fully realise that all desire is pain; real contentment comes about when desire is removed.

The near equivalent to this power in Western correspondences is that of the 'magical memory', placed with the twenty-ninth path of the letter *qoph*, the zodiacal sign of Pisces and the Tarot trump called the Moon XVIII. Some of the means used to develop this in occultism make the realisation and operation of the real power impossible; firstly, practices are limited by the theory of 'reincarnation', which must inevitably rest on fantasy owing to the falsehood implicit in the theory. Secondly, other practices go no further than attempts made to develop quite ordinary mental powers; however useful that might be, it has nothing to do with the Supernormal and certainly does not touch on anything supernatural or even 'magical' in the sense of real traditional sciences.

---

[191] See 'Transmutation'.

How to Read Minds

This aphorism is not about telepathy exactly, as it is exclusively concerned with mind-reading, not transmission. The means is, as always, Samyama, though it is understood that some persons are born with the ability to read the minds of other people and so they do not get the power from yoga. If Samyama is practiced on any idea of the mind, that idea is fully realised. One must be able to do this before applying concentration on the thoughts of others. The idea, thought or 'notion' is then isolated from all other thoughts and concentration is brought to bear on it.[192] In order to realise the thoughts of another, the reader holds only the sense or 'view' of the other person, restraining all other thoughts entirely, effectively then producing a mental vacuum. Thoughts arising are then the thoughts of the other person. A reader may also know a feeling long forgotten.

We had this demonstrated to us once by a person that was born with the ability. They were able to retrieve thoughts and feelings from long ago, and which were quite exactly correct. Nonetheless, the mind-reader did not understand the power or know if it had any real use; neither were they able to tell from where in the person's life this originated, and whether the kind of thought was in any way still active. The mind-reader did not need to be in the presence of the one whose mind they were reading but only needed to be able to quietly concentrate on the 'view' of the person, as it is put in the aphorism. In this case, the mind-reader only seemed able to read thoughts and feelings from long ago with precision; she used the power to a certain extent even in a social situation, and without disclosing what she was doing, perhaps because it had become habitual; however, her ability to do this with any degree of accuracy was impaired by psychological and other bias.

The yogin may learn the nature of such an idea, for example as one of attachment or desire, but is unable to know the basis, the object. This is because it is the mental modification only that is observed by the yogin. Fear is given as an example: fear may be observed, as mental modification, but that fear is independent of the tiger that generated the sense of fright. The aphorism is emphatic: 'The prop (support or basis) of the notion remains unknown because that is not the object of the (yogin's) observation.'

---

[192] The word 'notion' is used in translation, presumably to distinguish this kind of thought from the higher Idea, which transcends the level of the ordinary mentation and cognitive faculties.

Power of Invisibility

The Supernormal Power of making the body disappear so it is completely invisible to others is perhaps one of the most well known of all the powers. It is known about, though scarcely believed in, through the popularity of the legends of King Arthur and the wizard Merlin, for example, who made full use of such powers. We are here looking at special applications of Samyama Yoga. Unless a person has practiced and experienced Samyama then no doubt all of these powers will seem to them as no more than fantasy. However, we intentionally placed the three chapters Samyama, Transmutation and Phenomena to serve as a kind of introduction before describing the Supernormal Powers. If that is understood perfectly well then the reader—who will no doubt also be a practitioner—should have little difficulty in seeing that what is being described here has nothing to do with 'tricks' or stagecraft, and is not being written for the purpose of entertainment only.

The *Yoga-Sutra* is very brief as the method owes mainly to the use of a highly trained will, such as comes about through yoga, which involves prolonged control of body and mind towards a goal that far transcends the acquiring of *siddhis*.[193] The visual link between the body and the sensory perceptions is suppressed by use of an effort of will. To put it another way, the body is placed beyond the sphere of perception of the eye. First one must perform Samyama on the visual appearance of the body; the yogin is accustomed through long practice to passing beyond the physical and subtle senses and even the cognitions, for the five *vrittis* are modifications of the I-sense.[194] Thus it will be seen by those who have succeeded in yoga practice to at least the realisation of the pure I-sense how the visual link can be suppressed, even in the faculties of other persons, thus rendering one invisible. In the words of Vyasa, 'the body ceases to be an object of observation by another person'. In fact, it is not only the visual faculty but also the audio and other faculties, so for example the yogin will not be heard either.

Magicians, or more accurately *fakirs* in the East, are able to exert their will so that others only see what the *fakir* wants them to see. In this case, no knowledge of any real kind is implied, as *fakirs* are not yogins. They develop their powers over long and arduous training, often involving extreme and torturous methods.

---

[193] Patañjali Aphorism III: 21.
[194] See *Thunder Perfect Gnosis*, p. 144.

Such a *fakir* could turn a man into an elephant or a snake into a house and yet have no knowledge of any transcendent principle; the difference must be noted that they do not do this by yoga power. There may be an analogy drawn between the use of this power by a *fakir* and the use of it by politicians and other advertisers who seek to profit from the manipulation of minds so that others see only what they want them to see. Likewise, the previous Supernormal Power that was described, the reading of minds, might be comparable on a very degraded level with the Western magical power of 'political and other ascendancy', or exerting influence over others, which is there a correspondence of Jupiter.[195] A politician must at least have a sort of instinctive sense of the kind of direction the mind of the populace is leaning, and the extent to which it can be given a 'push' in the desired direction.[196]

The power of invisibility exists in the Western correspondences, and is ascribed to the twentieth path linking Chesed with Tiphereth, the letter *yod* and Virgo. Interestingly, the further correspondence of the Tarot Atu the Hermit IX introduces the notion of the 'cloak of concealment', which we will describe later. The Hebrew letter *yod* is sometimes analogously taken as the power of will, and the sage or the hermit is seen as one who practices the necessary austerities by which such a will is made possible. The attribution of the zodiacal sign of Virgo lends to this another aspect, for a further power of the path is parthenogenesis, which links it to the ancient Egyptian Isis, to whom the power of both concealment and pristine conception of a divine 'child' (Horus) belongs. This takes us away altogether from any kind of tricks or deception, for we are back on the ground of the yoga powers developed through silence and withdrawal from the world of appearances. The 'child' is then emblematic of that aspect of the devotional path complemented by the 'warrior', and where the child as a yogic state is the superior of the two and not to be confused with any sentimental notions.

---

[195] Key Scale 21, Jupiter, the letter *kaph* and Tarot Atu X named 'Fortune' or 'Destiny'—those two things not being in any way the same.

[196] 'Majority rule' makes this easy. Such a 'push' often involves very sordid and criminal acts set up by the various covert arms of the State. A great deal now of course depends on data collection and this in turn forges links with the world of *asuras* or demons, the *sub-infra* human level, barely inside of manifestation. By the increasing use of data and machines, decisions are made that affect the lives of many persons and that have no real intelligence behind them. All of this is a symptom of the final phase of the Kali Yuga.

The warrior 'clings' to wisdom by his own volition whereas the child does not act or will, resting wholly upon divine ordinance. Horus nonetheless carries both attributes, the former indicating the active mode (*rajas*) and the latter the non-active (*sattvic*) mode.[197]

Finally, mention might be made of a very elaborate attempt to gain the power of invisibility through magical means that was at one time circulated among members of the Golden Dawn. This made use of the notion of a cloak of concealment, and rested upon the theory that the astral light could be 'densified' and woven into a shroud and worn for a temporary period of time by the magician, so as to make him invisible. This was sometimes supported by the use of talismans, which are themselves usually concealed or wrapped up. The whole operation is placed under the governance of Saturn, though some might find it worthwhile considering there is an analogous relation between Saturn and the Moon.[198]

---

[197] Sri Ramakrishna said there are two kind of *bhakti* devotees, the monkey and the child. The monkey clings to the tree while the child is like a kitten, completely helpless without its mother—i.e., Kali Ma, for Sri Ramakrishna likened himself to the child at a certain stage of his life. Called Balya in the Hindu tradition, it is an advanced stage of the solitary *sannyasin*; it has nothing to do whatsoever with any Western notions of infantalism. Cf. 'The Deliverance of Horus', Part One.

[198] When Isis is associated with the Moon, the power of invisibility becomes very obvious. As 'throne' or Shekinah, the abode of Isis is Saturn.

Knowledge of Omens

The knowledge of omens really concerns *karma*, a word very widely misconstrued in the modern world owing to the efforts made by neo-spiritualists to link it with morality, whereas the word only means 'action' in the most general sense.[199] The aphorism is mostly concerned with foreknowledge of death although the nature of omens can include wider applications.[200] We will take as our basis the particular use as indicated in the *Sutra*. The span of a person's life is described as a fructification of *karma*, and this is governed by time as a measure. The span of a life can pass either quickly, like a consuming fire blown by the wind, or slowly, as in the case of a wet cloth rolled up that takes long to dry out. Thus according to the aphorism there are two ways to know the span of a life, one is by practicing Samyama on the underlying *karma* of that existence, and the other is by knowing how to read omens or portents. Karma, more precisely the *karmasayas* or ongoing fruits of action, comes about with varying length of duration as previously indicated, as according to the nature of the *karma*. Therefore some actions will be slow to fructify and some others quick. Some will be active and some will be dormant until activation.

Of the ominous signs three kinds are given: personal, elemental and divine. Personal portents include not hearing sound from within the body when closing the ears and not seeing any effulgent light when closing the eyes (with the fingers). This may well be meant quite literally and it seems so from the wording of the text, which we have here paraphrased, but those who have practiced yoga for long enough to gain special knowledge will understand that *pratyahara*, 'withdrawal of the senses', first indicates the gross or physical senses and later the subtle senses. Elemental portents involve seeing the angels or messengers of the Lord of Death or in some other cases the ghosts of the ancestors. It should be noted, while it is not mentioned in the commentaries, which are very brief, that seeing such a portent does not necessarily indicate the imminent death of one's self but may indicate the death of another person. In some cases the person may not even be known to the seer, or may become known to them later. One should also bear in mind that death is cognate with any change of state in the being.

---

[199] See 'The Key of Magick', *Way of Knowledge*, and also 'Karma and Sin', *Nu Hermetica.*
[200] *Yoga-Sutra* III: 22.

The divine portents include suddenly having a vision of the heavenly or celestial world, with its creatures (Siddhas or 'etherials') as well as seeing all things in a contrary-wise fashion. A further note might be added here that this latter portent is sometimes seen at a time of tremendous import, as when a great revolution or change of world affairs is imminent.[201] In the wider sense, where this power is not necessarily about the death of a person, there is comparison with the Western magical power of prophecy, which is corresponded to the seventeenth path of Gemini, the letter *zain* and Tarot Atu VI the Lovers (or twins). The power of prophecy involves the foretelling of any event that comes to pass at a later date, and so is particularly concerned with the future. It should be made clear that there is no relation between prophecy and 'prediction', though the two things are commonly confused. While the latter involves making a guess or forecast, a prophecy means 'giving voice before', and if it is genuine prophecy and not ordinary charlatanism then this is not usually very detailed. There are exceptions, though, as in the case of the Prophecy of Hermes, written down sometime in the 2nd century AD and which is quite explicit and very accurate in telling of the decline of the Egyptian civilisation and even that of the whole world up to the present time.[202]

Although it does not involve omens as such, there is a further power attributed to the Geminian intellectual mind, which is that of 'being in two places at once'. This has two levels of interpretation. The first is that time is a determining factor of the human state but is not involved in other states than that of the human. In reality, or with the supreme principle, there is simultaneity, non-sequential. From the corporeal human point of view, this can appear as a bi-locational manifestation and to all intents and purposes it is that. The literal interpretation is not entirely separate from the principial but it will raise the immediate question as to how can it be in any way possible for a body to be in two places at once? Many will find this to involve stretching the mind further than it will reach, but it is not that complex. As we have already mentioned, a change of location or place, which is a matter of spatial determination, is a change of state in any object or creature whatsoever.[203] Thus the power as such really involves existing in two states or modalities of being simultaneously. Furthermore, particular conditions can bring this about unwilled.

---

[201] Such a vision of the 'world upside down' was seen by some in late 2019.
[202] See *Nu Hermetica*, 'The Prophecy of Hermes'.
[203] See 'Transmutation'.

Power of Strength

There are many different kinds of strength but of course the overriding concern of the *Yoga-Sutras* is strength to assist the practice of Samyama Yoga. Friendliness, compassion and goodwill are essential to yoga strength and while this becomes self-evident to the long-time practitioner that remains true to the goal and the path (these two not really being separate) it is needful to supply some explanation. This is especially needful for those who do not know of any Self other than what is superimposed on the Real by the mind and its faculties, producing all self-identifications of 'this is mine'—I am the knower, I am the one who enjoys or suffers, and so forth. A person who is angry, which comes about through attachment and aversion, mistakes misery for happiness owing to the fact he takes a certain pleasure in being angry. In that, he might produce justifications for this even while knowing, from what he has learned, that anger is driven by *tamas* 'inertia' that belongs to the world of demons and drags the soul down to inferior or sub-human states of being.[204]

We must first make a careful distinction and rule out completely the 'mindfulness' that has been borrowed from heterodox modern Buddhist schools of thought and propagandised.[205] Such notions as these have their origin in true knowledge but have become degraded and even totally inverted by the modern mentality, which seeks to reduce everything through popularisation to something 'anyone' can do. This attitude is so deeply embedded that anything that clearly is beyond the capability of 'anyone' is regarded as worthless.

Mindfulness had its origin with the *Yoga-Sutras* though the term is rarely used there. It is the practice of discrimination as a constant vigilance. When it is removed from the context of the discipline of yoga and devotion to God, it means nothing. The word 'compassion' also cannot be used without qualification. Compassion owes directly to the *Yoga-Sutras*. The Buddhists used this, and it is from there that the term gradually became known and misused in the West.

---

[204] While terms such as *asuras* or 'demons' lend a sense of reality to what are really non-sentient things, the use of words denoting sub-human states that weaken the practitioner is to remind ourselves of the latter.

[205] Compassion, often used side by side with 'mindfulness', is now used by governments and corporations to control minds as well as the bodies of the 'work-force', so there should be no resistance to official policies.

The original meaning of what is here translated 'compassion' is more akin to telepathy than anything that can be 'practiced'.[206] It is a *siddhi* or magical power that corresponds to Nirvikalpa Samadhi. Nirvikalpa Samadhi is even further advanced than ordinary Samadhi, if union with God can even be called 'ordinary', because of course that is an extraordinary thing in the present times. So no one can 'practice' compassion in the highest sense of what that means. In fact, if they could truly experience it and were not prepared by valid yoga practice it would derange their minds perhaps permanently.[207]

What kind of compassion is really meant then in relation to the acquiring of strength in yoga? *Yoga-Sutra* 3: 23 declares,

> Through Samyama on friendliness (amity) and other similar virtues, [yoga] strength is obtained therein.

The commentary of Vyasa then goes on to mention 'three kinds of sentiments', which are the aforementioned friendliness, compassion and goodwill. While these are considered as virtues, it is only so from the point of view of the mind that knows virtue and vice, of which vice has been qualified previously as 'vicious' thoughts and actions.[208] In practice vice weakens the yoga power while virtue can strengthen it. It has to be understood this should not be a matter of imagining that one is 'doing good' and accruing merit, although there are some schools of thought that will have it that way. Why not? Because that is egoism, which is one of the great afflictions! If, instead of the term 'sentiment', which is given in translation and which has emotional connotations, we said it was about cultivating an attitude of mind, we would be less inclined to make an error here. An attitude can be construed as one meaning of Sanskrit *mudra*, which is a 'seal' or 'impression', often mirrored in a physical ritual gesture. It makes a *samskara* retained impression that is helpful to the practice. While a person might still feel (mistakenly) that they are doing or thinking 'good' in the hope they will get a reward for it, with practice and knowledge the relative truth of such a cultivated attitude becomes self-evident. We desire tranquility so meditation is possible, hence 'forbearance', but in the highest kinds of *samadhi* tranquility is not striven for, and neither is the *samadhi* itself; one does not need to encourage rain to fall or morning dew to precipitate.

---

[206] Cf. 'How to Read Minds'.

[207] No doubt there have been countless cases of persons having what is now thought to be 'mental illness', treatable by mind-destroying drugs, that in reality had the Supernormal Power of compassion latent from birth.

[208] See 'Knowledge of Previous States of Existence', footnote on first page.

The meaning of compassion as intended here is then not much different from amity or friendliness but is further qualified. Amity towards happy beings eliminates envy, resentment and so forth. The same if practiced towards unhappy beings is compassion, and this eliminates possible afflictions such as disgust (aversion), anger and other *klésha* disturbances. Very often the student, reading such instruction, will imagine he is beyond it already and does not need it, which is really egoism because we all suffer from *karmasayas* owing from previous states, even the most advanced yogin, and these do not stop until the most final and permanent liberation (*moksha*) comes about.

Becoming engrossed in amity and goodwill is not there so as to puff up the pride with false notions of virtue; the purpose is the total opposite of that, which is to lose all sense of self in absorption in the meditation, to the extent that he passes on to the state of *samadhi*. Furthermore, according to the Bhāsvati commentary:[209]

> Samyama renders his strength of amity (etc.) infallible, removing all hindrances to their attaining perfection. As a result, contrary thoughts (i.e., contrary to amity or goodwill) do not even rise in his mind. Others come to rely on him, looking up to him as a trustworthy friend.

Now there are other kinds of strength and one that is most often misconstrued in the West is that of physical strength, such as 'having the strength of an elephant' (*Sutra* III: 24). This has direct frame of reference to what is often listed as the (Western) magical power that corresponds to the sixteenth path of Vav and Taurus, to the extent that one modern Tarot deck depicts elephants woven about the figure of the Hierophant.[210] However, the import of the *Yoga-Sutra* is that Samyama Yoga meditation on the power of strength is the highest form of strength. Vyasa goes on to speak of the strength of the King of Birds (Garuda) and the power of the wind acquired through yoga on the strength of Vayu (as air, wind). If there is weakness in either the body or mind of the yogin then meditation on elephants and birds is perfectly plausible. It should hardly need to be added that yoga requires at least reasonable bodily health and sound state of mind, so we are here looking at development not cure for sickness.

---

[209] Bhāsvati of Swami Hariharananda, his commentary on *Sutra* 3: 23, *Yoga Philosophy* [ibid p. 99].

[210] *The Hierophant V*, Crowley-Harris *Thoth Tarot*. While the use of will-power on the bodily muscles as used in physical culture is used for analogy, it is curious to note how the Western mentality first took this literally then removed it one step further to a notion of 'athleticism' applied to yoga.

Power of Knowing Distant Objects

This knowledge is about the light-ray of the higher intellect or *boddhi*, by which even the pure I-sense devoid of mind comes about as reflection of Purusha or 'essence', and which Itself is no different from the Atma as considered from the point of view of the being or individuality. The mind and its faculties resting upon sense perceptions is therefore but a secondary reflection of this ray. The kind of knowledge included here is of very subtle objects, or of things that are completely obscured from view or otherwise placed at a great distance.[211]

It is first needful to recapitulate on this kind of knowledge that is received from the *boddhi* ray.[212] This perception is radiant and free from pleasure and pain as experienced by the self cognised as the doer and enjoyer of things. It is said that by this—by prolonged meditation in this state—the mind becomes steady, or fixed (in the knowledge free from pain). This comes about through the meditation on the 'cave' or 'void' centre of the heart lotus, and is also boundless, resplendent, effulgent, luminous, jewel-like and so forth. It means that the mind is really stopped, at least partially and temporarily, so that there is perception of the pure I-sense 'like a waveless ocean, placid and limitless'.[213] This is called reflective meditation, not to be mistaken therefore for direct knowledge (Purusha or Atma), but which is nonetheless quite advanced practice and not an easy thing for practitioners to get who are still for the most part immersed in a modern world filled with objects of empty amusement and diversion. The meditation is of two kinds. The first is the meditation on the pure I-sense and the second is the meditation on objects of whatever kind but both involve the 'effulgence', which is not an imagined light but what comes about when the mind is at least partially arrested.

This effulgence is really the knowledge itself and it is that which comes about through what is called Sattvika enlightenment (owing to *sattvas* predominating). Thus, this knowledge 'manifests things that are subtle, covered from view or situated at a distance'.[214] The light or effulgence is not the I-sense itself but remains present or oscillates or fluctuates until there is total engrossment in the I-sense.

---

[211] *Sutras* III: 25–28.

[212] *Sutra* I: 36.

[213] Commentary of Vyasa on *Sutra* I: 36.

[214] Commentary of Swami Hariharananda on *Sutra* I: 36. See pp. 123–124 of *Thunder Perfect Gnosis*, on the practices of this.

In meditation on an object, such as one described as being very obscure or placed at great distance, the effulgence is directed towards that object and the object will be known. This comes about through the contact of the object with the power of *boddhi*, all-pervading. It is pure knowledge, and so must not be thought of as in any way like ordinary knowledge about a thing, or subtle knowledge in the sense of the reflections of the psyche, and which are no more than dreams.

This yoga can be extended to the cosmic regions, hence the 'great distance'. This is done by following the ray or light-thread that leads out through the *brahmarandra* 'located' so to speak at the top of the skull. In the *Yoga-Sutras* this is naturally associated with the summit of Mount Meru, the primordial axis of Hinduism. From the summit and beyond the stars and planets to the Pole star is a region called Antariksha ('space between'); the heaven worlds have their names and regions in all the traditions and it matters not which is adopted so long as we are consistent in that. There are also hell worlds, of which the lowest in the Hindu tradition is called Avichi, where no light can reach at all ('waveless'). Above and beyond that and the abodes of terrible suffering are also various Dvipas, islands or countries, filled with heavenly beings and men. These are curious beings. Some are totally absorbed in various kinds of *samadhi*, for example. They can also know of the higher and the lower realms. Some retain a sense of the body while others have no need for it though all are discarnate.

The yogin that is able to pass through the solar door can know all this in utmost detail. It should be mentioned again that this begins in the heart lotus or 'cave' but *sushumna* or the 'thread of light' can be followed out through the solar door, situated, if we use a manner of speaking, at the top of the skull. By this, total knowledge of the whole universe can be obtained. The more the senses are transcended, then the more powerful *boddhi* becomes, as it is less and less restricted. The *boddhi* knows nothing of distance as it is not within time and space, as is the human modality, so it can then easily be inferred how knowledge of subtle things or objects placed at a great distance can be known. This is likened to the removal of the coverings or veils upon the *boddhi*, and which correspond to the various *lokas*, places or worlds of existence. One may think, by way of comparison, of the Babylonian Ishtar, who descended into the underworld to rescue her son Tamuz, at each level removing one of her veils. In the Egyptian and Babylonian traditions the underworld is more or less the same as heaven, only illuminated with stars and not the sun—as the day or waking state is symbolised by the diurnal sky, so the night and the dreaming or subtle state is symbolised by the nocturnal heaven.

It is important to understand that while we speak of the *lokas*, abodes and places of heaven or hell, these are not places as such in reality but are states of consciousness. What is earth, water, fire and air to one person is hell from the point of view of a being that is trapped in the prison of mind corresponding to hell. Even the highest heaven is a place of utmost suffering to the one whose consciousness is in hell. In some of the nether regions, where desire is strongly retained in the altered discarnate state and the memory of human life continues, intense suffering comes about because one does not have a body to perform actions with. The word 'altered' is used here as a denizen of the nether regions may be a former human being but is now in a different state, which cannot be called 'human' (especially because there are subtle perceptions but no physical organs). It is also the case that those who dwell in the upper regions, the places of the *devas*, gods or angels, are able to retain memory of a human life. It is emphasised that the value of such knowledge is to appreciate the joy of final liberation. From that, called *moksha* or *kaivalya*, there is no return to any of the worlds whatsoever; liberation is final.

There is also the lunar door or entrance, and by which the stellar regions are known. The lunar door is a term used not to indicate the Moon as such, in the same way the solar door does not indicate the Sun. It is to indicate that the soul passes out of the body by one of the senses, for it is reflected knowledge. It is also said sometimes that the lunar entrance is by way of the roof of the palate.[215] Essentially, it is by the subtle senses that an object is made luminous by the reflected light and in this case one knows the subtle arrangements of stellar systems. This is helped by accomplishment at meditating on gross objects. One may also practice Samyama Yoga on the Pole star and by that is known the 'motions of the stars'. In fact, it is the space that the stellar regions occupy that is the ground for the meditations and is what is called the 'vehicle' in the *Yoga-Sutras*. The key to this, which might otherwise seem quite obscure, is that the movement of any stellar body is known by one's own stillness.[216]

It follows that by practicing Samyama on the various nerves of the body, organs and so forth, knowledge is thereby gained, and from this was derived principles of the (real) medical science of Ayurveda.

---

[215] In Hatha Yoga.

[216] The Pole star is called Dhruva in Sanskrit, literally 'fixed', but implies the primordial tradition as the 'unmoved mover' of Aristotle. The space that is the ground for meditation is called Urdhva-vimāna, literally 'upper vehicle' or measure (of sky), but the implied meaning is 'empty space or void of sky'.

Knowledge of Purusha

T he *Yoga-Sutras* are not called 'weaving' for nothing. The silken thread winds back and forth, passes through and out and back again. While deeply immersed in the considerations of Supernormal Powers the question of how to know Purusha, which is Itself the Seer or Atma, arises.[217] We must anticipate that there comes a time when such powers are nothing but an impediment to *samadhi* and we must prepare for that, even while there is yet more to know so far as the acquisition of such powers goes.

The *Yoga-Sutras* are emphatic that distinction must be clearly realised between the knowledge of the *boddhi* or higher intellect, the principle of sentience and knowing, and Purusha, which is absolute pure consciousness. Also, that error comes about from not realising the difference.[218] There comes at a certain point in the path of the yogin a definite stage where he realises that the *boddhi* cannot 'know the Knower', or apprehend the Real as Purusha. How then to make this considerable leap from the knowledge of the pure I-sense to that of the absolute consciousness of Purusha? This is not easy for minds to grasp that have not yet known the I-sense for more than a fleeting instant, so we shall proceed very carefully.

Everything called 'experience' is of the knowledge of *boddhi* or its modifications. Purusha cannot be experienced in that sense, cannot truly be known as an object. While Purusha is 'known' by the *boddhi* as experience then a dualism remains in the knower of things. One must establish firmly in the mind that all experience is of the *boddhi* as 'presentation' and that Purusha is distinct from all experience and is absolute. It is possible to make Samyama Yoga meditation on that. It is most important to know, if it has not already been realised by entering into the equivalent state, that such knowledge is intellectual conception and is not the realisation of Purusha as such. Vyasa, in his commentary on *Sutra* III: 35, thus quotes from the *Upanishads*:

What will the Knower be known by?

---

217 Purusha is Atma when considered from the point of view of Being, which is the point of view of the *Yoga-Sutras*. Cf. 'The Vayus and Integral Being'.

218 Certain Buddhist schools of thought have not realised this difference and have mistaken the *boddhi* for the absolute, which means that, as according to Vyasa, Buddhist sages are unable to enter into final liberation (*moksha*).

The highest that can be reached through the *boddhi* is called *viveka-khyāti* or discriminative enlightenment, and this is very advanced in itself, for it comes about only when most of *tamas* and *rajas* has been eliminated and only *sattva* remains, called the *sattvika* state. This *sattvika* state, most desirable, is a form of the discriminative knowledge but the *boddhi* is mutable and the Purusha is quite other than that—there must be no mistake here. It is possible to have the conception of *boddhi* and Purusha simultaneously but this is still in the realm of experience as it is a fluctuation of the *boddhi*. As such, it seems to be a knowable object and one remains in the domain where pleasure and pain is suffered or experienced. This is the reason why such emphasis is placed on this, the ultimate discrimination. When Samyama Yoga is made on the *boddhi* having knowledge of Purusha then it is as if *boddhi* takes on the appearance of Purusha, and this is why it is easy to make the error as previously referred to, which is nonetheless a very subtle one.

It is possible then to know Purusha 'in a certain sense' or in a manner of speaking, but that is not the Purusha—there must be no mistaking of absolute consciousness for conceptual knowledge even if it is of the highest intellectual order. The knowledge of Purusha as separate and distinct from the mind is only grasped by *samadhi*. This is compared to a threefold division of knowledge: on one side of it there is Purusha, the absolute consciousness without objectivity. On the other side is experience, which is reflected or as it is put, 'working on behalf of another (i.e., Purusha).' The pure I-sense, which is more readily attained by concentration of the mind over time, following all the practices as given, is in the middle of these two and it is that which is the object of Samyama meditation. The state of 'being-in-itself' only comes about when the *boddhi* vanishes away, and that amounts to *kaivalya* or *moksha* liberation. The advanced nature of what is being written about here must then be appreciated.

It was stated at the outset that Purusha cannot objectively be realised by the *boddhi*. Through the *boddhi*, there is knowledge of Purusha owing to *boddhi* taking on the likeness of Purusha, and this is attained through Samyama Yoga meditation on the pure I-sense (as object)—and by pure I-sense it is meant that the *boddhi* is stripped of all other 'knowables'. This is no different in effect from what is called *sa'asmita samadhi*, in which the duality of the knower and the known yet remains. Yet *sa'asmita samadhi* is relatively very far along the path. Nonetheless, so far as the Real, Purusha or Atma is concerned, even this high state, which is the 'immaculate faculty of knowing', which is the *boddhi*, amounts to a pseudo-Purusha, which is not different from *prakriti*. One must know this.

158

Immaculate Faculty of Knowing

Now it follows that one does not reject the knowledge of Purusha referred to in the previous chapter, even if it has been relegated to a pseudo-Purusha. It is in fact the building of the bridge that makes the great leap possible; and so we must continue with Samyama Yoga meditation. The *boddhi's* immaculate faculty of knowing cannot be gained while the mind is restless and in a state of disturbance by the urge to action (*rajas*) or the covering of ignorance (*tamas*). While the Gunas are not eliminated entirely the two that prevent further knowledge can be suppressed. It is only by the dominance of the *sattvika* state that Purusha can be known as distinct and different from *boddhi*. The persistent idea that 'I am the knower' arises from not knowing the difference, and that notion is in the way of the further knowledge as it is in the realm of 'experience', as previously pointed out. Purusha is the witness of all that but does not participate or act in it, and so it is said that such experience is presented to Purusha (by the modifications of *boddhi*) and that in reality Purusha owns it. Thus 'I am the knower' is relative ignorance, though when Purusha and the I-sense are present simultaneously it amounts nonetheless to 'experience of Purusha'. This focussing on the Purusha is a type of modification of the mind but it is one that is needed. By maintaining total engrossment in this, the real knowledge of Purusha from the 'Purusha point of view' (*atmadarshana*) then is possible or within reach.

One must first know the pure I-sense. In that, it becomes possible to know that however exalted, that is not Purusha and that Purusha is completely distinct from it. However, this 'simulation' of Purusha that takes place through the simultaneous appearance in the likeness of the *boddhi* is known by the Seer of All (Purusha) as it is presented. Here then is the tenuous bridge that has been alluded to. Some of Purusha is revealed from this 'middle state' of knowledge.

We can now return to the Supernormal Powers. The kind of knowledge of Purusha that has been described as a pseudo knowing is that which gives rise to foreknowledge, already described, and the Supernormal senses—hearing, touch, sight, taste and smell.[219] Such powers arise spontaneously from this state without being 'worked on' through Samyama meditation. Also knowledge of distant objects, and so forth, all of which have been described. Of the senses, these are divine sounds, touch, light, taste and fragrance.

---

[219] Foreknowledge is described in 'Knowledge of Omens'.

However, the Supernormal Powers are impediments to *samadhi* from the point of view of the one that wants to know the absolute, and such powers are only 'accomplishments' to the ordinary mind. So far as the state of the Self-in-Itself goes, the mind is naturally excited and disturbed by such powers and they are a real obstruction. All the same, as the powers arise spontaneously when reaching a certain elevation, it is needful to know something about them. The kinds of powers now discussed are of a different kind and are to do with action (*karma*). Firstly, the five *vayus* are as follows:[220]

> Prāña is not to be confused with the *prana* undivided or chief principle. The action of *prāña* is centred on the heart and its movement the mouth and nose. Inspiration.
>
> Apāna *vayu* is concerned with elimination of waste products and extends from the pelvis down to the soles of the feet. Expiration.
>
> Udāna *vayu* is the upward direction and leads, by a sort of 'nerve' as it were, from the throat to the top of the head. Aspiration (also speech).
>
> Samāna *vayu* gives nourishment to all parts and its action is focussed at the naval.
>
> Vyāna *vayu* permeates the whole body. Circulation (on all levels).

When *udāna* is mastered one may exit the body without becoming ensnared by *karmas* owing to previous actions. These are described in *Sutra* III: 39 as 'immersion in water or mud', or the 'entanglement in thorns'. This has its equivalent in the ancient Egyptian tradition, where such traps bar the passage through the *duat* or underworld, which is the body. Thus to make the exit from the body upon death, the mastery of *udāna* is needed. Becoming Horus typifies mastery of the upward *prana*. Meditations on the attributes of Isis, for example, align the self with *udāna*, for Isis has total power over the forces of the underworld. By it death may occur at will, which implies one enters higher states of being. All meditation on the cultivation of the *sattvika* state assists in gaining such power.

As mentioned previously, the *vayus* should not be taken as only pertaining to the gross body; they are interpreted in the widest possible sense.[221] By mastering the vital force called *samāna* for example, the body becomes light by it, and this leads sometimes to the perception by others that the body of the yogin is luminous. In this condition of radiance one is not affected by muddy water, sharp thorns or snares.

---

[220] The five *vayus* involve inspiration, expiration, aspiration, digesting food and circulation. See also 'The Vayus and Integral Being'.

[221] This is explained in 'The Vayus and Integral Being'.

Danger of Celestial Beings

The yogin is warned against the seductive powers of celestial beings. Yogins are classified as according to four types by Vyasa. The first consists of those who are engaged in *bhakti* devotion and in whom the supernatural powers are emergent or dawning, and have not yet been brought under control. The second have attained a measure of wisdom from continued practice. The third have acquired mastery over the five elements and sense faculties. The fourth class of yogin has passed beyond all desire for attainments and only wishes to enter the Arrested State permanently, which is the total subjection of the mind.

It is the second class of yogin that is particularly susceptible to the seductive glamours and tricks of the celestial beings. Having developed their intellect, this brings them to the attention of such beings, whose abodes are relative to that intellectual realm. It then follows that the celestial beings will invite the yogin to partake of the pleasures afforded by their regions. This work to undo the yogin is described by Vyasa as flattery first and foremost, for the yogin is addressed as 'Great Soul'. Then a very beautiful woman is offered, or many women in the form of obedient nymphs, or an elixir of life that gives immunity to old age and death. Or otherwise, a celestial chariot that will enable the yogin to ride the skies, or a Tree of Wishes that fulfils any desire. Then there is the Holy River, where it is possible to see all the perfected souls or Siddhas. The Supernormal Powers are also offered, such as adamantine strength and lustre, along with the promise that all are everlasting and much loved by the deities.

The yogin must reflect that desire brings not everlasting joy but everlasting sorrows, owing to perpetual births in different worlds of being, where one is tossed about helplessly between life and death. The yogin must realise that he has acquired illumination from yoga but all this attachment is antagonistic to that light, and nothing but delusion. Most especially the yogin does not give way to egoism from having realised this, and so fall prey to feeling superior to those who still crave sensuous pleasures. He blesses them and wishes that they may enjoy happiness. Also, the yogin must not in any way fall prey to the seduction of feeling special because he has won the attention of celestial beings—such gratification gives rise to complacency. Thus what is really promised is *pramāda*, the inability to control the mind, following one object after another. The consequence of this for the yogin is the need for constant correction of errors.

Divine Hearing and Light-Travelling

Akasha, the fifth element sometimes likened to 'space' as it is all-pervading, has the property of sound vibration. Some confusions have arisen with the use of the word 'void' in relation to *akasha*, but the word only denotes that there is nothing to obstruct *akasha* or the formless, all-pervading nature of its property, of which sounds that are heard by the ears are only an indicator (*linga*).[222] The Supernormal Power of hearing is developed by the yogin who meditates on the subtle relation between the ear, as organ of hearing, and *akasha*, the sonic principle. Akasha is the principial source of audio perception but is not in itself that which is heard. The confusion alluded to above comes about because 'emptiness' or 'void' is only a verbal means of imagining what *akasha* might be like, but there is no such thing as a void in reality or in nature. For vibration to take place there must be space so that can happen.[223] Akasha is thus 'full of sound', or to be more exact, is pure vibration—or at least, that is one way it can be thought of or imagined. All sense organs have affinity with that which they perceive; thus the ear is able to hear by the space defined by its labyrinthine shape.

We next consider how the I-sense is related to *akasha*, given all that has been said here. By meditating on the subtle relation between the ear and *akasha*, as just mentioned, there is a development of the knowledge of the I-sense. The *sattvika* state encourages this through the property of *akasha*, defined as non-obstructiveness. Realisation of the I-sense is thus able to intensify or to put this another way, becomes purer. This is what can lead to the divine sense of hearing. One may recollect that all the five senses are modifications of the I-sense and so the sense of hearing is sometimes called the highest of the faculties. The subtle sense of hearing must not be confused with the gross or bodily sense, however, for all the reasons given.

---

[222] A violin string, for example, acts as a support for the manifestation of the sonic principle—vibration is not the property of the string as such. It is likewise the same with all things that can carry sound vibration. Vibration is the source of sound, light and heat through transference.

[223] It is mentioned in the commentary of Swami Hariharānanda on *Yoga-Sutra* III: 41 that there can be comparative voidness or vacuity as in the case of a gas or liquid being more of the void nature than a solid, but absolute void is inconceivable.

The meditation is sometimes likened to the 'unstruck sound', and yet it is emphasised in Raja Yoga practice that Samyama is done on a real object or entity, and not a hypothetical mental concept. Thus it begins through the relation between the ear of the gross body and the *akasha*, and from there to the body as 'void' but filled with sound or vibration, or otherwise as a light-filled space without limits.[224]

Through yoga union with *akasha* comes forth such well known powers as flying through the air, levitation and so forth, all derived from the lightness of body owing to its identification with 'void'. As *akasha* has no limitation of size, distance and so forth, one can then travel anywhere. In the Hermetic source texts we are told of Aridaeus being led by a hermit and travelling a vast distance at great speed, or in an instant, which owes to the Supernormal Power being described here.[225] It can be explained, for those who might find this hard to grasp, that for a body to exist at all it must occupy space, and that the principle of space as *akasha* is not limited or obstructed by anything, which owes to its very nature otherwise it would not be space. The material constituents of the physical body, the 'flesh and blood' that is all that is known by most persons, are modifications of the I-sense. Commenting on *Yoga-Sutra* III: 42, the sage Vyasa has mentioned some of the possibilities available to the yogin who realises this:

> By becoming light he can walk on water and then on cobwebs and on rays of light. Thereafter he can fly across the sky at will.

Furthermore,

> There is a deep truth underlying the statement that the body becomes light by contemplation.[226]

It must not be thought from this, however, that the purpose of Samyama Yoga is to transform the body. As we have said, the body is but a modification of the I-sense. The purpose of this yoga is thus to transform the ego.

---

[224] One may develop divine hearing but it cannot result in liberation, as with all Supernormal Powers. Furthermore, while Samyama Yoga on the relation between the ear and *akasha* can produce the divine sense of hearing, this is subtly different from the *akasha tanmatra*, which is beyond the sensations of pleasure, pain or delusion. The *shabda-tanmatra* is the subtle root of the *akasha* element.

[225] See 'The Vision of Aridaeus', 'Alexandrian Gnosticism'.

[226] The Commentary of Swami Hariharānanda on *Sutra* III: 42, p. 319, *Yoga Philosophy of Patañjali with Bhāsvati* [University of Calcutta 2012].

Before leaving this subject something more must be mentioned about the 'divine hearing', which in a way is far more important than the other powers associated with *akasha*, however fantastic or even improbable they may seem.[227] It has been said previously that the practitioner forms a sort of bridge.[228] On the far side of it is the absolute, on the near side the modified knowledge of experience, and in the middle between these is the pure I-sense. By engrossment in the pure I-sense the tenuous bridge is strengthened. This is perfectly true but it omits something else, called the 'celestial ray', a word that is not only descriptive of the *boddhi* and its knowledge but is also the cult of the Virgin or Holy Mother and the Shakti in Hinduism, which has a near equivalent in the Shekinah of the Hebraic tradition, and a veritable multitude of feminine deities across ancient traditions. All these are intermediaries or 'bridges' between the absolute and man. So while it can look as though the *sadhaka* is busily engaged with 'bridge-building', as though it were something to be accomplished by his own effort alone, that is not strictly in accordance with traditional knowledge, especially wherever *bhakti* devotion and the cults of love are involved. The same particularly applies to chivalric orders such as once existed in the West.[229] When the ability to remain fixed in the pure I-sense is gained, and where this is supported by the devotional attitude, which will most often already exist in the practitioner, then a certain 'Knowledge and Conversation' is entered into, which can sometimes involve received oracular wisdom as from the holy mouth of the Virgin direct to the recipient. This is not 'heard' in the ordinary sense, by the organ of hearing, but belongs properly to the realm of the Supernormal—which as mentioned is only such when considered from the point of view of the ordinary mind. As it is what is termed in Sanskrit *para-vak*, 'beyond (normal) speech', if it is written down a certain 'translation' has to be effected from one mode to the other. It is to be carefully distinguished from all forms of psychism.

---

[227] Accounts of yogins and even of saints being witnessed as having such powers occur frequently enough in scripture and other testaments. One can hardly overlook the miracles of Christ Jesus recorded in the Gospels, of which walking on water is perhaps one of the best known, along with the transfiguration on the holy mountain. It is notable that these two powers were witnessed only by his disciples. Also the sequential context, where they occur in the narrative, is something all too easily overlooked. The powers are soon after renounced and a full withdrawal takes place. The only use of them was to assist the conveyance of knowledge to the disciples in a form that they could apprehend, even if it terrified them or they did not believe it.

[228] See 'Knowledge of Purusha'.

[229] See René Guénon, *Insights into Christian Esoterism*, p. 4 footnote 11.

Forms of the Elements

Continuing with the meditation on the all-pervasive *akasha*: the idea of the mind as existing outside of the body is called 'discarnate fixity', which is to say, such exteriorisation is to be brought about by concentration of the mind. However, while this can be imagined, the *Sutras* are emphatic that exteriorisation can be actual and not imagined. The imagination, however, acts as support to the actual experience. One begins by concentration on an exterior object and feels 'I am there'. While there is a sense of being both inside the body and outside it in another place, it is imagination. But when all sense of being in a body is removed, the discarnate fixity is the new state of affairs, and this can be understood by the fact that the 'fixity' refers to deep engrossment of concentration, which is now removed to another place outside of the body's confines. By this same means, a yogin can enter the body of another person and influence their mind, or fill their mind with their own mind. This may seem rather strange but the real purpose from the point of view of Samyama Yoga is that it removes the most serious veil or covering of ignorance that obscures the illumination of *bodhisattva* knowledge. Thus, one escapes the illusion 'I am this body'. As Vyasa has put it, the power of this *samadhi* removes the afflictions (*kléshas*), actions (*karma*) and fruition (*vipāka*) from *rajas* and *tamas*.

The first form of the *bhuta* elements is gross, which involves shape and spatial location.

The second form consists of the essential attribute or generic character such as hardness of earth, liquidity of water, the heat of fire, the mobility of air and the all-pervasiveness of *akasha*. These show the distinction of one element from another. Note that the senses are derived from these. Smell is derived from the substantial nature of earth; taste is experienced through liquidity and light usually involves heat, which is the character of *tejas* (fire), as with the sun, which is also the source of colours (vision). The *vayu* (air) element gives rise to sense of heat and coolness, through the contact of the skin with air, which is mobile. Sound, as has been described previously, owes to the unobstructed, all-pervasiveness of *akasha*. These differences define one object from another, so that a pot is not the same as a piece of cloth or a cow. In the case of mass objects such as a forest of trees, a shelf of pots or a group of men and so forth, these are collections of distinct combinations whereas in the singular each forms a whole, which is no different than a substance.

The third form of elements is called subtle, and these are the *tanmatras*, the subtle roots of elements. The five *tanmatras* are both generic and specific, and are compared to the smallest thing imaginable, such as an atom, which is of course analogous and not actual. They are very subtle, a trace, not perceptible to the gross senses at all. The *tanmatras* do not have parts and so they form an indivisible wholeness. They are not known by space, therefore, but they are known by sequence or mutation in time—a 'momentary apprehension'. One should not forget also that the *tanmatras* are a subtle modification of the I-sense, as are all the five forms of the elements.

The fourth form of the elements equates to manifestation or knowability, action and retentiveness, and these inherently sentient qualities relate in turn to the three Gunas, of which the elements are a modification. These are the constituent qualities of the elements, and that is to say, 'made of the Gunas', which is how they can be knowable through the sentient I-sense.

The fifth and last form mentioned by Patañjali is the objectivity, which is relative to the state of being. Both experience and the escape from that illusion is held in the three Gunas, which are inherent in *tanmatras* and *bhutas* as well as physical or material objects. This is not to say of course that the Gunas confer liberation (*moksha*) as that is entered into through renunciation alone. It is that all experience of happiness and misery owes to the properties arising from the Gunas and it is through renunciation that freedom is gained.

By Samyama Yoga meditation on the five elements and realising all their aspects, mastery is obtained through gradual realisation and thereafter the elements follow the will of the yogin. One is able to work changes upon the elements in this way, through the knowledge of them, which differs from magick in the degree of knowledge being applied. However that may be, such is not the goal of yoga, which is freedom from the joys and sorrows that arise from attachment to objects so as to gain the infinitely greater bliss of pure knowledge. In fact, it is from the fuller realisation of the nature of objectiveness in all things that the power to renounce all objectification for the spiritual goal is gained.

All objects have the undifferentiated *prakriti* as their ground or basis for emergence into manifestation and being knowable. While it is said sometimes that *prakriti* is their 'cause', *prakriti* does not really cause anything but things come about (become manifest) through one very small change or mutation, whereas in *prakriti* the Gunas are in a state of equilibrium and so unmanifest.

Forms of the Senses

The five forms of the elements or *tattva-bhutas* are naturally mirrored in the senses that perceive them. Thus, one may at length become the master of the elements but it is of no avail unless there is mastery of the senses that perceive them, and this means one must first have knowledge of the forms of the senses or to be more exact, the sense faculties.[230]

The first form of the senses is receptivity. That is to say, the sense is the channel through which a sound or object is 'knowable'. The ear, by which is really meant *hearing*, is receptive to sound. Receptivity is nonetheless the active state of the senses. Taking sound as example, as with *akasha* (described in the previous chapter), it has generic or general aspects as well as particular aspects. Together this makes up receptivity, which then includes reflective thought, which is involved in the knowing of particular aspects. Note that different kinds of cognition are being described here, of which the first only is direct.

—The generic principle of sound is not the same as the sound of a note played on a piano or blown through a horn. In each case it is the same principle but the particular aspects distinguish the sound of a note played on a piano from a note blown through a horn, or the sound of wind blowing through trees, and so forth.

The second form of the senses is essential character. The senses are able to produce knowledge owing to sentience inherent in them, which is a modification of the *boddhi*; this makes up a whole thing, and which is the essential character.

—Just as the ear, fitted to receive sound, is quite different from the eye, fitted to receive light, so the senses have essential character.

The third form of the senses is the I-sense, itself a modification of the *boddhi*, and which gives rise to the notion of existing as a separate self or individuality. The I-sense is referred to as the 'cause' of the senses but it is more accurate to understand the I-sense as their principle, of which the senses are a further degree of substantial modification. The I-sense active in each sense is the cognition that is active within the sense—otherwise nothing could be known.

---

[230] The faculties are often referred to in the source text translations as the 'organs', which is not wrong but leads the English speaking reader to think that it is the organs of the corporeal body being referred to whereas it is not the nose or ear that is meditated on, for example, but the sense of smell and sense of hearing—which in this chapter is gone into in some detail.

The fourth form of the senses is their qualities. These consist of sentience, mutation and receptivity. This can also be put otherwise as *perception*, *movement* and *retention* (as related to receptivity). The faculties are mutations of the I-sense, which is in itself a mutation of the three Gunas via the *boddhi*, the knowing principle.

—It will be remembered that the mind (*manas*), as with the I-sense, which is its higher principle, exists only owing to the weaving, change or mutation of the three Gunas by which all things in the universe appear. Thus the senses are different arrangements or modifications of the *boddhi*. Pure knowledge is modified as sound, touch, sight and so forth.

The fifth form of the senses is their objectiveness, by which the senses are the objects of the Self. They are instruments of pain and pleasure but are also instruments of salvation, otherwise liberation, through knowledge and renunciation.[231]

By mastering totally the five forms, faculties can be made or modified at will by the yogin to suit different purposes. That is to say, external and internal senses are shaped and modified at will to a desired level or 'frequency'.

It may be noted that the power of the senses to enthral, even to mesmerise, is common to all men but the ability to cognise, that is to say, to gain knowledge, of what the senses convey whether as objects or the faculties themselves as instruments of the Self, varies to a very considerable extent in each individual. This owes to the action of the I-sense. Although the I-sense must be present in the senses or else they would convey nothing it is clear that the I-sense is active in different individuals to different degrees. One could also say that this is because the delusion is greater or less. While all can sense things, especially pleasure or pain derived from objects, the ability to know something of the principles involved, as has been set forth here, is latent in some but not at all in others. While reflective thought is part of this, it is also the ability to cognise directly (*pramaña*) that is the basis for knowledge of more than an ordinary kind. What is meant here by the latter is mere 'information', plus inferences and so forth.

---

[231] The words 'salvation' and 'liberation' are frequently treated in texts as though they are interchangeable terms but they are very different. Salvation is a kind of temporary prolongation of the individuality in other states of being whereas liberation is the total and final (permanent) release from all worlds of being—and the ending of all delusion or bewilderment forever and ever.

Mastery of Time

Time appears to us as sequence, passing from one moment to the next, each 'moment' being infinitesimal, in a continuous flow like a river. In fact, in this sequential 'flow of time' there is no real aggregate of moments. Such aggregates as there are, for example a second, a minute, an hour, a day, are nothing but mental conceptions. Thus time itself is a *vikalpa*, not real at all save as a verbal construction—it is not substantive reality. Our concept of time rests on objects that are knowable, and from there the notion of a sequence of moments arises. Thus, as Vyasa puts it, time only appears to be real to the ordinary person, or the person that only has ordinary knowledge. In reality the present is the only 'moment' as such and it is unbroken, though the present seems to replace the past and then be replaced by the future, all of which is an illusion. In fact the past and future are nothing but an indication of mutability, and which takes place in the present. But when a mutation disappears back into the unmanifest *prakriti* from whence it emerged, we think of it as 'the past', though the past does not exist. The future does not exist either, as it has not emerged from undifferentiated *prakriti*. The emergence of the present is not from the past, as we can easily believe, but from *prakriti*, and this comes about through mutation of the Gunas. In *prakriti* the Gunas are in perfect equilibrium and so nothing manifests, but when there is even one minute change then there is an appearance, which we like to call the 'present moment'. In that moment, such as it is in our minds, the universe experiences a change—that is, the entire universe experiences it. All characteristics of what we think to be the past, present and future are in reality in the present or 'present moment'. Samyama Yoga can be made on this 'moment' and 'sequence', which can give rise to knowledge of time.

While this consideration might seem a digression, or a detail for the sake of forming a complete science, the real use of this forms a valid part of gaining transcendence once the mind has learned of the reality of the *tanmatras*, which are themselves sometimes likened to an 'atom' or a very minute trace, like a 'moment'. In fact they are not known by spatial awareness but they are subject to time. Both 'atom' and 'moment' are here used in an analogous sense, as the smallest 'whole' that is indivisible and yet cognisable to the yogin. Movement of such an object is known 'sequentially' or by the apparent passing of one moment to the next. Those who have persisted with Raja Yoga practice at length will recognise this in terms of experience. Knowing the *tanmatras* involves perceiving them as a series of perceptions.

The All-Powerful Yogin

I t follows then that by gaining supreme mastery of such powers as has been described, and which involves the ability to cause the elements, *bhutas* and even the *tanmatras*, to appear and to disappear at will, or to modify them, the yogin becomes invincible to the extent his powers are almost (though not completely) unlimited. He is able to make himself so small he cannot be seen or so great that he eclipses a mountain. He can touch the moon with his fingertips, and can swim down inside solid earth and come up again as though it were water. He is not obstructed in any way and so can pass through solid stone. Water does not make him wet and fire does not burn him. Even a hurricane does not move him and he can hide himself in *akasha* so as to affect total invisibility so that even the Siddhas or magical beings cannot see him.

In fact the only limitation is that as there can only be one Lord of the Universe (Ishvara Saguna), the all-powerful yogin cannot do anything that would change the natural order of things. He does not use the powers outside of his domain, as it were. This involves an aspect of yoga philosophy that is little known about or understood, especially in the West, while it seems to be quite controversial among the Hindu scholars. Hiranyagarbha or the Lord of the Universe is effectively a type of magical being, a Siddha, who attained perfection through countless births in all possible states of existence. It follows there can be other Siddhas, such as those who become total masters as described here, supreme renunciationists and so forth, but that these other Siddhas cannot or will not change the order of things as ordained by the previous Lord of the Manvantara.

This may be beyond the scope of modern day readers but we include it without apology; indeed, to do that would be to bow to the kind of 'positive criticism' so loved by the profane world. It might be difficult for those who even doubt the existence of God (Ishvara) to then consider the Lord as a magical being but the universe and the mystery of Maya, without beginning or end, appears by his Shakti power. The word Siddha includes the idea of a universe made of five elements, a liberated or perfected being, an immortal, and one that has attained all of the Supernormal Powers. To go further requires that we do Samyama Yoga meditation on Ishvara 'himself'. We will leave it with one further thought, though, which is that the Egyptian Isis holds the attribute—it forms part of her hieroglyphic name—of Hiranyagarbha in the form of the 'world egg'.

Omniscience

The discussion on all these Supernormal Powers always leads back to the consideration of the ultimate goal of yoga, which is final liberation (*moksha*). Earlier, the importance of clearly knowing the difference between the knowledge of the *boddhi* and the Purusha, the absolute consciousness, was made clear.[232] The *boddhi* knowledge, when purified from the actions and *kléshas* ('afflictions') arising from *rajas* and *tamas* is called *bodhisattva*.[233] Liberation involves first knowing the difference between this, however exalted it may be, and Purusha.[234] The one that truly knows this difference, which is only known from the Purusha 'point of view' (*darshana*), acquires power over all phases of existence. Hence, the title of this chapter is 'omniscience', which may cause surprise to some. What is meant by this, technically, is that there is simultaneous knowledge of the mutations of the three Gunas in past, present and future states of existence. And by this is also meant that the yogin becomes all-knowing as well as free from all afflictions or sorrows.

What is being described then is the ultimate of discriminative knowledge and is called in the commentaries 'transparently clear sentience'.[235] The knowledge of the *boddhi* is no longer reflected and modified; it is known as the Self, and this is where the importance of the final discrimination concerning Purusha comes into it, because Purusha is the true Self whereas the *boddhi* is still a mutation of the three Gunas, which bring *boddhi* about as the first production from *prakriti* unmanifest ground. This knowledge of the *boddhi*, though exalted, does not bring final liberation. Omniscience comes about when Purusha is fully realised. The *boddhi* and all else is only then below the feet of the Master. The yogin sees himself in all objects, as everything is directly and simultaneously perceptible. However, since all knowables are indefinitely multitudinous, there is no end to such knowledge; the yogin does not seek after a sort of 'final' all-knowing conclusion therefore, in spite of gaining this omniscience.

---

232 See 'Immaculate Faculty of Knowing'.

233 This term *bodhisattva* will be familiar to those who have studied various schools of thought relating to perfected beings that in some cases are able to assist human beings to realise the Self.

234 According to the teaching of Vyasa, some schools of Buddhism do not make this distinction and are unable to pass beyond the *bodhisattva* state to final liberation, called *kaivalya* in the *Yoga-Sutras*.

235 In the words of Swami Hariharānanda, commenting on *Sutra* III: 49.

This omnipotence and omniscience is called Great Self, when the adjuncts (i.e., powers) and the Seer are considered as one.[236] What comes next, in fact, is the renunciation of all Supernormal Powers, of which omniscience is the last as it comes about with the acquisition of all of them. The ultimate power is to renounce all of this. Even the jewel-like *bodhisattva* then becomes an object to be disposed of along with all else. Even the *sattva* Guna is not the immaculate Purusha. When the yogin begins to lose desire for the *bodhisattva* knowledge then he is truly a step away from final liberation. In this, all afflictions, of which sorrow is the foremost of all that is brought about by past actions and deeds, melt back into the undifferentiated ground and cease to exist as such. No further *kleshás* are generated as they are unable to produce new modifications. Even the Gunas return to the unmanifest *prakriti* so far as the mind is concerned. Purusha then stands inviolate as unmixed, unmodified consciousness absolute. It is no longer 'known' as the false reflection of *boddhi*. Furthermore, the establishment of absolute knowledge is the Self-in-Itself and this cannot be changed or altered by anything; it is for all of time.

---

[236] Mahān-atmā is the Great Self. The powers as such are called Mahat-tattva or Vivekaja-siddhi, 'all embracing (power)'.

PART THREE
MISCELLANEA

I n an earlier work we put forward a novel interpretation of the function of the three outer planets Uranus, Neptune and Pluto.[237] When combined with the luminaries or angular houses in a natal horoscope they become Outer Gateways, as we termed it, exerting a powerful influence on the native. This involves special powers latent in an individual who carries these marks in their natal horoscope. It will be useful then to reappraise the subject.

In astrology, it is not the planets as such we are concerned with. All of nature is a symbol and it is what the planets symbolise that interests us. The names of Greek gods that were given the outer planets were chosen in a more or less arbitrary fashion but over time the attributions have proved to be curiously apt, as are the symbols of the planets. The glyphs were drawn from traditional sources, even if that was done without knowledge. If we are to believe, for example, that the original symbol of Saturn (♄) was simply the first two letters of the Greek word Kronos, that does not render the symbol itself insignificant. It is commonly thought that the names of the Greek letters have no meaning whatsoever other than being indicative of the letters and sounds they represent. It can hardly be denied, however, that the Greek letter *alpha* is remarkably similar to the Hebrew *aleph* and the Arabic *alif*—and these letters are certainly not without meaning in their traditions.

We have first to dispel the error of modern astrologers in replacing the traditional planetary rulerships of Aquarius, Pisces and Scorpio with the three outer planets.[238] This disrupts the harmony of the ancient cosmology; apart from the fact that the seven planets including the two luminaries are visible to the eye while the outer planets are not, sacred geometry and the science of numbers play an important part in the astrological placements; the numbers and relations between stellar powers and principalities are not arbitrary assignments. The disruption to order that comes about through the modernist substitution is typical of the times in which the outer planets were 'discovered', when there was everywhere a loss of all true principles.

---

[237] *Hermetic Astrology.* This book was revised and republished in 2024.
[238] The traditional rulers are respectively Saturn, Jupiter and Mars, for which modern astrologers, unknowing of the perfection of the traditional and true governances, have rudely substituted Uranus, Neptune and Pluto.

The outer planets are then outside—to be more precise, *below*—the traditional cosmological scheme. In keeping with the times in which astronomers first tracked them, the outer planets represent a disruptive anti-traditional force, at least in their first manifestation. They form part of the 'signs of the times' as we near the end of the Kali Yuga.[239] We will attempt to show to some extent how the outer planet principles, as they manifest in the human and cosmological environment, may at the same time play a part in initiation and spiritual realisation in some rare cases. As indicative of the forces coming to bear on the ending of an age, we must at the same time be wary that outer planet configurations will frequently be found in the nativity of charlatans and fantasists.[240]

The conventional notion of the outer planets is that they indicate collective traits influencing a generation, and so are different from the so-called 'personal planets', Mercury, Venus, Mars, Jupiter and Saturn; the Sun and Moon are also included. The rather strange expression 'personal planets' means that in natal astrology these planets, apart from their cosmological aspect, may also symbolise the structure of the individuality.[241] The generational influence of the outer planets is a reasonable supposition; this easily becomes evident to anyone that lives astrology on a daily basis over a number of years. It is also true, however, that when outer planets are found in angular signs of a natal horoscope, or they otherwise form a conjunction with the Sun or Moon, they can indicate something quite other than that. However, it is not our present purpose to venture far into natal astrology. While natal astrology has its practical uses, becoming overly preoccupied with that aspect tends to obscure the real purpose of what was originally a traditional science that was not in any way separate from spiritual knowledge, and the associated ancient doctrines. The symbolism of the outer planets can be viewed in the light of traditional knowledge and without the accretions of modern 'psychological' interpretations—for the latter necessarily limit us to the egoistic sphere.

---

[239] See 'Cosmic Cycles', *Nu Hermetica—Initiation and Metaphysical Reality*.

[240] These easily gain influence in various fields, including politics, business, the occult and the various New Age 'healing' domains. Having done so, they will work tirelessly to spread more confusion and disorder in the world. The ambiguity of symbolic inversion is often used to gain influence over those predisposed to agree with all that attacks and subverts true knowledge.

[241] The word 'planet' is derived from the Greek, *planētēs*, 'wanderer', which is indicative of the apparent motions of the celestial bodies, not their physical structure.

The general idea of the Outer Gateways schema is that when one or more of the outer planets forms a conjunction with the Sun, Moon or Ascendant, or otherwise falls in the first house of a nativity, special powers dominate the individual, influencing them subversively, as well as the lives and affairs of others they come into contact with.[242] Some placements of the outer planets are 'transmissive' while others are more 'magnetic' in their action. When the powers are latent or unrealised, they tend to be destructive. The notion that the Outer Gateways are beneficent when realised and developed, however, owes to a psychological interpretation, which we will treat here with some reservation. The outer planets are conditioning factors that form no part of the individuality unless the latter has become so degraded as to have entirely succumbed to demonic or inferior forces, and in that case, there is no question of any 'development'. While the special powers are deemed to include the supernatural, this should not be confused with what are called Supernormal Powers in the traditional yoga aphorisms of Patañjali. These powers (siddhis) involve far more than the degraded forms of them as known to occultists; their proper context is Samyama Yoga.[243]

The outer planets have been linked with extraterrestrialism, in which case they are called 'Alien Powers' when they are active in the individual.[244] This is an error typical of neo-spiritualists; apart from the fact that nothing in the universe can truly be 'alien', all planetary bodies as well as moons and stars are literally 'extraterrestrial' if seen as existing outside or beyond the range of the earth itself. However, this confuses what the planets symbolise with the planetary bodies as material objects appearing to the corporeal senses, which in any case are very much terrestrial, as exclusive to the human domain.

---

[242] A wide orb is allowed, up to 15°, for a conjunction between any outer planet with the Sun, Moon or Ascendant. There is also an influence when outer planets occupy any of the angular houses, but it is not as powerful as when it is the first house that is occupied. An outer planet may then fall in the twelfth house and be considered an Outer Gateway if it is within 15° of the Ascendant. A conjunction with the MC is also very significant. There are other ways in which outer gateways may form a subtler influence, for instance through mutual reception or aspects.

[243] See Part Two, 'Yoga Power'.

[244] Extraterrestrialism covers a wide field, from the ravings of those who think that God is a spaceman (Erich von Daniken), to occult fantasists that produce subtler interpretations; but these always rest on the intervention of forces from 'outside', which, when understood correctly are really forces from a sub-infra level. That is to say, below the level of actual manifestation.

Ancient astrologers wisely insisted that all celestial influences are made perceptible by the action of the Moon, which by analogy is as a mirror or lens to the earth.[245] To the ancient sages, the Moon always symbolises the mind and the Sun the heart, which denotes the special intelligence of higher intellectual intuition. The extraterrestrial link, along with the designation Outer Gateways rests on the notion that anything supra-human must be 'outside' or experienced through a passing out of the self. The word 'experience' itself means 'taken out', whereas the spiritual is only known through inward concentration, as in the yoga practice of meditation. It can then be seen how dangerous it is to use such terms unthinkingly, for the mind is shaped by its own cognitions and the perceptions then can easily make things appear in accordance with false notions.

Nonetheless, while it is certainly empirical evidence, study of the horoscopes of students and practitioners as well as those of infamous occultists and worthy sages alike leaves little doubt that the outer planet conjunctions are significant in those who seek knowledge of a non-ordinary kind. Those with a will to persist have the marks upon them from birth, so to speak, and those who lack them are rarely able to muster the sufficient fortitude, at least not without considerable assistance from others in possession of the powers, so-called. René Guénon never mentioned the outer planets and it is said that Hindu sages would simply laugh at the mention of them, as they are not visible without a telescope. Guénon, nonetheless, had a configuration of the Moon and Saturn in his horoscope accentuated by Neptune and Pluto closing in on his natal Ascendant.[246] We must treat Saturn as a special case if it is to be regarded as an outer planet, for Saturn was known and figured since ancient times; its very nature indicates tradition and discipline, which is the opposite of what the outer planets symbolise. Saturn is a key factor in the initiatic possibilities of an individual and we might see in the horoscope of Guénon deep involvement with traditional knowledge combined with the exposure of the anti-traditional forces that have accelerated exponentially in modern times.[247]

---

[245] For this reason aspects formed between the planets and the Moon are considered to be of first importance in traditional astrology.

[246] It might also be mentioned that the position of the Moon's Nodes in Guénon's ninth and third houses indicates one who teaches higher wisdom. In fact, he is seen by some as a very unique type of the avatar.

[247] See as one example 'Uniformity against Unity', *Thunder Perfect Gnosis*, and for another, the Author's Preface and opening chapters of *The Way of Knowledge in the Reign of Antichrist*.

So what are we to make of these invisible, oftentimes sinister wanderers of the heavens? Firstly we must re-evaluate what the outer planets symbolise, as that which modern astrologers have deduced amounts to little beyond a psychological 'collective' consciousness that explains nothing. Historically, Uranus was identified by William Herschel in Bath, Somerset 1781, six years before the beginning of the French Revolution. From our point of view, the most significant factor in that violent upheaval, of long lasting consequence, was that the new social ideas accelerated the anti-traditional movement. Although other European nations did not replicate the bloodshed involved in the French Revolution, all would eventually move power away from the kings and nobles into the hands of the bourgeois and merchants, in the name of 'the people'. Along with the very bloody revolution in France, and the fear of it everywhere else, came the exaggerated sentimentalism that is part of the rejection of tradition and real spirituality in favour of individual expression—or at least, that is how it appears, for the loss of all knowledge of governing principles and the symbolism that alone conveys them must always eventually result in total suppression of individual qualities, as we have seen in very recent times.

Neptune was identified in 1846. It was not actually seen, even through a telescope, but was known by mathematical calculations based on its gravitational effect on Uranus. This time was marked by what would amount to a huge upsurge in spiritism, hypnotism and mediumism; by the end of the nineteenth century Sigmund Freud's psychological theories based on bizarre and extremely invasive and manipulative experiments would place the power to gain influence over the masses in the hands of governments and corporations to devastating effect.[248]

Pluto was identified in 1930, a time that marked the rise of totalitarianism and that would see Europe and the rest of the world devastated yet again by industrial weaponry on a massive scale. Strangely, the particular kind of totalitarianism that came to rise in the 1930s might easily be seen as a reactionary movement against the 'progressive' anti-traditionalism, yet it was much in agreement with the latter, tearing down institutions and redirecting finances and assets into the hands of the new rulers.

---

[248] See *Way of Knowledge* [ibid].

Stranger still is the fact that something very similar has taken place in recent times but without arousing the least suspicion in the minds of the populace, by now totally mesmerised by new hypnotic technological devices and global media networks, which are in turn fully controlled by the ruling class of merchants and financers and their faceless multinational conglomerates, a situation that is best described as plutocracy, but where the ideal is neo-socialism.[249]

The outer planets symbolise demonic or *sub-infra* agencies that manifest in the universe near the end of time to bring about final dissolution of a cycle of humanity designated as a Manvantara in the Hindu doctrines. Although it might seem astonishing to some, and will scarcely be believed by those enthralled by conventional science and its arbitrary measurements based on discontinuous number, the outer planets did not exist until their 'discovery', which coincides with the malefic influence that is now exerted upon humanity, and by humanity against itself.

Uranus figures the breaking apart of all conventions that hold meaningful or lasting value, and the substitution of false or inferior knowledge for the 'benefit' of the degraded mentality that must then follow in the wake of the disappearance of true and lasting principles. This is typified by compulsory education of the young, which is only a cover for the instilling of scientistic evolutionism and 'progress', a type of education that is in every way anti-traditional, and that is even fiercely aggressive in the assertion of its 'truth', a truth that is nonetheless updated frequently to fit with new theories and new inventions. It is a curious coincidence that one of the symbols used for Uranus, consisting simply of an 'H' with a planetary circle below ♅, looks exactly like an early television aerial, of the sort that once sat on top of the equipment in the living room of every home. The letter stands for Herschel, who built the high-powered telescope by which the planet could be viewed. It may seem strange to name a planet after a person, but the rise of individualism and its subsequent inversion typifies the modern era in which Uranus was discovered. The alternative symbol of Uranus ⛢ is thought to have been derived from combining the alchemical symbols of the planetary metals gold (Sun) and iron (Mars) to create a symbol for platinum. However, this was done in ignorance of all traditional symbolism. The base metal is transformed into gold, or is otherwise used to purify gold, through heating; the two metals cannot be combined to make something finer.

---

[249] *Way of Knowledge* [ibid].

The Greek God Uranus is the Lord of the Sky, or heaven. The Greek name also has the meaning of a veil or covering. In the fragmentary remains of the Orphic tradition, Uranus can be an attributive, as all nouns once were, and can indicate the 'heavenly order' or harmony of the Cosmos. The veiling of heaven is something peculiarly related to the present Dark Age or Kali Yuga, for in this time rites that were previously carried out openly or on mountain peaks were withdrawn into the earth, in caves or subterranean vaults. At a still later time, in the relatively recent historical period, the vaults were used as places to keep the dead, and this has led historians and the like to imagine that the sole purpose of such places was to serve as tombs.

Neptune symbolises the great dissolution, called *mahapralaya* in Sanskrit, which, while perfectly natural and inevitable, has a wholly negative effect in the loss of mental and other faculties as we near the end of a Great Age.[250] Even the memory and ordinary senses of the 'average person' are much degraded as a consequence of reliance on technological machines and data, the mesmeric influence of films and television, the destruction wrought upon body and mind by 'new' pharmaceutical drugs and the stupefaction brought about by belief in contradictory and false knowledge. All of this was brought in by the fixation of the Uranian powers.

The Neptune trident Ψ is identical to the Hindu trident of Shiva, which is also the attribute of all forms of Shakti, including Parvati, Durga and so forth. It is the power of the 'three worlds' as well as the Hindu Trimurti; also the past, present and future. The cross is the drum of Shiva, which is the sonic vibration of the mantra as well as AUM, also threefold. The Greek God Neptune is associated with the deep sea or ocean. Modern minds have associated this with the absurd psychological theory of the 'unconscious'. The ancients, on the other hand, used mutual symbolism and nouns for 'sea' and 'sky', so that the word 'firmament' for example is descriptive of either. Space is the garment of Shiva. 'Space', in Sanskrit, is closely related to words for 'black' or 'dark', also *akasha*, commonly translated as 'spirit'. Thus, while Uranus can in one sense symbolise radiation, Neptune is the space that is needed for radiation to take place in. At the present time, space is one thing that is vanishing away quickly.

---

[250] Dissolution has both a superior and an inferior aspect. The dissolution of the ego self is one of the aims of traditional Laya Yoga, for instance, which means 'dissolving union'. The negative or inverse of this is the dissipation of the individuality, loss of memory and degradation of the mental faculties that takes place collectively, and which is strikingly evident today.

Pluto, since the 1990s, has been regarded by astronomers as a dwarf planet among many others on the outskirts of the asteroid belt that circles the solar system. In many ways this is fitting as the ending of the Kali Yuga has obscurity as its main characteristic. Pluto symbolises excess of concentration on egoistic attachment to wealth, property and temporal power, and the actual worship of individuals supported by the hypnotic fascinations of the Neptune powers.

The 'PL' monogram ♇ commonly used for Pluto means nothing symbolically. The alternative symbol of Pluto ♀ is thought to have been derived from the bident, a weapon or attribute of the God Hades (sometimes shown as a trident), who is closely identified with Pluto. The circle merely symbolises 'a planet' in this case, while the lunar crescent is accidental, owing to refinement of the letter style from the original 'v'. While the sign of 'two' is anciently a symbol of the Great Mother, in this context it can only refer to the division that takes place in the self when all higher principles are abandoned and only the demonic vices of anger, greed, lust, envy, pride, malice and selfishness remain.

The Greek God Pluto gained a malefic reputation over time, to the extent he became the God whose name could not be uttered—or at least, that is one particular view of it. Originally, as in the case of Saturn, Pluto was associated with gold, firstly in the spiritual sense, where it symbolises eternity, and later, with treasure, money or coins. It is worth bearing in mind in this case that coinage in ancient times bore sacred symbolism and was regarded very differently from the way that money is now, which has in fact reached the final phase of meaninglessness in the digital age. The underworld or chthonic aspect of Pluto, acquired late in historical terms, is well known. The withdrawal of the 'heaven' in the Age of Kali Yuga, as typified by Uranus, means that the earth and men are deprived of the beneficial aspects of the 'radiation' of spiritual influence, so that the negative influence of Pluto is at its maximum. What is 'radiation' in regard to Uranus becomes 'magnetism' in the case of Pluto. While radiation has very negative physical connotations, the negative magnetism of Pluto manifests, for example, through the power of a wealthy elite to enslave entire populations through promotion of a constant state of anxiety, even fear and terror, to ensure the continuance and predictability of its capital. It is also the power that keeps the soul bound to the earth ('earthbound') while sealing shut the ways that lead out of what is effectively a prison. In this way Pluto typifies all anti-initiatic forces.

The most deadly radioactive poisons that have been unleashed by man's insatiable craving for power and destructive force have the same names as two of the outer planets.[251] The glyph for Neptune is identical to the Greek letter *psi*, which is also used to represent the psyche, now seen by many as an outer reach, with nothing else existing beyond it. As the absolute negation of all true principles, the infernal triad of outer planets cannot properly be described in principial terms, but when an individual sees through the illusions they generate, the triune spiritual principles are no longer obscured and become fully visible: Knowledge, Wisdom and divine Will or ordinance. The initiatic function of the outer planets then becomes clear. Taken together, they can be symbolised by the inverse trident of the Antichrist or anti-spiritual force in man that is now the dominant force in all world systems. The Adversary must be overcome within the sphere of any individual before initiation and spiritual realisation is in any way possible. Those born with the outer planet configurations, as previously described, have a great advantage but an equally great disadvantage should they succumb to the machinations of the System of Antichrist. The knowledge of the implications of the greater and lesser Cosmic Cycles was with them at birth, and remains latent until it is 're-discovered' at the end of time, in a sense, recollected.

Conversely, the fatal attraction of the negative or 'anti-qualities' that the outer planets symbolise, owing to their intensely magnetic force of restriction, can easily drive the person to destruction or otherwise hoodwink them into conforming with the covert new world order, which amounts to the same thing. This can come about through enthralment by continuous new inventions, the perpetual 'improvement' of technological and other products, hypnotism, or even joining in with, or leading the campaigns to instil fearful ideas into the minds of the populace to control their behaviour and isolate them to ever greater degrees.

Such conformity can also be subtle. For example, there are those who wish to 'save the planet'. Some will buy up land to form what they think to be 'sustainable communities', at the same time wholly accepting the 'facts' of conventional science, including evolutionism and 'progress'. Others simply strive to become pure in the body by special diets or abstinences. This leads to dispersion of mind and will, and the state of Stupefaction much liked by the System of Antichrist. The attention is placed on that which is wholly exterior and outward.

---

251 Uranium and Plutonium.

Fear of a threat to survival is an exterior object, and fear itself is one of the three great afflictions of humanity. The anti-Christian evangelists that are foremost among populist movements, including 'eco warriors' and health and therapy faddists, are certain to have the outer planets placed in key positions in their natal horoscopes. While sincerely believing they work for the betterment of humanity, they are no more than puppets or dupes for the System of Antichrist, which easily accomodates them. These will never suspect the truth, as that truth is unacceptable to all they believe, and such belief has shaped their minds permanently in what is called the 'image of the beast' in the Revelation of St. John, 14: 11.[252]

> And the smoke of their torment ascendeth up for ever and ever: and they have no rest day nor night, who worship the beast and his image, and whosoever receiveth the mark of his name.

This is an apt description of what is called in the *Yoga-Sutras* the 'Restless' mental state, which is directly under the control of the Asuras or Demons. However, the triumph of the anti-spiritual force is seeming and short-lived, as mentioned in the New Testament book of 1 Corinthians, 15: 51–52:

> Behold, I tell you a mystery; we will not all sleep, but we will all be changed, in a moment, in the twinkling of an eye, at the last trumpet; for the trumpet will sound, and the dead will be raised imperishable, and we will be changed.

These Christian verses are remarkably exact in their accordance with the ancient Hindu doctrine of the Cosmic Cycles, in particular, the ending of the present Kali Yuga where all manifestation is dissolved and withdrawn at the *mahapralaya*. The language is very specific. The first person plural 'we' always denotes in these scriptures the elect, that is those who follow Christ, whose second coming is to judge the world at the ending of all. It indicates that all will be changed but there are those who sleep, which is to say they are ignorant of spiritual reality or even opposed to it. The 'moment', which is as the 'twinkling of an eye', figures the return to the present, which is the simultaneous instant of withdrawal, when time is ended and there is no more past or future. The sounding of a trumpet is the vibration of the angel Israfel, signifying the call to awaken to the primordial 'sound'. Those who have waited for the coming, having attained the 'second birth' into the life of spirit, are raised from the dead, as it were. They are able to resurrect as Christ, for they are one with him in body at the last moment. Thus they enter eternity.

---

[252] See also Revelation 13: 14–15; 15: 2; 16: 2; 19: 20 and 20: 4.

In Sanskrit, this primordial 'sound' or vibration is the divine word OM or AUM. The three parts of the word AUM symbolise and actually are, in a certain respect, the entirety of the universe of three worlds, plus a fourth indivisible reality, the ineffable or supreme principle by which all is accomplished.[253] The word is thus everything that the anti-spiritual force, symbolised by the three outer planets, fears and rejects.

The outer planets are not principles, as previously stated, as they symbolise the negation of spiritual reality, but they can then be seen as the obscuration of the divine Word that is symptomatic of humanity at the end of its cycle. In so far as they have been called 'Outer Gateways', the question has not been answered as to where do such gateways lead? It has been explained that it is the error of men in the present times to seek a continuation of mortal life in that which is 'outside' or exterior, which nullifies all possibilities of knowing the Real, as that can only be known directly through inward concentration, in which all exterior things are closed off. In so far as the infernal triad forms a kind of portal or gateway to the 'outside' of manifestation, then that can only mean a very final death of oblivion for those who follow Antichrist, which involves dispersion of body and mind to its elements. This always seems harsh to those with modernist inclination; in fact to the latter it is quite unacceptable for they bear the mark of the beast upon them, so to speak, which we have referred to above. It is a way of saying that they are bound to the appearance of things, unknowing of any reality. In yoga practice it is said that the mind is shaped by its own cognitions, and that shape is also the image of Antichrist if the negation of truth—that truth is relative and can be 'either this or that', for example—has been accepted wholly. Salvation, as it is put in Christian terms, is no longer possible at the end of time, but even if it were, in the case of the damned there is nothing to save. One must mark clearly the difference between 'salvation' and 'liberation' or final deliverance. Salvation is the perpetuation of a being, called 'immortality', until the end of time. It is comparable with the abiding in Amentet of the Egyptians, or a celestial paradise.[254] As such, it is not eternal but is limited to the duration of a Cosmic Cycle such as a Manvantara. Liberation (Sanskrit *moksha*) is final deliverance, with no return to a manifest state of being.

---

[253] See 'AUM: Reality and Unreality', *Thunder Perfect Gnosis*.
[254] Abydos in Egypt was in some ways the construction of a terrestrial paradise or Eden. King Seti I had an impressive temple complex built there to commemorate the earliest dynastic kings. The purpose there seems to accord with the way of Pitriyana as opposed to Devayana (see p. 89).

Looked at another way, the infernal triad symbolises the entire force of the System of Antichrist and those who choose to believe in its subterfuges. The Initiates or 'elect', or those who have achieved salvation and who are waiting, in a manner of speaking, do not then pass through such a gateway at all, for it is the passage to hell. The notion of 'hell' is subject to as much confusion as any other aspect of theological doctrines, let alone the metaphysical, but let it suffice to say here that in the present context hell does not denote any 'place' of eternal punishment but oblivion. This is not to deny the regions of the netherworlds, which are a prolongation of psychic elements.[255] The notion of eternal punishment, however, has no proper place in Christian theology. It is an absurdity as that which is eternal does not admit to duality and so is beyond 'good' and 'evil' altogether.

Those who know or even suspect what life truly is and what it can be, with all of its unlimited and vast possibilities, will follow the way of truth, for that truth has its seed within them, and for that reason the 'mark of the beast' will never gain entrance to the citadel of their souls. These have mastered the power of the infernal triad, and know that Vincit Omnia Veritas, 'truth triumphs over all', is no abstract or idealistic saying, but is immutable and certain as the principle that it represents.

It remains then for something to be said about the action of the infernal triad in the natal horoscope. It would not be profitable to list all combinations, as the secondary possibilities are too numerous to mention. Also, that would amount to systematisation. What might be more useful would be to make some general notes on the function of the outer planets when conjoined with the Sun, Moon or Ascendant; those with skill to do so can easily work out the rest.

When Uranus is conjoined with the Ascendant (or otherwise is located in the first house) the person is able to gain influence over others through sheer force of personality. It is then needless to say that unless they have overcome the infernal aspect of the power in themselves, they are liable to persuade others that new inventions or technologies, whether in the conventional realm or that of occultism, neo-spiritualism, psychology, hypnotism and so forth, will greatly benefit them.

When Uranus is conjoined with the Moon, the native is very susceptible to the machinations of those that are able to exert the Uranian force. Their minds are easily moulded by the anti-spiritual notions of our times.

---

[255] See 'Power of Knowing Distant Objects', pp. 155 and 156 in particular.

186

When Uranus is conjoined with the Sun, the person is able to exert a powerfully disruptive force without appearing to do much in the way of action; their very presence is sufficient, and they are also able to transmit to others across time and space. That is a kind of parody of the *siddhi* or magical power of some yogins, if the native does not understand the force, or is afflicted by it. Mastering it, however, may enable such a person to become a cosmic mediator.

When Neptune is conjoined with the Ascendant, then there is easily a dispersion of the self through succumbing to illusions of every kind. The position is typified by the neo-spiritual 'follow your intuition' mode of thinking, which rejects all order and authority and is completely impervious to learning anything of real value. It is also what is termed in the yoga of Patañjali the state of mind called Stupefaction, where one object after another is followed for its own sake. This position may lend the person a certain charisma but in most cases their influence on others will be of an evil nature.

When Neptune is conjoined with the Moon, the native is much drawn to occultism or psychism, and the phenomena associated with such practices carries an overwhelming power to captivate and enthral. The person may be mediumistic, and while this can have some uses in spiritual organisations, there will always be antagonists that will want to exploit any weakness to gain power, and this can lead to the destruction of the medium or otherwise cause a great deal of harm to them. They are also susceptible to what Guénon has termed 'wandering influences', which can spring from a variety of sources but are generally part of a subconscious milieu of ideas particular to a people and time.[256] There are the 'spirits' of the Goetia that are evoked by occult experimenters, and which can then become attached to a person's sphere; there are also what can be best be termed as the dissociated psychic remnants of former human beings, and which neo-spiritualists and experimenters imagine to be 'higher intelligences'.[257]

When Neptune is conjoined with the Sun, it is easily possible for a complete disintegration of the soul to be effected even quite early in life. Such persons who survive are rarely able to overcome the forces of the System of Antichrist as they personally identify their self with the whole spectrum of anti-spiritual thought and activity.

---

[256] See Guénon, *The Spiritist Fallacy* Part Two Chapter Two.
[257] See 'Shadow of the Wings'.

The solar-Neptunian native may nonetheless profit in the world becoming successful in the popular domain of astrology, for example, where they are able to spread anti-spiritual notions in the guise of 'helping and healing others'. Such a person will also adopt 'disguises' or in other ways hide their real intentions. They will readily form affiliations with occult or even spiritual organisations in order to gain information that they can turn to their own use.

When Pluto is conjoined with the Ascendant, or is located in the first house, then powerful influence is brought to bear, although this is not usually suspected by the recipients and in many cases of course, the transmitter of such force is not aware of it. So it is the case that this native may find that whenever they become involved in a relation with a person, group or organisation, it is only a matter of time before all hell breaks loose in the way of bizarre or sinister behaviour from those concerned. This can produce supernatural phenomena in some cases, so that a person without knowledge might suffer from severe nervous strain or even mental breakdown.

When Pluto is conjoined with the Moon, there is a real danger of actual insanity or otherwise a state of wilful Stupefaction, which can lead to the same result especially if the person is totally unable to make use of any spiritual discipline that would teach concentration. This is all the more so if the configuration also coincides with the Ascendant or the Midheaven, for example. Those who are able to survive this may be found in occupations such as psychotherapy or other related 'healing' trades, where they are able to do considerable evil to others under the pretext of helping them 'spiritually'.

When Pluto is conjoined with the Sun, there is danger of insanity, as with the above placement, owing to extreme attachment to the objects of mind and imagining. The magnetic power of Pluto then compels the native to pay continual attention even to the most harmful of *karmasayas* or recollected past deeds. Such a person may develop an interest in the occult, in which case the chances are the condition may be worsened through exposure to mediumism or 'psychics'. For this reason the ability to influence others is in most cases weakened and, on the contrary, they may themselves be subject to the influence of the Pluto power received from others. If the native is fortunate enough to find their way to a spiritual organisation that could help them they often refuse the help offered, either because they are simply unable to overcome the compulsions that overwhelm them, or because they are unable to see what is spiritual in the real sense and what is merely counterfeit. All of this can amount to what might be called a disorder of the will.

In all cases, when the infernal powers are understood for what they are, genuinely beneficial agencies are brought in. This is rarely the outcome, however, as the anti-spiritual notions are by now so deeply imbedded across the whole of the postmodern world. In those rare exceptions, which include the person finding their way to an organisation affording a kind of 'protective umbrella' that allows spiritual development to take place, then purification of the malefic outer planet forces makes way for the influence of all that the latter had previously obscured and confused. And that is to say, spiritual influences are at last received and assimilated by the person that had the latent possibilities in them from their birth.

Selected Works of Oliver St. John

Hermetic Astrology (2015)

Magical Theurgy (2015)

The Enterer of the Threshold (2016)

Liber 373 Astrum Draconis (2017)

Hermetic Qabalah Foundation—Complete Course (2018)

Babalon Unveiled! Thelemic Monographs (2019)

Ritual Magick—Initiation of the Star and Snake (2019)

Nu Hermetica—Initiation and Metaphysical Reality (2021)

The Way of Knowledge in the Reign of Antichrist (2022)

Thirty-two paths of Wisdom (2023)

Thunder Perfect Gnosis—Intellectual Flower of Mind (2023)

The Law of Thelema—Hidden Alchemy (2024)

Advaita Vedanta—Question of the Real (2025)

Egyptian Tarot and Tarot Cards (2025)

The dates given are of first publication. All of these books prior to 2021 have been revised and new editions published in 2024.

Contact the O∴A∴

Universal Gnostic Collegium: Contact details and information is posted on our website at www.ordoastri.org

www.ingramcontent.com/pod-product-compliance
Lightning Source LLC
Chambersburg PA
CBHW060418100426
42812CB00030B/3222/J